Lives of Early Buddhist Nuns

Lives of Early Buddhist Nuns

Biographies as History

Alice Collett

With a foreword by Jonathan S. Walters and an
afterword by Martin Seeger

OXFORD
UNIVERSITY PRESS

OXFORD
UNIVERSITY PRESS

Oxford University Press is a department of the University of Oxford. It furthers the University's objective of excellence in research, scholarship, and education by publishing worldwide. Oxford is a registered trademark of Oxford University Press in the UK and in certain other countries.

Published in India by
Oxford University Press
YMCA Library Building, 1 Jai Singh Road, New Delhi 110 001, India

First Edition published in 2016

ISBN-13: 978-0-19-945907-0
ISBN-10: 0-19-945907-X

Typeset in ScalaPro 10.5/13
by Tranistics Data Technologies, New Delhi 110 044
Printed in India by Rakmo Press, New Delhi 110 020

For Auntie Eve,
who loved a good story,
and was looking forward
to reading this book.

We miss you.

Contents

Foreword

The scholarly study of Buddhist women was arguably born at the Ninth International Congress of Orientalists in 1892, where two young Pāli scholars delivered what I believe were the first-ever professional papers dedicated to the topic. Inspired by the still-recent (1883) edition and publication of ancient Buddhist poems (in Pāli) ascribed to the accomplished monks and nuns of the Buddha's own community (the *Theragāthā* and the *Therīgāthā*, respectively), and by advanced copies (it was published in 1893) of the Pāli commentary on the *Therīgāthā* (by Dhammapāla), composed about a millennium later than the poems themselves, these two young scholars, Caroline Augusta Foley (later Rhys Davids, 1857–1942) and Mabel Haynes Bode (1864–1922), had come to a shared discovery that this biographical tradition represents an extraordinarily rich and valuable record of women's lives, hopes, and achievements in a particularly and compellingly Buddhist idiom.[1] With lengthy translated excerpts and excited anticipation, Foley and Bode independently announced their discovery to the Congress, in the explicit

[1] The commentaries explain how to read difficult passages in the collections of poems, and contextualize them within centuries of supplemental material.

hope of inaugurating a comprehensive study of—as each titled her paper—'The Women Leaders of the Buddhist Reformation'.

Today, more than a century later, these biographies remain a major stimulus to and a source for scholarship about Buddhist women, thanks especially to the much-republished (under various titles and in differing formats) translation of the original *Therīgāthā* poems, with synopses of major commentarial contributions, by Caroline Augusta Foley Rhys Davids (1909; now supplanted by the more reliable but non-poetic 1971 translation by K.R. Norman). This provision of widespread access to the primary evidence through translation was clearly part of the future study anticipated in the 1892 papers. Though it took a century to appear, Dhammapāla's commentary is also now available in English translation (by William Pruitt, 1999 [1998]).

But their titles, frameworks, and interspersed comments make clear that Foley and Bode wanted to catalyse more than that. They saw and wanted to champion Buddhism as having given women an unusual degree of freedom, equality, and agency for an ancient (or even modern) religion, not only liberating them from gendered oppression but welcoming them as equal co-participants in a Buddhist 'Reformation'. Both went on to produce important contributions to Pāli and Buddhist Studies, but the unpacking of this insight—that the Pāli texts bear important witness to Buddhist women's comparative well-being—was left to their younger colleague, and Foley Rhys Davids' later successor as President of the Pali Text Society, Isaline Blew Horner (1896–1981). Horner's monumental *Women under Primitive Buddhism* ([1930] 1990) processes this whole biographical literature and indeed all the major early Pāli texts into an argument in extenso that, by and large no matter what their station, Buddhist 'almswomen' (nuns) as well as laywomen (she devotes separate chapters to 'The Mother', 'The Daughter', 'The Wife', 'The Widow', and 'The Woman Worker') were better off than their non-Buddhist counterparts in ancient India, and in fact lived 'under' a remarkably open-minded and egalitarian 'Primitive Buddhism'. As careful to note discrepancies and counter-examples as it is comprehensive, and like Foley Rhys Davids' *Therīgāthā* translation—much-republished and widely cited in subsequent scholarship—I think it is fair to say that

Horner's book has remained the standard authority on ancient Indian Buddhist women to this day.

But the standard itself belonged to a very different era from our own, dominated by proudly unapologetic colonial administration, imperialist rumination, Orientalist 'Othering', 'kings and battles' historiography, philological determinism, Christian mission, patriarchy, and other practices and presuppositions so far from twenty-first century academic culture as to render increasingly in need of explanation the fact that scholars of the day embraced (or rejected) them so concertedly (or even at all). Foley, Bode, and Horner were women of their day, who not surprisingly spoke to it and within its idiom.

Thus, for example, their shared title placed Foley and Bode's original contributions firmly within a very particular (and peculiar) reconstruction of Buddhism as a 'Reformation' of ancient Indian religion. This 'Reformation' supposedly entailed missionary zeal and self-sacrifice on the part of Buddhists to convert Hindus (and others) to the new-founded revelation; social and political reconfiguration in the direction of egalitarianism and enlightened rulership; self-deprecation of 'vile' customs (especially, in this context, gendered ones), even to the point of abandoned loyalty to family and forebears. The striking parallelism here with then-contemporary Christian self-understandings and, in particular, Christian missionary writings about then-contemporary India, was of course no accident. The question of how well off women were in various religions was a matter of considerable discourse during the second half of the nineteenth century, because self-congratulation by Victorian Christian missionary ladies on their own liberation from gendered oppression very much depended upon their abhorrence of and activism against the purported abuses of women in other religions (and classes); nineteenth-century Christian missionaries in both Hindu and Buddhist 'fields' often called out gendered abuses in their larger critiques of the target religions. Foley, Bode, and Horner's presentation of Buddhism as 'good' for women was made against the grain of this dominant discourse—they were radicals themselves, in their way (Foley and Bode were the only 'lady members' who presented papers in the Aryan and Indian sections of the Ninth Congress, and their papers alone dealt with women;

Bode's paper, only published in excerpt in the proceedings of the Congress itself, subsequently broke the glass ceiling for women at the *Journal of the Royal Asiatic Society*). However, whether this was the intention or not, their view, grounded in *ancient* Buddhism, was easily absorbed into missionary rhetoric: it allowed missionaries to argue that Hindus had been criticized for caste and gender oppression (as well as for excessive ritualism, elitism, superstition, and other mainstays of missionary writings on Hinduism) even since the time of the Buddha. Buddhists too could be portrayed as having sunk far from the supposedly almost-Christian virtues of their founder and from his original, revolutionary social vision, fallen back as it were into Hinduism. Not only among missionaries, this proved to be a claim with staying power which has multiplied in subsequent scholarship too—where the supposedly superior status of women in Buddhism has been portrayed as evident in comparison with Confucianism, Shinto, or, much later (and ironically enough), with Christianity or Judaism as well. The same calculus sometimes has positioned Mahāyāna Buddhism as the solution to lingering (or increasing) misogyny in the Pāli texts and the Theravāda tradition, or Tantrayāna as the solution to the same in both. Among Buddhists this view has helped crystallize revivalist and nationalist movements as well as mass liberationist conversions to Buddhism during the twentieth century.

'Women', in all these cases, were framed as 'better off than' within a discourse that levelled centuries of development and change and whole continents in its sweeping generalizations about hypostasized entities like 'Buddhism', 'Hinduism', and 'Christianity'. This same, then-widespread tendency to vast generalization and essentialism similarly shaped Foley, Bode, and Horner's focus on 'women' (levelling variation in women's experiences to examples of a single type or a handful of types) and their conceptualization of the biographical literature itself (telescoping the texts, which span a thousand years, several genres, and the entire subcontinent, into singular biographies confined to the early period as the sources for its history, even though only the original poems actually date from that period).

It is no criticism of their own work to acknowledge that in these ways (and certainly others as well) Foley, Bode, and Horner spoke to the issues and within the idiom of their day. Given that caveat we may even admire the conclusions that they reached about the issues, as well as the generative impact that their decision to thus locate their discovery within that idiom has in fact achieved (though it has not perhaps attained the unity Foley and Bode envisioned, nor entirely confirmed all of their sometimes overly rosy interpretations, their dreamed-of comprehensive study of Buddhist women is certainly a reality today, increasingly for all periods, genres of literature, and different cultural traditions). Likewise they cannot be blamed for ignoring texts that had not yet been edited (or in some cases discovered) or theoretical and methodological developments since their day; they did not have the last century of scholarship (and feminist theory) behind them, and they can hardly be expected to have asked (or even to have been able to formulate) questions that drive our interests today.

The distance between our questions and theirs becomes a problem, however, to the extent that a formative work like Horner's has shaped and continues to shape the discussion, ultimately grounding it in long-since-irrelevant fights by and with missionaries, or historical positivism. Its continuing indispensability today lies in laying bare that effect so that we can extricate the evidence from its entanglement in long forgotten debates and look at it anew from our own perspectives and for answers to our own questions, taking advantage of advancements in both theory and substantive knowledge over the last century. If these Pāli biographies of Buddhist nuns remain an invaluable source for reconstructing this piece of women's history, how can that value be realized by twenty-first century scholars?

Alice Collett's answer to this question is two-fold. On one hand she returns to the texts themselves, spending the first half of this book teasing out the differences in different layers of the Pāli biographical tradition, and among different women's biographies. This functions to introduce non-specialists to the actual sources and to greatly enlarge even specialist perspectives on them, in part because Collett draws on sources (notably texts from other Buddhist traditions and epigraphic records) and secondary scholarly works which were not even available to Foley, Bode, or Horner. But her reading is largely new because she approaches the Pāli texts themselves so differently than did these forebears. Rather than boil a vast literature down to a few generalized nuggets, Collett starts from the biographies of just six nuns and proceeds to explode them outward, developing their texture across time and across Buddhist traditions. Having thus introduced the literature itself, in all its complexity, Collett proceeds in Part II of this book to track the contexts of meaning within which Buddhists themselves understood these specific nuns' biographies. Paying special attention to the particular virtues which these particular nuns were said to embody, Collett creatively reconstructs the backdrops against which these claims were made and the ways in which they developed and changed through the centuries. Though the starting place is, again, but a small group of nuns, as she tracks them across time and Buddhist imaginations she points us to crevices and alleyways and intriguing possibilities now open for investigation into the lives of Buddhist women, as well as the process of composing texts about them, from the very inception of the tradition. And she demonstrates in that same tour through the Pāli texts that the lives of Buddhist women, in turn, bear on central questions of Buddhist history, practice, and thought.

This book thus claims not to be a new final word, but rather a first one, a new beginning for a new century of scholarship on Buddhist women made possible by the existence of this extraordinary record. In addition to highlighting numerous gems in these six biographical traditions that will continue to be examined and faceted by the next generation of scholars, Collett's work also exemplifies a methodological approach which will usefully be adopted by scholars who want to re-examine any of the many additional biographies of Buddhist nuns—and of monks—preserved in the Pāli texts.

Jonathan S. Walters, Ph.D.
Professor of Religion and George Hudson Ball Chair of Humanities, Whitman College,
Walla Walla, Washington, USA

Acknowledgements

The research for this book was done under a fellowship grant from the Arts and Humanities Research Council of Great Britain. I would also like to thank The Spalding Trust for a preliminary grant for materials.

My interest in gender politics began with my grandmother, who, when I was a child, used to tell me, 'Don't ever let anyone tell you you can't, just because you're a girl.' My grandmother and many other members of my family are very important to me, and I would like to thank them for their ongoing love and support.

I would also like to thank my friends and some (international) colleagues for continued support, guidance, and advice, and for giving up some of their precious time to help with this project. I would like to thank Bhikkhu Anālayo, for all his ongoing support and advice, on this and other projects, and for his close and detailed reading of a draft of this book. I would like to thank Jon Walters for being an inspiration to me as a postgraduate through his work—before I knew him—and since as a friend and mentor, and, lastly, for agreeing to write a foreword to this monograph; it is such a privilege for me to have someone I so admired as a student now supporting and being interested in my work. I would also like to thank Martin Seeger for agreeing to write his afterword, at very short notice, and for his patience with me through an untimely dose of flu. I would also like to thank my students Matt Coward and Tom Mitchell for kindly agreeing to read a draft and give me a student's perspective on the work. And lastly, I would like to thank Ruby the dog, for all those welcome moments of distraction!

Abbreviations

AN	*Aṅguttara-nikāya*
AN-a	*Aṅguttara-nikāya* commentary or *Manorathapūraṇī*
Ap	*Apadāna*
ĀpDS	*Dharmasūtra of Āpastamba*
AŚ	*Avadānaśataka*
AV	*Atharvaveda*
BDS	*Dharmasūtra of Baudhāyana*
Dhp-a	*Dhammapada-aṭṭhakathā*
DN	*Dīgha-nikāya*
GDS	*Dharmasūtra of Gautama*
JA	*Jātakatthavaṇṇanā*
MBh	*Mahābhārata*
MDS	*Mānavadharmaśāstra*
Mil.	*Milindapañha*
MN	*Majjhima-nikāya*
MN-a	*Majjhima-nikāya aṭṭhakathā*
Pv	*Petavatthu*
Rām.	*Rāmāyaṇa*
SN	*Saṃyutta-nikāya*
SN-a	*Saṃyutta-nikāya aṭṭhakathā*

Tha	*Theragāthā*
Tha-a	*Theragāthā* commentary or *Paramatthadīpanītheragāthā-aṭṭhakathā*
Thī	*Therīgāthā*
Thī-a	*Therīgāthā* commentary or *Paramatthadīpanītherīgāthā-aṭṭhakathā*
Ud.	*Udāna*
Ud-a	*Udāna-aṭṭhakathā*
Vv-a	*Vimānavatthu* commentary
Vin.	*Vinaya*

General introduction

...the vision of higher things was within their grasp. It needed but their effort and determination and choice, their will to kindle it, in its burning to consume what had been.

—Horner ([1930] 1990, 185)

With entry into the Order the almswoman was not expected to begin with a clean slate, and to become a different person, new, disconnected from her past mental history. The struggle was not pitched in the effort to forget, but in the effort to develop and advance from a lower to a higher state.

—Horner ([1930] 1990, 187)

The Indian Buddhist tradition furnishes us with narrative biographical accounts of important figures from the past who, for the tradition itself, are considered to have been living people. This book is concerned with narrative accounts of important nuns from the Pāli tradition. I have structured this book around biographies of six of the best-known nuns who are considered to have been direct disciples of Gotama Buddha: Dhammadinnā, Khemā, Kisāgotamī, Paṭācara, Bhaddā Kuṇḍalakesā, and Uppalavaṇṇā. I have chosen biography as the platform for the study for two reasons: first, the biographies are central within the Pāli corpus with regard to the amount that they tell us about—if not actual historical nuns—the historical memory or historical idea of venerated early nuns. Further, the biographies are a rich source to tap because they provide us with details of some of the most salient and poignant issues in relation to (real or imagined) women's lives in the historical milieu under discussion. That the biographies are, at the very least, an attempt to tell us about women's lives makes them one of the best tools with which to assess the position of and situation for women in the Pāli tradition.[1]

Women in Buddhism, and women in early Indian Buddhism, as seen through the Pāli sources, are a much-debated subject, but the biographies—that are richly detailed and of which there are a plethora—have not often been centred as the foundation from which to view attitudes towards and portrayals of women in the Pāli canon and commentaries. But the biographies are important as they are ornately woven with the fabric of women's (apparent) lives in ancient India. And that there is a treasured biographical tradition for Pāli Buddhism at our disposal—that became imbricated into the canon early on—is of great value. Notwithstanding counterparts and parallels in the texts of other Buddhist traditions, the biographies from the Pāli canon provide us with an impressive multitude of stories of women's lives when compared with what is preserved by most other contemporaneous ancient cultures and civilizations.

To what extent can the accounts be taken to be attempts to transmit stories of actual lives? That is a difficult question to answer. In both the oral and manuscript traditions that preserved the biographies, either conscious and/or unconscious editing, redacting, dramatization, fabrication, occlusion, and so on, took place. This question is addressed in the introduction to Part I. Here, some obvious problems with Pāli accounts of Paṭācārā are discussed, as an example of how difficult it can be to rely on texts as a source

[1] The general understanding these days is that the extant Pāli texts have come out of the Mahāvihāra tradition of Sri Lanka. However, as there remain north Indian elements to the texts, there are obviously some Abhayagiri elements still present (see Kieffer-Pülz 2013 and Cousins 2012), and they demonstrate influence from Indian folk narrative traditions, I have decided to keep the term 'Pāli Buddhism' to demonstrate an awareness of the broad influences on the development of the extant texts.

for history. While attempts at preservation might have been high on the agenda of reciters, compilers, manuscript scribes, and so on, the extant textual record nonetheless attests to problems with attempts at both oral and textual transmission. As might well be the case with Paṭācārā, stories associated with one nun in the historical memory of the tradition come to be linked to another, and even the personal names of nuns change as the corpus is transmitted down the centuries.

The biographies that form the basis of this book are found, in the first instance, in the *Apadāna*, a late canonical work.[2] While this text contains the first biographical accounts of these nuns, they are mentioned in earlier canonical literature, some of which relates incidents involving one nun or another, while others are verses apparently composed by them. One text that is a collection of verses, the *Therīgāthā*, is considered to have been the main source for the biographies, and contains a few narrative accounts of one or two other nuns.[3] The biographies next appear in the Pāli commentaries (*aṭṭhakathās*), the extant forms of which came into being between the fourth and sixth centuries CE, although they are based upon earlier, now lost, Sinhala works.[4]

Historically, in relation to Pāli biographies of Buddhist nuns, the evidence of the canon and commentaries have been taken together. The best early unerring example of this, and a precursor to what followed, is Caroline Rhys Davids' 1909 publication of the

[2] The *Apadāna* narratives are presented as autobiographies, that is, they are in the first person; however, I term them 'biography' throughout rather than 'autobiography' as there is little reason to assume they are autobiographical, not least because they are dated to a later period than the nuns whose stories they tell.

[3] I use *Therīgāthā* when I am referring to only the nuns' section, and *Thera-Therīgāthā* for the text overall.

[4] Although all these accounts are biographies, and therefore apparently based upon true life events, many of them have strong hagiographic features. In the case of Indian Buddhism, this manifests as from the 'outsider' perspective—concerns with past lives and magico-supernatural events and elements. These elements are imbricated into the drama of the biographies of the lives of early nuns.

Thera-Therīgāthā.[5] In this work, Caroline Rhys Davids prefaces her translation of each set of verses with a prose narrative on the life of the nun or monk to whom the verses are ascribed. She uses biographies from the commentary on the *Thera-Therīgāthā* to recount their stories. During the period in which Caroline Rhys Davids was writing, using commentaries to augment comprehension of the canon was vital. During this period of burgeoning studies of both Pāli and other forms of Buddhism, the early exemplary translators and scholars used whatever they could to advance their understanding of the Pāli canon, and we remain irrevocably indebted to them for their efforts. The first translator of the *Therīgāthā* into a European language—Neumann (1899), into German verse—did not utilize the commentaries to help him. Caroline Rhys Davids notes this, along with noting that it could be—for herself and her contemporaries—difficult to get hold of manuscripts of commentaries. Of Neumann's translation of the monks' ('Brothers') and nuns' ('Sisters') verses and his method, she writes:

> He translated without aid of any commentary on the Brothers' verses (a task bristling with difficulties), and with a 'thorough scepticism' as to the value of the commentarial chronicle about the Sisters. And in view of the shortness of life and the length of the literatures, there is no doubt much to justify immediate translation of what we have, instead of waiting, to enrich and improve our work, for materials that we have not yet. To what extent such materials as I wait for do enrich and improve, the educated reader of past, present and future translation must judge. (Rhys Davids [1909] 2000, xv)

Since Caroline Rhys Davids wrote these words, scholars have judged that the commentaries can and do improve comprehension of Buddhist canons, and of course this is, in essence, their

5 Caroline Augusta Foley Rhys Davids became a scholar of Buddhism prior to her marriage to T.W. Rhys Davids in 1894. The majority of her work was published subsequent to her marriage, so although in discussing her earlier publication in the Foreword, Jonathan Walters calls her by her maiden name of Foley, or Foley Rhys Davids when discussing her activities after her marriage, in the remainder of the book I will refer to her as Rhys Davids, as I will be discussing only works published after her marriage.

expressed raison d'être after all. However, the commentaries that contain the biographies of nuns—like most commentaries—were compiled centuries later. They are based upon earlier Sinhala commentaries, now lost, which were translated back into Pāli to be used for the extant commentaries. Thus, their geo-linguistic and historic milieu needs to be considered when assessing them. Rather than simple aids to comprehension of the earlier canon, the commentaries can be regarded as historical documents in their own right, born of another socio-historic milieu, and even though of a patchwork origin, still a rich source for the historian of religion.

Following Caroline Rhys Davids, two distinguished publications that discuss the biographies came out within eight years of one another: 1930 saw the publication of I.B. Horner's seminal work, *Women under Primitive Buddhism*, and some years later Malalasekera produced his *Dictionary of Pāli Proper Names* (1937), in which he offers brief biographical accounts of the named individuals who populate the Pāli literature. These two works followed Caroline Rhys Davids temporally and also mirrored her work methodologically. Horner begins the first of two chapters of her book devoted to the *Therīgāthā* with reference only to the verses in the work itself, but then moves seamlessly on to discuss Paṭācārā's biography, without acknowledging (in-text) that her evidence is from any other work ([1930] 1990, 173–4). A few pages on, she does more than this in relation to Uppalavaṇṇā, when she states that 'Uppalavaṇṇā ... did not marry ... because she had too many suitors' ([1930] 1990, 179). At times, Uppalavaṇṇā is portrayed as married, at other times not. However, in the *Therīgāthā* itself, contrary to Horner's comment, Uppalavaṇṇā's verses begin with the mention of the plight of her marital status.[6] Horner does sometimes differentiate between which texts say what; in her discussion of Khemā, for example, she notes differences between different versions of her story ([1930] 1990, 180), but then in the very next paragraph presents the later commentarial story about Dhammadinnā obtaining consent from her husband to join the Order as normative. But this is

[6] She is said to be a co-wife; see the discussion in Chapter 6, and for these verses, see page 70.

not specified in the *Therīgāthā* and is only one possible interpretation of her *Apadāna* account.

Taking the same example of Dhammadinnā to illustrate Malalasekera's method, Malalasekera again conflates the canonical and commentarial versions to produce an overarching narrative of Dhammadinnā. He reports that she was the wife of Visākha of Rājagaha, and when her husband

> ...having heard the Buddha preach, became an anāgamin, she left the world with the consent of her husband who sent her to the nunnery on a golden palanquin. (Malalasekera 1938, 1142)

While Malalasekera's version of Dhammadinnā's biography is not incorrect, he fails to note significant differences between canonical and commentarial accounts. Dhammadinnā's relationship with her husband does not feature centrally in canonical accounts of her. The canonical discourse that becomes the basis for her biography—the *Cūḷavedalla-sutta*—does not even mention that the interlocutor is her husband, and the *Apadāna* version of her biography only mentions him in one verse. In the canon, Dhammadinnā is portrayed as an illustrious teacher, whereas in the commentarial accounts she is first and foremost a subservient and sometimes disrespected wife, who renounces because she was rejected by her husband. The two characterizations of her could hardly be more different.

Subsequent to the (invaluable) works of these esteemed early scholars, this conflation of the evidence of the canon and commentaries in relation to the biographies continues. It is evident in Sharma's article, published in the 1970s, about how and why early Buddhist nuns decided to renounce. Further, Rita Gross (1993), in her popular and influential book of the 1990s, *Buddhism after Patriarchy*, uses Caroline Rhys Davids' translation of the canon and commentaries together, and does not differentiate between the texts. More recently, the same approach has been used in the Wisdom publication *Great Disciples of the Buddha: Their Lives, Their Works, Their Legacy*, which includes a chapter on nuns (Nyanaponika Thera and Hecker 2003), and in Kumkum Roy ([2003] 2010).

Part I of this book contains detailed versions of each biography, specifying variations in each textual (re)telling. The introduction to Part I offers a detailed survey of the texts for the general reader or student. In Part II of this book, rather than taking the accounts of the canon and commentaries as one, I attempt to differentiate between texts of—what I broadly define as—three periods: early canonical, late canonical, and commentarial (aṭṭhakathās).[7] The earlier and later canons are both north Indian in origin, with some parts of some of them perhaps dating back to the time of the historical Buddha. The commentaries are considered to have come into their extant form between the fourth and sixth centuries CE, in either Sri Lanka or south India. They are based upon earlier, now lost, Sinhala works, and attempts to differentiate which parts of which commentaries might be earlier, later, Sri Lankan, or south Indian are just beginning. With the state of play as it is, attempting to situate the Pāli texts historically, geographically, and temporally is indeed another task 'bristling with difficulty' and might elicit a 'thorough scepticism' from some. Nonetheless, dividing the texts in this way can enable us to grasp a clearer understanding of attitudes to women and how they differ between the Pāli canon and the commentaries. Overall, what I argue in this book is that the canon is more favourable towards women than the commentaries. Therefore attempts—such as those undertaken in the past—to assess the question of women in relation to the Pāli tradition that try to answer it by taking the canonical and commentarial accounts together, or by using the commentaries to augment the canon, dilute the evidence of the canon itself.

The structure of the book

The focus of the book is the biographies and an examination of themes and issues arising from them. Part I contains the biographies, retold with differences between different versions noted. Part I begins with an introduction to the texts used, and each section begins with a few short paragraphs on Pāli and other sources on the nun in question. Part II discusses themes, focusing on

7 I am also interested in authorial intention, in instances in which it is possible to discern an author (that is, with regards to some commentaries).

analyses of themes and issues in socio-religious and cultural contexts. I look at differences in relation to these themes and issues across Pāli texts and then, through comparative analysis with texts of other Buddhist schools, the evidence of archaeology and epigraphy, works of art, and the texts of Brahmanism and Jainism. My primary objective is to explore broader social history; so my focus is on a range of texts and sources, and not only texts composed for or with the monastic community in mind. Although women in ancient India is a topic that has received a great deal of scholarly attention—and continues to do so—there remain resources that have not yet been fully utilized in relation to this and other issues. Work on translation of the Chinese Buddhist canon continues in earnest, and Gregory Schopen and Shayne Clarke continue to produce excellent work on the Mūlasarvāstivāda *Vinaya* and women. The evidence of inscriptions in both India and Sri Lanka has never been fully unearthed for what it can tell us about women of the period—although again Schopen's work has been invaluable. Nonetheless, the sources we have to date can offer a rich tapestry to work with.

Summary of the chapters of part ii

Chapter 7

The theme in this chapter, exemplified and inspired by Dhammadinnā's biography, is female teachers and pupils. A survey of evidence reveals two threads running through the early tradition. On the one hand, in both texts and inscriptions, we find esteemed female teachers: teachers of other nuns, of individuals and groups, and of men and women alike. Also, the evidence of epigraphy points to situations not so envisioned in the extant texts. These are that individual teacher–disciple relationships existed between monks and nuns. On the other hand, in the formalized (Pāli) canon, we find records of more institutional and officially sanctioned teaching relationships between monks and nuns.

In this chapter, I document examples of both well-known and lesser-known female Buddhist teachers, analyse the evidence of inscriptions, and discuss the role of monk advisors to nuns. The extant Pāli canon is the most edited of the canons, and also the most formalized, and I engage with these aspects of it in this chapter.

Chapter 8

As the most salient feature of Khemā's biography is her obsession with her own appearance, this chapter focuses on female beauty. The notion of beauty discussed is circumscribed around the relationship between beauty and adornment. I argue that, rather than the *Thera-Therīgāthā* saying, as Lang (1986) has claimed previously, that women per se are the snare of Māra, it is in fact the adorned and ornamented body that is conceived of as that which entraps, and this body can be male or female, as men also adorned themselves in this historical milieu. As the preoccupation with bodily adornment can be seen, fully formed, on the earliest Indian sculptures, circa 150 BCE, it would appear that these social constructs were formulated before then. So, ironically, the *Thera-Therīgāthā* verses which talk of rejecting the adorned, sexualized body are some of the earliest attestations of this view. We see the same ideas in other early books of the canon, but much less so in the *Apadāna*. In the *Jātakatthavaṇṇanā*, in stories that were around in some nascent form prior to the Common Era—as evidenced by the stone reliefs and *stūpa* railing art—a similar interest in adornment and ornamentation is evident, although it is less present in other commentaries. Reconceptualizing craving for the female form as in fact desire for the ornamented and adorned body refigures these passages from the early canon as concerned not with women and their bodies in and of themselves, but with the doctrinally endorsed problem of sexual desire more broadly.

Chapter 9

This chapter looks at wandering women, as although Kisāgotamī's biography focuses on her life prior to ordination as a nun, she is distinguished as a wearer of coarse robes, and thereby as an accomplished renouncer. I assess the evidence for wandering women in the earliest texts, the question of whether women did, in fact, ever wander alone, and of the seemingly ever-present fear of sexual assault. As the question of sexual assault appears related to a not-yet-established social identity, I compare the position of nuns to that of other women who existed outside of the parameters of normative, domestic roles for women: courtesans and other prostitutes. While the early texts are concerned with the question of sexual assault on nuns, the *Apadāna* shows no similar concern, and neither do the commentaries. This suggests that prior to the *Apadāna*, the social identity of nuns was not yet fully formulated, such that as they did not clearly belong to any man they were considered sexually available. Courtesans (*gaṇikās*), like nuns, also undergo periods of more or less established social identity. In the early canon, courtesans are valued and no moral comment is passed on them. However, by the time of the *Apadāna*, life as a gaṇikā is proffered to have been caused by bad *kamma*.[8] In the earlier texts, gaṇikās are regarded positively and it is only other types of prostitutes who are considered lowly—and it is these sorts of low-grade prostitutes that nuns are likened to and made to bathe alongside. In the *Apadāna* it is the opposite; nuns are revered and prostitutes reviled. In the *Apadāna* all types of prostitutes come under fire, including gaṇikās, as the types are undifferentiated and the different words used as synonyms. The *Jātakatthavaṇṇanā* has views on gaṇikās similar to those in the earlier texts, but the *Dhammapada* commentary treats prostitutes in a much more misogynistic, or at least gynophobic, manner.

Chapter 10

This chapter focuses on social status, a discussion borne from Paṭācārā's decision to elope with an unsuitable man. Social class is conceptualized in the canon, the nuns' *Apadāna*, and the commentaries as focused around family (*kula*), as previously noted by Uma Chakravarti (1987). However, the authors/compilers of the monks' *Apadāna* appear to have attempted a manoeuvre away from social status circumscribed around family—which has its origins in Brahmanical ideology—positioning its protagonists

[8] Bad *kamma* (karma in Sanskrit) in this context refers to actions done in the past, that have consequences in the present.

within the Buddha-lineage of the twenty-four Buddhas instead. In relation to specific families, classes, or low occupations, in the historical memory of the nuns, few are said to hail from low-status families and none—with the possible exception of Paṭācārā—to marry those from socially excluded groups. Also found across the corpus of texts is that while women leave their husbands to go forth, they are never presented as abandoning a brahmin husband in favour of the Buddha—except on two occasions in which they follow either a husband or father into the Order—and the notable absence of this suggests it may have been considered taboo.

In this chapter, I also look at female agency with regard to marriage and women's prerogative to choose their own spouses, which is a feature of both Paṭācārā's biography, and that of Bhaddā Kuṇḍalakesā.

Chapter 11

The theme discussed in Chapter 11 is conversion. The conversion account of Bhaddā Kuṇḍalakesā changes significantly between the canonical and commentarial versions. Conversions of former Jains like Bhaddā Kuṇḍalakesā in the early canon are discussed alongside those of other renouncers (*samaṇī/samaṇa*).[9] Within both the later canon and the commentaries, as the notion of kammic trajectory becomes more prevalent there is less interest in conversion, which itself begs the question as to why then Bhaddā's conversion account varies as dramatically as it does. Whatever the reason for the variation, Bhaddā Kuṇḍalakesā's story appears to be connected to south India in a way none of the other biographies is. Bhaddā's story looks to have been the basis for a Tamil text—the now lost *Kuṇṭalakēci*. Just like the account of Bhaddā now extant in the commentaries, Tamil texts dated later than the commentaries present vibrant and robust female debaters of Buddhist and Jain doctrines, who mirror south Indian heroines more generally. The figure of Bhaddā Kuṇḍalakesā in the commentarial accounts seems to be a precursor to these.

9 A difficult term to translate; see the discussion on pages 189–90.

Chapter 12

In this final chapter, male and female characteristics are explored. In the canon, Uppalavaṇṇā is a model of all that a woman can achieve—she is a chief disciple and a shining example to others. In the commentaries, she maintains a positive standing, depicted in various ways to exemplify gentle and/or virtuous aspects of womanhood—as a caring mother, altruistic helper, benevolent goddess, and upholder of the teachings. The jealous wives that feature in some of the commentarial biographies of Uppalavaṇṇā exemplify the worst attributes of women. Initially met with in the later canonical *Petavatthu*, types of jealous and scheming women who plot the downfall of others can end up, according to the *Petavatthu*, as horrifying ghouls who devour the flesh of children. In this chapter, I compare these depictions of female characteristics with those of men, and conclude that the canon and commentaries provide us with examples of the best and worst of both men and women. Men and women, at their best, can both be exemplars on the path, and have the ability to teach others. Across the texts, but caricatured more in texts with folkloric elements, the worst women can be are manipulative and jealous, while the most ignoble of men are idiotic, aggressive, or greedy for wealth.

Readership

Part I of the book is aimed at the student, general reader, and/or Buddhist practitioner, anyone who has not had access to these biographies previously. My retellings of the biographies are more detailed than previous attempts, and the detail provides the foundation for the thematic discussions in Part II. In addition to the detailed retellings, Part I contains an introduction to the texts that are the sources for the biographies. There is also a section following the introduction which delineates the problematic task of reading the biographies. This section, entitled 'Problems with Texts', examines the extent to which it is possible for us to say—with any degree of certainty—that the extant biographies bear any resemblance to the actual life of any historical figure they purport to be based upon and, second, raises the question of whether these nuns, who have become firm fixtures within the manuscript/textual tradition, were indeed historical figures at all.

Part II of the book is a discussion of themes from the biographical accounts. It is aimed at the same readership as Part I, but may also be of interest to academics. In this section, the themes outlined above are explored in more detail, with the central aim of demonstrating the differences between canonical and commentarial accounts. The canon as it stands offers a rare insight into the position of women in ancient India, and there is a great deal in it that is very positive about women, which is noteworthy for a textual corpus from a traditional society. As the commentaries are more negative about women, and the transmission of the canon was for centuries in the hands of the commentators, scribes, redactors, and their contemporaries, it is crucial to note that the Pāli canon as we have it is visible only through the lens of such agents. Horner, writing some eighty years ago, with her extensive and comprehensive knowledge of the Pāli corpus, speculates:

> In the first place, the texts were written down later than the events they purport to record. In the interval much concerning the lives of women may have been forgotten ... and the task of repeating the material to the monks for incorporation into the texts which they were editing would fall mainly, if not entirely, to men. They would tend to remember chiefly events and customs concerning themselves, and let those concerning their women-folk fall into oblivion. ([1930] 1990, 61)

As we now know, things are not quite as simple as this, and indeed the preservers of the tradition may well have unwittingly let much 'fall into oblivion', on men and women alike. And, of course, not everything on women was relegated or tossed to the wayside; if that were the case, neither Horner nor I would have a book to write. However, it remains interesting to consider how things might have come down to us if the world of the commentators had been otherwise.

Part one

Pāli biographies

Introduction

Introduction to the texts

The canon

The *Therīgāthā* and *Apadāna* are the basis and beginning of the biographical tradition that records and recounts lives of female disciples, and although these are part of what is sometimes considered the more minor collection within the Pāli canon, their value to the historian of religion is far from inconsequential. These works prove crucial in providing insights into the potential lives of women in early Indian Buddhism. And that we have these records at all might be considered a stroke of good fortune.

The Pāli canon consists of five collections, or sections, called *nikāyas* in Pāli and *āgamas* in other traditions. These are:

Dīgha-nikāya	The collection of long discourses
Majjhima-nikāya	The collection of middle-length discourses
Saṃyutta-nikāya	The collection of connected discourses
Aṅguttara-nikāya	The collection of numerical discourses
Khuddaka-nikāya	The collection of miscellaneous discourses

The *Therīgāthā* and the *Apadāna* are part of the *Khuddaka-nikāya*, and although the formulators and preservers of the Pāli canon decided to rank the *Khuddaka-nikāya* as canonical, this was not the decision of the formulators and preservers of other Buddhist canons. In extant Chinese works, only the first four āgamas are preserved—the *Dīrgha*, *Madhyama*, *Saṃyukta*, and *Ekottarika*.[1] In the Sanskrit canon of the Sarvāstivādin tradition, the evidence and information from the *Kṣudraka-āgama* is utilized and referenced in the other four āgamas, as if the side-lined *Kṣudraka* had once been considered canonical in some way or other. Given the precarious position of the *Kṣudraka-āgama* in other traditions, it may come as no surprise to know that there are, unfortunately, no extant parallels to the Pāli *Therīgāthā*.[2] Neither are there any direct parallels to the *Apadāna*, although the genre—*apadāna*[3] in Pāli and *avadāna* in Sanskrit—branched out in its own right in texts connected to other traditions and flowered into a full and rich genre.[4]

[1] The fourth of these has a different name in Pāli—*Aṅguttara* in Pāli, *Ekottarika* in other traditions. The slightly different spellings above are the Sanskrit spellings.

[2] There are extant fragments of a *Sthaviragāthā* transcribed and discussed by Bechert (1958a). See also Anālayo (2010c, 75n40) for some mentions of *Therīgāthā* parallels. Further, the text is mentioned in lists of what constitute the *Kṣudraka* that belong to other traditions (see Lamotte [1958] 1976, 177–8).

[3] Although there obviously exists a Buddhist genre of apādana/avadāna literature, attempting to assess the parameters and boundaries of it has been, and continues to be, a matter of debate. Part of the problem is to do with whether the term 'apādana'/ 'avadāna' is or has been used with an intention to indicate actual historical events (and so should be seen as biographies or autobiographies) or more fictitious stories of heroic deeds.

[4] Salomon's publication (2008) of Gāndhārī fragments of an *Anavataptagāthā* includes reference to some parallels with three apadānas from the monks' *Apadāna* (*Therāpadāna*). However, Salomon does not suggest that this is an indication of a parallel to the *Apadāna* but instead, following Bechert, that in two cases it appears the *Apadāna* has borrowed from an *Anavataptagāthā*, and in the third case the direction of borrowing is less clear, and the two might be borrowed from a 'common but unknown source' (Salomon 2008, 29).

Dating the texts of the Pāli canon is notoriously difficult, and remains a subject of controversy. According to intra-traditional accounts the canon was 'closed' to additions in the first century BCE, but within modern scholarship there is a spectrum of responses to this. One end of the spectrum would be Schopen's ([1985] 1997, 23–4) assertion, some time ago, that it is not possible to know anything definite about the Pāli canon prior to the time the extant commentaries were compiled, as the commentaries delineate the form of the canon when they reproduce it to comment upon it. Alternate to that is the view of Anālayo in an article that criticizes Schopen, in which he concludes that it 'seems ... reasonable to consider the Pāli discourses as fairly closed, in doctrinal terms, by the 1st century BCE ...' (2012, 246).[5] My own view is that the Pāli canon consists of layered texts, such that some parts or sections of each text are earlier and others later. As an example of this, scholars such as Witzel (1997) and Quintanilla have used archaeological evidence to assess the way towns and cities are conceptualized in the Pāli canon.[6] For example, Quintanilla notes that although Mathura is recognized in Buddhist literature as an important city, archaeological excavations reveal that it 'did not emerge as a cultural and economic center until the third century BCE at the earliest', and that prior to that it was 'a hamlet of little consequence' (2007, 1). The evidence of such excavations does certainly demonstrate that in relation to particular locations such as Mathura, the sections and passages of text on them in the extant canon can be dated to later periods—but it does not necessarily follow that any entire *sutta* that then ensues should be called into question.[7] Schopen, elsewhere (2004, 194–208),

5 In this article, Anālayo reassesses the story of the *stūpa* of Buddha Kaśyapa that Schopen uses as the basis for some of his assertions.

6 According to Witzel, in relation to the Videha area, the Pāli texts 'describe the area as characterized by the fully developed town civilization (represented by the archaeologically attested culture of a luxury pottery, the Northern Black Polished Ware, NBP)' (1997, 311).

7 This is not what Quintanilla herself is arguing, but can be adduced also from the textual prescriptions from other traditions about what to do if memory fails and you cannot recall a setting for a sutta, and so on (Schopen [1997] 2004, 395–407).

demonstrates that the frame-story for a Pāli *Vinaya* account on monastic ownership of servants and slaves is likely Sri Lankan in origin. He argues this in part on the basis that it seems that the preamble is concerned with the clearing out of a natural cave, and there is more evidence of this in ancient Sri Lanka than India.[8] However, evidence such as this—identifying a frame-story as late—does not itself necessitate that an entire episode/account is late.[9]

Dating the *Thera-Therīgāthā* is as problematic as dating the rest of the canon, although attempts have been made to do so in the past. Many of these attempts demonstrate that the text is composite, coming into its extant form over a long period. Lienhard's contextualization argument (1984) exemplifies this. Setting the poems within the overall context of the development of classical Indian poetry, Lienhard argues that at least some parts of some poems are old, and thereby should be considered to be some of the earliest examples of single stanza poems in existence. Similarly, in his survey of Pāli metre, Warder (1967) concludes that the text developed over a long period, as it includes a range of different metres. Concurrently, in his discussion of the date of the text, Norman ([1969/1971] 2007) examines different bases for assessment, including following the commentary, which states that, for example, the verses of Vītasoka and Ekavihāriya are late, as these two were brothers of King Asoka, who lived some centuries after the time of the Buddha.

The *Apadāna*, by contrast, is later, likely dating to the post-Asokan period (Walters 1997). Unlike the *Therīgāthā*, which has been a focus for the study of women in Indian Buddhism, the *Apadāna* has received relatively little attention. In fact, it has not even been translated in full into any European language yet.[10] There

8 If this is indeed what *pabbhāraṃ sodhāpeti leṇaṃ katthukāmo* means in this context (2004, 197).

9 Again, this is my interpretation of the Sri Lankan frame for the account, and is not what Schopen himself is arguing.

10 Most of one recension of the nuns' *Apadāna* has been available in English translation for some time, as it is included in Dhammpāla's commentary on the *Therīgāthā*, translated into English by Pruitt in 1999. At the time of writing, Jonathan Walters is completing his full translation of the text—which is to be available at www.whitman.edu/penrose.

are three known recensions of the *Apadāna*, that is, versions of it (von Hinüber 1996, 61). First, there is an apparently complete version, although as Walters (2013) notes, the Pali Text Society's (PTS) edition and the Buddha Jayanti Tripiṭaka Sinhala edition differ somewhat, not least in that they do not have the same number of monks' apadānas. A different recension of the monks' and nuns' *Apadāna* appears in the extant Pāli commentary to the *Thera-Therīgāthā*, although this seems to have been added to the commentary at a subsequent time, as noted by Norman (1983, 135). The third recension has been used in a commentarial text, the *Paramatthajotikā* (Bechert 1958b, 18).

The relationship between the *Thera-Therīgāthā* and *Apadāna* has been commented upon by several scholars. Warder, for example, suggests that the biographies of the monks in the *Apadāna* are 'almost a commentary on the *Theragāthā*'.[11] Bechert (1958, 14) delineates the *Apadāna* collection as 'pre-birth stories' of the monks and nuns of the *Thera-Therīgāthā*. Von Hinüber (1996, 61) calls the *Apadāna* 'a supplement' to the *Thera-Therīgāthā*, while Norman suggests it is 'almost an appendix to the *Therīgāthā* and *Therāgāthā*, since it connects together the past and present lives of the *theras* and *therīs*' (1983, 89). Evidently, there is a close connection between the two texts, although it is not the case that all the same monks and nuns appear in both, as Norman notes:

> [The *Apadāna*] ... includes many *theras* [monks] who do not appear in the *Theragāthā*, and does not include all the *therīs* [nuns] who are in the *Therīgāthā*. On the other hand, there is an *Apadāna* for Yasodharā, although there is no poem for her in the *Therīgāthā*. (1983, 90)

The issue of the *Apadāna*'s relationship to a female lay audience has been raised by Jonathan Walters. Walters argues that, in the post-Asokan world when Buddhism was flourishing in north India, the existing tradition that was primarily renunciate began to change:

> The early paradigms—saints who renounce the world and attain *nirvāṇa*—were not immediately appropriate for the bulk of society newly included within Buddhism's post-Aśokan universal embrace,

[11] Introduction to Bhikkhu Ñāṇamoli's translation of *The Path of Discrimination* (1982, xxxviii), translated by A.K. Warder.

> who would not renounce the world in the present life but would instead continue to produce karma and, consequently, future existence. The early paradigms seemed relevant only to those near the end of the path, who were already putting an end to karma and rebirth; how did they apply to common people who would remain in the world of attachments, unwilling to leave it? The answer demonstrates a remarkable logic: if biographies of the Buddha and his monks and nuns in this life provide models of and for the end of the path, then biographies of their previous lives, the stories of what they did when they too were commoners, should provide models of and for a person at the beginning of the path. This insight of the second and third centuries B.C.E. stimulated the composition of the Apadāna stories, which focus on the previous lives of the monks and nuns in light of their present achievements. (Walters 1995, 113–14)

More recently, Walters (2013) has proffered a convincing argument for female authorship of the nuns' *Apadāna*. If Walters is correct, this indicates an interesting scenario in which biographical accounts of early disciple nuns were themselves composed by women, which then became enshrined into the tradition as part of the canon and then, from that sacrosanct position, were furthered, and sometimes augmented, by the later male commentators.

The commentaries

Fairly early on, a commentarial tradition developed in relation to the Buddhist canon within which new texts were written as exegesis on the canonical works. The main Pāli commentaries are the aṭṭhakathās and the *ṭīkās* (sub-commentaries). In this volume I focus on the aṭṭhakathās, the extant versions of which belong to the Mahāvihārin tradition of Sri Lanka, but some parts of some of them, at least, are Indian in origin, and were transmitted along with the canon to Sri Lanka. The commentaries that are the focus in this volume are the ones that contain the biographies of the nuns, and are as follows:

Aṅguttara-nikāya commentary
Therīgāthā commentary
Dhammapada commentary[12]

[12] The *Dhammapada* is another text of the *Khuddaka-nikāya*.

Other commentaries are made use of as well, as is the *Jātakatthavaṇṇanā*. The *Jātakatthavaṇṇanā* has an unusual place within the textual schema, as some parts of it are considered canonical and others not.[13] In general, all these commentarial works (except the *Jātakatthavaṇṇanā*.) are word-by-word or phrase-by-phrase exegesis of the canonical texts. Some of the exegeses are hyper-short, being just one synonym of the word or phrase in question, and sometimes appear virtually redundant. In other places, the exegesis is several words long, including both synonyms and rephrasing, such as in the exegesis on the nun Sīhā's verses, which tells us that the phrase 'afflicted by desire for sensual pleasures' means 'oppressed by passion and desire through the strands of sensual pleasures'.[14] Further, a paragraph-length exegesis of a word can be proffered, such as in the explanation of the beautiful woman who speaks to Nanda, the (half-) brother to the Buddha, as he leaves to become a monk. The explanation of the word used to describe this woman—*janapadakalyāṇī*, 'the most beautiful in the region'—goes into some detail as to the nature and manner of the woman's earthly charms, an extract from which tells us she was

> ... supreme in beauty, lacking in the six blemishes of body, endowed with the five beauties. She is not too tall, not too short, not too thin, not too fat, not too dark, not too pale.... She is endowed with the five beauties; beauty of skin, beauty of flesh, beauty of nails, beauty of bone, and beauty of youth.... Her four hands and feet and her lips, as if they had been prepared with the essence of lac, were like red coral or red woollen cloth. That was her beauty of flesh...[15]

[13] For more on the *JA*, see Appleton (2009) and Anālayo (2009).

[14] *Thī* (v. 77) *kāmarāgena aṭṭitā, Thī-a* (78) *kāmaguṇesu chandarāgena pīḷitā.*

[15] *...rupena uttamā cha-sarīra-dosa-rahitā pañca-kalyāṇa-samannāgatā. Sā hi yasmā nātidīgha nātirassa nātikisā nātithūlā nātikāḷī nāccodātā... chavi-kalyāṇaṃ maṃsa-kalyāṇaṃ nakha-kalyāṇaṃ aṭṭhi-kalyāṇaṃ vaya-kalyāṇaṃ ti imehi pañcahi kalyāṇehi samannāgatā... Cattāro pan' assā hattha-pādāmukha-pariyosānañcalākhā-rasa-parikamma-kulāviyaratta-pavāḷa-ratta-kambalena sadisā honti. Ayam assā maṃsa-kalyāṇatā* (*Ud-a* 170). All translations are my own unless otherwise stated. Many of the texts studied in this volume have been translated previously, and in creating

The word-by-word (or phrase-by-phrase) exegesis can be difficult to comprehend, such that early scholars who published Pāli editions of the commentaries, such as Rhys Davids and Estlin Carpenter, note that they feel at a loss because they do not fully comprehend the commentator's exegetical method. Of the commentator Buddhaghosa, they write, 'we are in constant want of Buddhaghosa's learning to help us to understand the exact meaning of what is said' (*Sumaṅgalavilāsinī* [1886] 1968, vii).

Further to this, the commentarial explanations can include narratives to make their point. This happens, for instance, in the commentary to Uppalavaṇṇā's verses in the *Therīgāthā* commentary (see the following sections and Chapters 6 and 12). Here, a narrative account about relatives of a monk, Gaṅgātīriya, is included to explain why Uppalavaṇṇā's verses are the way that they are. Also, biographical accounts of monks, nuns, laymen, and laywomen can form a major part of a commentary. This happens particularly in commentary on verses attributed to a monk or nun, or as exegesis of those listed as distinguished monks, nuns, laymen, and laywomen (such as in the commentary on the *Aṅguttaranikāya*, which includes such a list). Further, narrative tales can be given as explanations of canonical verses. This is the essence of what the *Jātakatthavaṇṇanā* and the *Dhammapada* commentary are in their extant form. In the *Dhammapada* commentary, there is word-by-word exegesis as well, but this forms only a small portion of the extant text, and the narratives that make up the majority of the commentary come sequentially prior to it in each chapter, with the exegesis tagged at the end.

A few early commentaries appear to have been brought to Sri Lanka along with the canon, and this is confirmed by a Sri Lankan Buddhist chronicle, the *Mahāvaṃsa*.[16] Some of them, such as the commentary on the *Vinaya*, became embedded into the text early and were transmitted alongside the canonical work. New

---

my translations I have often had recourse to the published translations of Horner, Norman, Bodhi, Bode, C.A.F. Rhys Davids, Pruitt, and other accomplished translators.

[16] See Malalasekera for a discussion of this issue ([1928] 1994).

commentaries were also written in Sinhala, and these form the basis of the aṭṭhakathās now extant in Pāli, although the Sinhala versions are no longer extant. Many of the compilations of the extant versions of the aṭṭhakathās are attributed to Buddhaghosa and Dhammapāla, although some of these attributions appear spurious. Buddhaghosa, who notes the names of many of these Sinhala works he based his commentaries upon, is considered to have lived in the fourth or fifth century, while Dhammapāla lived some time later, in the sixth century (Norman 1983, 130 and 137; von Hinüber 1996, 102–3 and 169). Thus, the extant Pāli commentaries, while based upon earlier content, are dated to these periods in their current form. However, examining the content, Mori (1989, 5) argues that

> ... all the datable Sri Lankans appearing in the Commentaries are restricted, with a very few exceptions, to those who were active in the period between the reign of King Devānampiyatissa (reigning: BC 250–210) ... and that of King Vasabha (65–109).

And he adds ([1988] 1989, 99):

> ... in the reign of Mahāsena (AD 276–303) the formulation of the sources ceases entirely; after that time nothing was added to them; and they were well preserved until the time when the Pāli commentators wrote their Aṭṭhakathā texts based upon those sources in the fifth to sixth centuries or thereabouts. Consequently the real and substantial date of the Aṭṭhakathā texts should be regarded not as the date of the writing of the texts, but as the date of their source material.

While it is the case that the source material for the aṭṭhakathās is earlier than their time of codification, it remains important to keep in mind authorial intention (or perhaps we should say in this case 'compiler intention'). As Norman has noted in regard to Buddhaghosa, and other Pāli commentators, they 'do sometimes state they are giving their own opinion about things' (1983, 125). As well as proffering one's own view explicitly, there can also be unintentional eliding, omission, or changes made based upon one's own predilections, and this is especially evident in that certain of the aṭṭhakathās are less favourably disposed to women than others. It is in the *Jātakatthavaṇṇanā* and *Dhammapada* commentaries, for instance, that we find particularly negative views on women, for which there is little canonical precedent.[17] This can be brought into sharp focus if we compare the *Jātakatthavaṇṇanā* with the earlier canonical *Cariyapiṭaka*, two works which share content, but the former of which displays much less negatively towards women.

Problems with texts

Issues with the Pāli accounts

The biographies that we have come down to us via an oral and then textual/manuscript tradition. If any part of any of them can be sourced from an actual historical nun, who was a direct disciple of the Buddha, then her story would have been retold orally and informally by generations of Buddhists in north India, until it become part of the *Apadāna* (if it did), at which point it became part of a corpus that was remembered and transmitted formally, in group recitation, until the Pāli canon was committed to writing. Once written, the canon forms the basis of a manuscript culture, whereby manuscripts are used, then copied when they age, and (ritually) discarded. During this preservation and transmission process, the biographies change. An account of one nun might become associated with another, may be lost, misconstrued, reformulated, relegated as less important, or lauded as an exemplary example of a moot doctrinal point. In this section, I illustrate some of these issues in relation to Pāli accounts of Paṭācārā.

These verses begin a section of the *Therīgāthā* devoted to Paṭācārā:

> Ploughing the field with ploughs, sowing seeds in the ground, nourishing wives and children, young brahmins find wealth.
>
> Why do I, possessed of virtuous conduct, complying with the teachings of the teacher, not obtain *nibbāna*? I am not lazy, nor proud.
>
> I washed my feet in the water and paid attention, observing the water for the feet flowing from the high to the low ground.

17 Von Hinüber argues that these two texts are related, and that 'an old independent *Dhp*-commentarial tradition has been modernized under the influence of the *Jātakatthavaṇṇanā*-commentary, when the 'new' *Dhp-a* was created' (1996, 134).

> Then I concentrated my mind, like an experienced, well-trained horse. I took a lamp, and entered my cell. I inspected the bed and sat on the couch.
>
> Then I took a needle and drew out the wick. The liberation of my mind was like the extinguishing of the lamp.[18]

Immediately following these verses are verses attributed to thirty nuns who pay homage to her. These recount that the thirty nuns heard her teachings and, as a result of Paṭācārā's teaching, made great progress. In the words of the nuns themselves, addressed to Paṭācārā, the text reads: 'We have taken your advice, we shall dwell honoring you like thirty gods honoring Indra...'[19] Immediately following these verses are verses attributed to Candā, a widow prior to her renunciation. Candā recounts that, as a result of Paṭācārā's teaching and encouragement, she was able to attain knowledge and insight and become one without defilements. Then come verses related to five hundred female disciples of Paṭācārā. In these verses, Paṭācārā speaks to the five hundred, who are understood to be mothers who have lost children. She offers them a teaching on the pointlessness of grief, setting loss within the context of Buddhist doctrine. Skilled teacher that she was, her words again struck a chord with her audience, and the responding verses attributed to the five hundred women rejoice in her ability to 'pluck out the dart' (*abbūḷhasalla*) in their hearts and minds. Later on, as well, Paṭācārā is mentioned in the verses of Uttarā (see v. 178), in which Uttarā recalls how she took Paṭācārā's advice. These verses in which other women and nuns pay homage to Paṭācārā, worship at her feet, take her advice, and are led to Awakening by her inspiration, make

[18] *Naṅgalehi kasaṃ khettaṃ bījāni pavapaṃ chamā, puttadārāni posentā dhanaṃ vindanti mānavā. Kiṃ ahaṃ sīlasampannā satthu sāsanakārikā, nibbānaṃ nādhigacchāmi akusītā anuddhaṭā. Pāde pakkhālayitvāna udake su karom' ahaṃ, pādodakañ ca disvāna thalato ninnam āgataṃ, tato cittaṃ samādhemi assaṃ bhadraṃ va jāniyaṃ. Tato dīpaṃ gahetvāna vihāraṃ pāvisiṃ aham, seyyaṃ olokayitvāna mañcakamhi upāvisiṃ. Tato sūcīṃ gahetvāna vaṭṭiṃ okassayām' ahaṃ, padīpasseva nibbānaṃ vimokkho ahu cetaso* (*Thī* vv. 112–16).

[19] *...katā te anusāsanī, indaṃ va devā tidasā...purakkhitvā vihissāma...* (*Thī* v. 121).

Paṭācārā the most prominent nun in the extant *Therīgāthā* in terms of her influence over others. However, there are issues with the extant *Therīgāthā* and the account of Paṭācārā's life within.

Immediately following the section in the *Therīgāthā* in which she features are verses attributed to Vāsiṭṭhī (vv. 133–8), a little-known nun, not well attested to in other literature. These verses attributed to Vāsiṭṭhī, more so than those attributed to Paṭācārā, appear as a potential nucleus for the life story that becomes Paṭācārā's. Vāsiṭṭhī's first two verses are as follows:

> Afflicted by grief for my son(s), with mind deranged, out of my senses, naked, and with disheveled hair, I wandered here and there.
> I dwelt on rubbish heaps, in the street, in a cemetery, and on highways, I wandered for three years, consigned to hunger and thirst.[20]

These verses of Vāsiṭṭhī resonate with Paṭācārā's biography. First, the affliction of grief suffered by Vāsiṭṭhī accords with the detail told of Paṭācārā in the commentaries at the loss of so many close relatives. Vāsiṭṭhī is described as a woman so distraught by her grief that she wanders naked, dirty, and dishevelled. This is just how Paṭācārā is described in the accounts of her in the later commentarial works, where she roams unclothed with a naked anguish, borne from intense grief. Because she wandered without clothing, the *Therīgāthā* commentary reports she was given the name Paṭācārā—'one who does not wander (*acaraṇato*) with a cloth (*paṭena*)'. The *Aṅguttaranikāya* commentary also records this as one reason, although not the only one, that she is given this name. Thus, the name Paṭācārā could indicate what came to be a central feature of her biography, rather than being the name of the protagonist.[21] There are many other examples of this in the *Apadāna*, for example, the biography of Ekāsanadāyikā (*Ap.* 525–6), whose name means 'the one who

[20] *Puttasoken' ahaṃ aṭṭā khittacittā visaññinī, naggā pakiṇṇakesī ca tena tena vicari 'haṃ. Vīthisaṅkārakūṭesu susāne rathiyāsu ca, acariṃ tīṇi vassāni khuppipāsāsamappitā* (*Thī* vv. 133–4).

[21] A pivotal relationship between a person's name and keywords in a narrative has been established as an aspect of the transmission process from early manuscript fragments. Waldschmidt has demonstrated, using the evidence of manuscript fragments from central Asia, that colophons

gives a single seat', recounts the merit the protagonist gains from having spread out a seat with a woollen cover for a recluse to rest upon. The verses attributed to Ekāsanadāyikā are recorded as those of the nun Ubbirī in the *Therīgāthā* commentary (52ff.).[22]

Vāsiṭṭhī is not, to my knowledge, known outside the *Therīgāthā*, apart from a brief mention of a woman called Vāsiṭṭhī in a narrative story (*jātaka*), which may or may not be the same person. She appears again, in an ambiguous setting later on in the *Therīgāthā*, in verses attributed to Sundarī (*Thī* vv. 312–37). In these verses, as with those above, Vāsiṭṭhī is linked with grief over the loss of children, in this case with the death of seven children. Another nun whose biography concerns grief, and is perhaps the best known of the Pāli biographies on grief, is Kisāgotamī, whose biography is narrated later and is the subject of Chapter 3. As discussed in Chapter 3, in the *Apadāna*, the *Aṅguttara-nikāya* commentary, and the *Therīgāthā* commentary Kisāgotamī's story arc remains relatively static and is the memorable story of the mustard seed. Kisāgotamī is distraught at the loss of her son, and goes to see the Buddha who skillfully asks her to get him a mustard seed from any home that has not experienced death, thereby teaching her about the impermanence of life and inevitability of death.

Kisāgotamī's story is well known, and may well have been in circulation prior to its mention in the *Therīgāthā*.[23] However, an oddity in relation to Kisāgotamī's verses in the *Therīgāthā* is

---

attached to texts can either contain the names of protagonists or keywords central to the story, or a mixture of both (1980, 136ff.).

[22] Similarly, the biography of Pañcadīpadāyikā (*Ap*. 527–8), 'one who gives five lamps', concerns just this very activity again, her making an offering of five lamps. In the *Therīgāthā* commentary the same verses are attributed to Selā (vv. 60–2).

[23] Kisāgotamī's story is referred to in the *bhikkhunīsaṃyutta* of the *SN* (I.129–30). In the section on Kisāgotamī, Māra approaches her and attempts to distract her. He asks her why, now that her son is dead, she sits alone with a tearful face. He further asks her if she has come to the woods alone because she is on the lookout for a man. Note that her interlocutor does not mention a deceased husband, reference to whom would surely be a better prelude to the question 'are you here searching for a new man?'

that some of them also, as is possible with Vāsiṭṭhī's verses, tell Paṭācārā's story. Four of Kisāgotamī's verses, spoken in the first person, quite clearly relate the story that has become Paṭācārā's. The initial five verses are unproblematic and while they do not directly recount the mustard seed story they relate to the story in that the words appear to reveal the ruminations of someone who has had the personal experiences that we associate with Kisāgotamī. This exemplifies a typical relationship between the *Therīgāthā* verses and the *Apadāna* narratives. Sometimes *Therīgāthā* verses tell the story, or aspects of the story, found in the *Apadāna*, but at other times there is this more thematic relationship. Kisāgotamī's verses can be found below (pages 41–2.). If we analyse Kisāgotamī's verses in relation to her biography, we can see that in the mustard seed story Kisāgotamī is indeed affected by 'the good friend' (the Buddha), and is herself released from pain by his wisdom. And this is how Dhammapāla glosses the first two verses in the *Therīgāthā* commentary, as her acknowledgement and gratitude for that. Thus the first three verses fit well with her story, as do verses 216 and 217, which lament the suffering endured by wives and mothers. Verses 218–21, however, are not her story but that which became Paṭācārā's. By the time Dhammapāla wrote the *Therīgāthā* commentary, it would appear that the two stories of the two nuns were fixed as they are now, as Dhammapāla attempts to gloss this section accordingly. First, rather than Kisāgotamī lamenting the state of women, in the commentary verses 216 and 217 are said to be uttered by a *yakkhinī* (demoness), who was finding fault with the state of being a woman. Next, Dhammapāla glosses verses 218 and 219 as Kisāgotamī talking with reference to Paṭācārā—even though these two verses are spoken in the first person, as if Kisāgotamī has momentarily become Paṭācārā. Although it is not uncommon to speak of oneself in the third person in the *Therīgāthā*, it is uncommon to speak as if one were another. Then, according to the commentary, in verses 220 and 221 the voice reverts back to being Kisāgotamī's, although there is a further mention of a 'family annihilated' and a 'dead husband', thus further referencing Paṭācārā's story rather than Kisāgotamī's. Dhammapāla's gloss, therefore, is not a convincing one. The most likely explanation for this confused placement of verses is that these verses are no longer in their original place and that they were initially in a section of the *Therīgāthā* on Paṭācārā. To draw a conclusion such as this accords with much of our current understanding of the process of oral and textual transmission.[24]

Turning now to one final point, on the number and authorship of verses. First, there is the question of the number of verses that should make up the *Therīgāthā*. According to three of the manuscripts used by Pischel to create the Pali Text Society (PTS) edition of the *Therīgāthā*, there should be 494 verses, spoken by 101 nuns in total ([1883] 1999, 121). Of these three manuscripts, only one is dated, with a date corresponding to the eighteenth century.[25] The extant text has 522 verses, which does not correspond to the transmitted number, but again this is nothing surprising, given what we know from early manuscripts. However (and perhaps this is more surprising), Pischel finds a way to align the number of 101 nuns to the number of nuns who 'speak' in the *Therīgāthā*. And here again we find ourselves back with verses related to Paṭācārā. Pischel notes that if the verses said to have been spoken by the 500 mothers are instead ascribed to Paṭācārā herself, then the extant text includes exactly the voices of 101 nuns. This again suggests some issues with the *Therīgāthā* verses associated with Paṭācārā.

24 The evidence from early manuscripts is that different versions of the same text can have verses in varying order or verses found in one chapter in one version and another chapter in another. As just one example of this, in his study of the Gāndhārī *Dharmapada*, which he compares with other *Dharmapadas* and 'Dharmapada-type texts', Lenz notes that although there is considerable overlap in the verses included in the various versions, 'the ordering and arrangement of verses are often considerably different'. He provides an example of two versions of the chapter on the Buddha, or Tathāgata, each of which contains 18 verses 'but have only one [verse] in common' (Lenz 2003, 13).

25 The Sakkarāj date is 1128, to which if 638 is added makes the date of the manuscript 1766.

1

Dhammadinnā

Summary of Pāli sources

The nuns whose biographies form the basis of this book are well known from the early literature, and Dhammadinnā is perhaps one of the best known. The most important Pāli source on Dhammadinnā is a sutta from the *Majjhima-nikāya*—the *Cūḷavedalla-sutta*. In this sutta, Dhammadinnā answers questions put to her by a lay follower, Visākha. She answers all of these questions on aspects of the Buddha's *dhamma* (teachings) fully and clearly and with some finesse. At the end of the sutta Visākha goes to the Buddha to report the conversation, and the Buddha says he would have answered just as Dhammadinnā did, thus sanctioning and endorsing her teaching. Dhammadinnā's skill in this regard is also noted on the canonical list of distinguished nuns, in which she is recorded as foremost of all (female) *dhammakathikā*, those who 'speak well on dhamma'. However, neither Dhammadinnā nor her reputation as a dhammakathikā is mentioned much more in the early literature.[1] If, for example, we compare the number of

[1] Dhammadinnā also does not appear in *JA*.

times Paṭācārā (see the earlier discussion on pp. 12–17 and see Chapters 4 and 10) is mentioned in the *Therīgāthā* as a teacher of other women, or as one from whom they seek advice and guidance, we can see there is a lack here in relation to Dhammadinnā, as she is not mentioned in the *Therīgāthā* in such a role. In the *Therīgāthā* she has only one verse attributed to her, which is much fewer than the other nuns that make up this volume. There is a biography of her in the *Apadāna*, but again this is fairly short, and does not champion her skills as a dhammakathikā as fully as it could. What came to be the biography associated with her in the commentaries, seemingly based on the *Apadāna* but expanding and dramatizing the role of her husband, appears in the *Therīgāthā* commentary, the *Aṅguttara-nikāya* commentary, the *Dhammapada* commentary, and the *Majjhima-nikāya* commentary. In these instances, in the commentaries, we see her innate skill repositioned somewhat as either significantly impacted by her husband or, in one instance, instigated by the Buddha's (divine) intervention.

Summary of other sources

Dhammadinnā appears more in the literature of other traditions than the Pāli literature, and seems to be more revered as well in the other traditions. She does not feature in the Pāli *Vinaya*, but does in the *vinayas* (monastic codes) of other traditions. In the Chinese vinaya of the Mūlasarvāstivāda, and a later commentary on it, she is said to be ordained by a messenger (Heirman 2001, 298–9). Heirman also notes that in the Mahāsāṃghika *Vinaya* a disciple of Dhammadinnā is said to receive ordination via a messenger. In the Tibetan version of the Mūlasarvāstivāda *Vinaya* (Finnegan 2009, 157ff.) Dhammadinnā is instead ordained by Uppalavaṇṇā (see Chapters 6 and 12 for more on Uppalavaṇṇā). In both these cases, this unusual ordination is agreed upon by the Buddha in order that Dhammadinnā does not have to be married (to Visākha). The *Cūḷavedalla-sutta* also appears in the Chinese parallel *Madhyama-āgama*, but here the sutta is named after its protagonist (see Minh Chau [1964] 1991, 269–78 and Anālayo 2011b, 6n6) and Dhammadinnā's interlocutor is not the male Visākha but the well-known female lay disciple Visākhā

(Anālayo 2011a, 277). This sutta also appears in Śamathadeva's commentary on the *Abhidharmakośabhāṣya* (see Anālayo's translation 2011b). Dhammadinnā also appears in the list of distinguished nuns in the Chinese *Ekottarika-āgama*. Here her quality is that she is foremost 'of those who analyse the meaning, widely discoursing on divisions and parts [of the teaching]' (Anālayo 2013a, 104).

Pāli accounts of Dhammadinnā

The verse attributed to Dhammadinnā in the *Therīgāthā* is:

> One should be eager, determinate, and suffused with mind; one whose thought is not attached to sensual pleasures is called an 'upstreamer'.[2]

This verse does not especially relate to what became the chief components of her biography. The account of her life, instead, is based around the discourse given by her in the *Majjhima-nikāya*. This sutta, the *Cūḷavedalla-sutta*, offers no biographical information on Dhammadinnā, nor on Visākha, focusing wholly on their discussion of some finer points of doctrine. This sutta comes to be the basis of Dhammadinnā's biography in the commentaries, and is also mentioned in the *Apadāna*—not by name, but through the statement that she answered questions from a lay follower—as the reason the Buddha bestowed on her the accolade of being the foremost of those nuns who teach. There is no mention, as we can see, in her *Therīgāthā* verse of her marriage, neither is there in the *Cūḷavedalla-sutta*, and although the *Apadāna* does mention that she was married into another family, few details are provided. However, her biography in the commentaries is shaped around her marriage to her interlocutor from the early canonical text, Visākha. In the Pāli canon, Visākha is not otherwise known, apart from in this exchange with Dhammadinnā but he is mentioned elsewhere is the commentaries, usually for his association with Dhammadinnā but once in his own right (*SN-a* III.223). The potential spousal relationship changes in vinayas of other traditions,

[2] *Thī* v.12, trans. Norman (Rhys Davids and Norman 1989, 167, the translations by Norman in the 1989 volume were originally published in Norman [1969] 2007 and [1971] 2007)) *chandajātā avasāye manasā ca phuṭā siyā, kāmesu appaṭibaddhacittā uddaṃsotā ti vuccati.*

as noted above. In these instances, Dhammadinnā is ordained by messenger/Uppalavaṇṇā in order that she is not forced to marry Visākha.

Just as the commentarial biographies of her do not expand on her role or life as illustrious dhammakathikā outside of the *Cūḷavedalla-sutta*, neither does her apadāna. The *Apadāna*, the *Therīgāthā* commentary, and the *Aṅguttara-nikāya* commentary each begin by recounting her past lives. According to all three, she was born at the time of Buddha Padumuttara as a servant in Haṃsavatī.[3] At that time she either did some service for or made an offering, of a cake according to the *Apadāna*, to one of the Buddha's disciples, Sujāta. The *Aṅguttara-nikāya* commentary notes here that her biography mirrors that of Khemā (see Chapter 2) who also makes an offering to Sujāta during the era of the same Buddha. According to the *Apadāna*, after Sujāta ate the cake she (Dhammadinnā) offered him more food, which he accepted, and seeing this happen, her master made her his daughter-in-law, marrying her to his son, we assume, due to the fact of either the offering made or the acceptance of it (or both). Following this, and again only in the *Apadāna*, she goes with her new mother-in-law to see the Buddha, who extols a nun as the foremost of dhammakathikās, and she aspired to that position herself. Buddha Padumuttara predicted this will be her role, during the era of Gotama. Neither of the other two commentaries repeat the prediction, but the *Aṅguttara-nikāya* commentary delineates this story as the same as Khemā's and by that token Dhammadinnā would, as Khemā does, articulate that she would one day herself like to be wise, as Sujāta is.

Both the *Therīgāthā* commentary and the *Aṅguttara-nikāya* commentary record that she was then born in the time of Buddha Phussa, and was known to be exceptionally generous; when told to give one thing, she would always give two. According to the *Apadāna*, following her birth under Buddha Padumuttara she then went to the Tāvatiṃsa realm, and then was born during

[3] *MN-a* also describes this life under Buddha Padumuttara, but it comes later, after Dhammadinnā has attained arahantship but before her return to Rājagaha.

the era of Kassapa. All three agree that during the era of Kassapa, she was one of the seven daughters of King Kīki of Kāsi. This is a previous existence Dhammadinnā shares with all the nuns whose biographies are told in this volume. The seven daughters are the six nuns who make up this volume as well as the well-known lay disciple Visākhā. In this existence, all seven daughters desire to go forth, but are not allowed to do so by their father; thus they are said to practice the holy life at home for 20,000 years (see Collett [2011] for more on the seven sisters). Then, in the *Apadāna* is another intermission in the Tāvatiṃsa realm, and in the other two accounts, in the interval between buddhas, she is said to have journeyed on in worlds of gods and men. In her final birth during the era of Gotama she was born in Rājagaha according to the *Apadāna* and the *Therīgāthā* commentary, although the *Aṅguttara-nikāya* commentary does not specify a birthplace. The *Therīgāthā* commentary and the *Aṅguttara-nikāya* commentary report that she was born into a good family, while the *Apadāna* specifically mentions it was a merchant family (*seṭṭhikula*).[4] The *Apadāna* then records that she was married while young, and her husband, hearing a discourse by the Buddha, attained to the state of non-returner. She then decided herself to go forth, and soon attained arahantship.[5] While this is reported with brevity in the *Apadāna*, the commentaries rather embellish it. Both the

4 See Chapter 10 on class, family, and birth for a discussion of this difference between the texts.

5 According to the texts of early Buddhism, there are four levels of attainment identified as the fruits of practice. These are (in ascending order) the stage of stream-entry (*sotāpattiphala*), the stage of once-returner (*sakadāgāmiphala*), the stage of non-returner (*anāgāmiphala*) and the state of *arahant* (*arahattaphala*). Attainment of the first stage means that the person has 'entered the stream' that leads to awakening/*nibbāna*, and their attainment of it is assured from that point on. In the second stage, the person will return to live one more life before awakening/nibbāna. In the next, they will attain it within this life, that is, they will 'return' or be reborn no more, and the last state, of arahant status, equates with awakening/nibbāna, that is, this is the state of having attained it.

Therīgāthā commentary and the *Aṅguttara-nikāya* commentary stretch this episode, and the entirety of the *Dhammapada* commentary account of Dhammadinnā focuses only upon the time from her husband's attainment to the end of her dialogue with him that makes up the *Cūḷavedalla-sutta*. Also, the *Majjhima-nikāya* commentary contains a narrative account that pivots on this episode, setting the context for the discourse between Dhammadinnā and Visākha by relating some of the same incidences as recounted in the other commentaries.

All four commentaries essentially relate the same story here, although some give many more words over to it than others. After Visākha had seen the Buddha, and become a 'non-returner', he returned home. According to the *Dhammapada* commentary and the *Majjhima-nikāya* commentary usually, if Dhammadinnā was looking out the window upon his return, he would smile at her but on this occasion he passed by without smiling. She wondered what she had done wrong. The other two accounts, the *Aṅguttara-nikāya* commentary and the *Therīgāthā* commentary, say that Dhammadinnā was standing at the top of the stairs when he returned, and he did not take her outstretched arm and, again, she wondered what she had done to cause this slight. In these two accounts she asks Visākha if she has done something wrong, and he tells her she has not—in the *Therīgāthā* commentary he tells her he has realized the truth, but in the *Aṅguttara-nikāya* commentary, he simply says they cannot live together in love anymore (and from this she comprehends why). In the *Dhammapada* commentary, she does not ask him outright, but is summoned to him and when he tells her to take all of their wealth she does then finally ask. In the *Majjhima-nikāya* commentary she is most patient, and most deferential to him. She thinks, 'I will know when it is time for going to bed', and waits only to find he does not come to the bedroom. But he does eventually tell her, 'Having heard the dispensation of the teacher, I understand the supreme *dhamma*.'[6] In all versions her response

[6] *MN-a* II.356 *sayanakāle jānissāmi*, *MN-a* II.357 *ahaṃ satthu dhammadesanaṃ sutvā lokuttaradhammaṃ nāma adhigato.*

to her husband's religious experience is the same—she decides that she will go forth herself, and soon enters the Order. In all versions but the *Dhammapada* commentary, Visākha sends her to the nuns in a golden palanquin. In the *Majjhima-nikāya* commentary, there is a full description of him preparing his wife for her departure:

> Having bathed her in perfumed water, adorned her in all her ornaments, sat her in a golden palanquin, surrounded her with a group of relatives, going to the dwelling of the nuns like one making an impression on the city by doing veneration with perfumed flowers. 'Noble Ones,' he said, 'give Dhammadinnā the going forth.'[7]

According to all four versions, she was not happy living amongst the nuns, and decided to go to the village to live in seclusion.[8] Once she did so, she soon attained arahantship. After this, she decided to return to Rājagaha, which she did accompanied by the nuns' community. Visākha, hearing of this, wondered why she had returned so soon, according to all except the *Therīgāthā* commentary, in which he is simply said to hear of her return and then decide to test her level of attainment. This he decides to do in each version, and it is the decision on his part that leads to the *Majjhima-nikāya* discourse. According to the *Therīgāthā* commentary and the *Aṅguttara-nikāya* commentary, she easily answered all his questions 'as if cutting a lotus stalk with a sharp knife'.[9] With the exception of the *Majjhima-nikāya* commentary, which then goes into a long exegesis of the *Cūḷavedalla-sutta*, the biographies then all end in a similar vein to the *Cūḷavedalla-sutta*, with the Buddha praising Dhammadinnā, and/or raising her to her pre-eminent status as an accomplished teacher. In each case, it is Visākha who goes to the Buddha to relate the interchange to him. In the *Dhammapada* commentary,

7 *Visākho dhammadinnaṃ gandhodakena nahāpetvā sabbālaṅkārehi alaṅkarāpetvā sovaṇṇasivikāya nisādāpetvā ñātigaṇena parivārāpatvā gandhapupphādīhi pūjayamāno nagaravāsanaṃ karonto viya bhikkhuni-upassayaṃ gantvā ayye dhammadinnāṃ pabbājethā ti āha* (II.357).

8 See Chapter 9 on nuns and living arrangements.

9 *...sunisitena satthena kumudanāḷe chindantī viya.*

Dhammdinnā recommends he go to the Buddha, telling him it is best to ask the teacher if he wants to know about arahantship. Each time, as in the *Cūḷavedalla-sutta*, the Buddha tells Visākha that he would have answered his questions himself just as Dhammadinnā did. However, the *Therīgāthā* commentary puts in a caveat that destabilizes this exposition of Dhammdinnā as a wise teacher. According to the *Therīgāthā* commentary, the Buddha had used his omniscience to enable her to know the answers to the questions.

2

Khemā

Summary of Pāli sources

There are verses attributed to Khemā in the *Therīgāthā*, and therefore also a biography of her in the *Therīgāthā* commentary. There is also an account of her life in the *Apadāna*. She appears in the list of distinguished nuns in the *Aṅguttara-nikāya* (*AN* I.25), and therefore has a biographical account in the *Aṅguttara-nikāya* commentary. Khemā, along with Uppalavaṇṇā, the subject of Chapters 6 and 12, is also noted as a chief disciple of Gotama Buddha in the *Āyācanavagga* of the *Aṅguttara-nikāya*. In addition, there is a sutta on Khemā in the *Saṃyutta-nikāya* (IV.374), in which a king visits her and questions her on religious matters. In this sutta, Khema and Uppalavaṇṇā are said to be chief nuns. Khemā is also noted in the *Buddhavaṃsa* as a chief female disciple of certain past buddhas; she is said to be one of two chief female disciples of the buddhas Dhammadassin: Sumedha, and Koṇḍañña.

In other later commentaries, there are two stories of Khemā in the *Dhammapada* commentary: first the usual biography (outlined later in the chapter), and a second one which emphasizes

Khemā's wisdom, as an illustration of a *Dhammapada* verse from the chapter 'The Brahmin' (v. 403) which contends that true 'brahmins' are those who are wise and know the path and what is not the path. The second story is very short, describing one moment, and is really little more than an acknowledgement that Khemā is the exemplification of a wise disciple. Continuing the theme of wisdom, there are five jātakas in the *Jātakatthavaṇṇanā* that include a narrative plot concerning a queen Khemā. In the concluding sections of two of these, in which the Buddha notes who the characters in the story are in the then-present, the Khemā of the past is said to be his disciple the nun Khemā. On the other occasions, the woman who is Khemā in the past life story is not mentioned in the end section.

Summary of other sources

Aside from the Pāli sources, Khemā (or in Sanskrit—Kṣemā) appears in the list of distinguished nuns in the Chinese *Ekottarika-āgama*, in which she is listed as distinguished for her wisdom and intelligence (Anālayo 2013a, 100). Also, Khemā and Uppalavaṇṇā are named as model nuns elsewhere in this *Ekottarika-āgama*. Among Mūlasarvāstivādin sources, Kṣemā's story is told in the *Avadānaśataka* (79). This story of Khemā is quite different to the Pāli accounts of her, differing in almost every detail (as outlined in the following section). The discourse on Khemā's discussion with the king in the *Saṃyutta-nikāya* also appears in the two extant Chinese versions of the *Saṃyuktā-āgama*. The biography of Khemā—the story of her obsession—is retold in the thirteenth-century Sinhala *Saddharmaratanāvaliya* (trans. Obeyesekere 2001, 202–4), which was intended as a Sinhala translation of the *Dhammapada* commentary.[1]

[1] However, as Obeyesekere notes, 'The authors-translators seem to have felt no compunction about adding to or cutting down the original in order to achieve their vision of what the work was intended to be' (2001, 2).

Pāli accounts of Khemā

The popular biographical account

The *Therīgāthā* verses attributed to Khemā are:

> 'You are young and beautiful, I am also young and in my prime. Come, Khemā, let us delight ourselves with music of five parts.'[2]
>
> 'I am afflicted by and ashamed of this putrid body, diseased, perishable. Craving for sensual pleasures has been rooted out.
>
> Sensual pleasures are like sword stakes, the elements of existence the executioner's block. That which you call delight in sensual pleasures, this for me is now non-delight.
>
> Everywhere love of pleasure is destroyed, the mass of darkness torn asunder. In this way know, Evil One, you are finished, Defeater.
>
> Revering the stars, tending the fire in the wood, not knowing it as it really is, fools, you thought it was purity.
>
> But revering the awakened one, best of men, I am completely released from all suffering, doing the teacher's teaching.'[3]

According to the *Therīgāthā* commentary, the first verse is spoken by Māra, who is seeking to seduce Khemā and entice her into lovemaking, so that she abandons her renunciation. With regard to both this verse and the next, this is not the only occurrence of them in the Pāli canon.[4] In fact, most of the verses attributed to Khemā can be found elsewhere in the canon, especially in other instances in the *Thera-Therīgāthā*. Nonetheless, these verses, while

[2] See the discussion later on *pañcaṅgikā turiya*.

[3] *Thī* (vv. 139–44). *Daharā tuvaṃ rūpavatī ahaṃ pi daharo yuvā, pañcaṅgikā turiyena ehi kheme ramāmase. Iminā pūtikāyena āturena pabhaṅgunā, addiyāmi harāyāmi kāmataṇhā samūhatā. Sattisūlūpamā kāmā khandhānaṃ adhikuṭṭanā. Yaṃ tvaṃ kāmaratiṃ brūsi arati dāni sā mamaṃ. Sabbattha vihatā nandi tamokkhandho padālito, evaṃ jānāhi pāpima nihato tvam asi antaka. Nakkhattāni namassantā aggiṃ paricaraṃ vane, yathābhuccaṃ ajānantā bālā suddhiṃ ammaññatha. Ahañ ca kho namassantī sambuddhaṃ purisuttamaṃ, parimuttā sabbadukkhehi satthu sāsanakārikā.*

[4] See, for example, the verses of Vijajā in *bhikkhunīsaṃyutta* of the *SN*.

to some extent generic, can stand as an appropriate foundation for the biography that came to be associated with Khemā in the Pāli biographical tradition. The story most often associated with her is a narrative in which she is obsessed by her own beauty. Once ordained, she reluctantly goes to see the Buddha, whom she knows to be disapproving of preoccupation with beauty. Understanding Khemā's problem, the Buddha makes manifest an apparition of a stunningly beautiful woman whom he then makes either old, decrepit, and/or ugly in front of her eyes, and this causes her to attain insight and become an *arahant*. Although this story is associated with Khemā in many Pāli texts, the same or a very similar story, with an identical story arc, is also associated with the nun Nandā (Collett 2013b). A second account of Khemā, on an entirely different topic, appears in the *Saṃyutta-nikāya*, in which she is depicted as an accomplished teacher (see page 36).[5] This is not a biography, but more a brief vignette: an account of a discourse between a king and a follower of the Buddha.

The four texts which recount the biography of Khemā are the *Apadāna*, the *Therīgāthā* commentary, the *Aṅguttara-nikāya* commentary, and the *Dhammapada* commentary. The version in the *Dhammapada* commentary is much shorter than the others, more a summary of the usual narrative, and therefore contains less detail. All four accounts record that she lived during the era of Padumuttara Buddha, and all but the *Dhammapada* commentary that she was born, or lived, at this time in the city of Haṃsavatī. The *Aṅguttara-nikāya* and *Dhammapada* commentaries do not mention her family background, but the *Therīgāthā* commentary and the *Apadāna* contradict one another in that the *Apadāna* records that she was born into the family of a wealthy merchant, while on the contrary, Dhammapāla, in the *Therīgāthā* commentary records that she was a servant and made her living through serving others.[6] Her conversion to Buddhism came about, according to the *Apadāna*, through

[5] This sutta has recently been studied by Krey (2010).

[6] *Thī-a* (121) ...*veyyāvaccakaraṇena jīvikaṃ kappentī*. Both recensions of the *Apadāna* that have this account record that Khemā was from a very wealthy family. Thus, the recension of the *Apadāna* now contained within the *Therīgāthā* commentary contradicts it.

paying a visit to Buddha Padumuttara and hearing the doctrine. However, the *Therīgāthā* and *Aṅguttara-nikāya* commentaries have a different conversion story. In these two accounts, one day she saw the monk Sujāta, one of the chief disciples of Padumuttara Buddha, on his alms-rounds. She offered him food and then also had her hair cut off in order to, according to Dhammapāla, make an offering of it to Sujāta or, according to the *Aṅguttara-nikāya* commentary, to barter it for gifts that she could offer up to the monk.[7] She then declares to Sujāta her aspiration to become, in the future, a disciple of great wisdom (according to the *Aṅguttara-nikāya* commentary only, as Sujāta himself was—'like you'). In a usual refrain—in relation to these aspirations for future positions within the *saṅgha*—in the *Apadāna* she invited Padumuttara Buddha to her house, after securing approval from her parents, and fed him for seven days. When these seven days had passed, the Buddha placed a nun as foremost of those with supreme wisdom, and seeing this Khemā herself aspired to that position. Padumuttara than predicts she will attain that position under Gotama Buddha. Apart from the version in the *Dhammapada* commentary, which has only one sentence on past lives, she is then said to journey on through various rebirths. The *Apadāna* gives the most in-depth account of her many lives, dedicating twenty-six verses to the detail of her rebirths in various realms and states. The *Therīgāthā* and *Aṅguttara-nikāya* commentaries, where they do provide any detail, essentially recount just the same remote past. Following her birth under Buddha Padumuttara, she was then reborn into different heavenly realms: the Tāvatiṃsa, the Yama, the Tusita, Nimmānarati, and Parinimmitavassavattī. The *Therīgāthā* commentary abbreviates this by simply stating that she took rebirth in the 'six heavens of sensual desires'.[8] Following the birth under Buddha Padumuttara, the *Aṅguttara-nikāya* commentary does not pick the trajectory until the time of Kassapa. The two texts that recount this continuum—the *Apadāna* and the *Therīgāthā* commentary—record that in each birth into a heavenly realm, she reigned as chief queen to the kings of the realms. Similarly, both record that once she passes from heavenly to human realms again,

7 This episode mirrors that in Dhammadinnā's biography—see page 21.
8 *Thī-a* (121) *cha kāmasagge*.

she is also chief queen to human monarchs.[9] Following these high-status births (during which she was 'happy everywhere')[10] she was born during the dispensation of Buddha Vipassī. Having heard his doctrine, she went forth and practised for ten thousand years. During this lifetime, she practised meditation and became one of great learning, and a skilled and brilliant teacher. According to the *Apadāna* only, following birth under Buddha Vipassī she then went to the Tusita heaven. During all of these births, according to the *Apadāna*, she was always reborn into a wealthy family and never had a husband who treated her with contempt. The *Therīgāthā* commentary says she was then born under Buddha Kakusandha, then Koṇāgamana, and both the *Therīgāthā* commentary and *Apadāna* note that during the time of Buddha Koṇāgamana she had a monastery built for the community.[11] Only in the *Apadāna* account does she do this with two friends—Dhanañjānī and Sumedhā.[12] Following this, according to the *Apadāna* only, she then goes to the Tāvatiṃsa heaven, and is pre-eminent. Next, she is born in the era of Buddha Kassapa, and it is here that the *Aṅguttara-nikāya* commentary picks up the story. All three then relate her time as one of the seven daughters of Kikī, the king of Kāsi. The *Therīgāthā* commentary adds that during this time (as with the previous Buddha), she has a monastery built for the community of monks. In her final birth, all three texts agree that she was born into a royal family in the Madda region, in the town of Sākala. According to the *Apadāna*

9 See Walters (2013) on the roles and privileges of chief queens.

10 *Ap.* 544 ...*sabbattha sukhitā hutvā.*

11 It is interesting to note the difference in the way the *Apadāna* and *Thī-a* record this. The *Ap.* describes the monastery as for the saṅgha (*sasaṅghe Ap.* 544), while the *Thī-a* records the monastery being built for the community of monks headed by the Buddha (*buddhappamukkassa bhikkhusaṃghassa Thī-a* 122). The equivalent to this phrase for nuns is not well attested in the early literature, although must be what is in the lacunae on a Gāndhārī fragment, recently translated and reconstructed by Strauch (2013, 17–45).

12 Dhanañjānī is not otherwise mentioned in the biographies of early Buddhist women, as far as I know. Sumedhā, on the other hand, features in the *Therīgāthā*, *Apadāna*, and commentaries. On Sumedhā see Collett (2011).

only, as soon as she was born, the city became peaceful and so she was given the name Khemā. All four texts agree that in her last existence she became the wife of King Bimbisāra, which is in accord with other commentaries which state that all wives of *cakkavattin* kings come either from the region of Uttarakuru or from a royal family from Madda (as noted by Malalasekera 1937, 433).

Khemā grew up to be a woman preoccupied with her own physical beauty, and her husband was rueful of this. As she knew the Buddha finds fault with those who delight in beauty, she kept her distance from him. Bimbisāra, himself a follower of the Buddha, conceived a plan by which to get Khemā in the presence of the Buddha, hoping this might impact upon her affectation. As attested to in the Pāli canon, Bimbisāra had donated his park—Veḷuvana—to the Buddha and his community and so, according to the commentaries, he had songs composed describing the beauty of Veḷuvana and, in all four accounts of Khemā, he had singers sing these songs to her. As a result of hearing them, she felt inspired to visit this glorious place which, according to the *Apadāna*, resembled an abode of the gods. The *Apadāna* describes the park in some detail:

> ... a blossoming grove with the buzz of many bees, filled with the song of the cuckoo and the dance of a multitude of peacocks. Free from noise, not crowded, decorated with terraced walks, filled with huts and festive pavilions....[13]

The accounts vary as to how she eventually comes into the presence of the Buddha at Veḷuvana, but in each case she does. According to the *Apadāna* she simply goes off in search of him herself once at the wood. The *Dhammapada* commentary assumes that once she sets off for the wood they will naturally meet, but the *Therīgāthā* and *Aṅguttara-nikāya* commentaries have the king insist to his attendants that if she does not happen to meet the Buddha at Veḷuvana, they must take her into his presence, by force if necessary. This becomes necessary in both cases, due to her reluctance to have the meeting. The Buddha, knowing she was coming, and

[13] *Ap.* 547. ...*phullapavanaṃ nānābhamarakūjitaṃ kokilāgītasaṅhitaṃ mayūragaṇanaccitaṃ. Appasaddam anākiṇṇaṃ nānācaṅkamabhūsitaṃ kuṭimaṇḍapasaṅkiṇṇaṃ....*

knowing of her intoxication with her own beauty, created an apparition of a stunningly beautiful woman, who was standing beside him fanning him. Khemā saw this woman and had a reaction to what she saw—but there is an important difference here between how the commentaries report this incident and what is said in the *Apadāna*. In the *Apadāna*, on seeing the woman she is surprised and it initially causes her to re-assess her assumptions about the Buddha. 'This is not a harsh bull amongst men,' she thinks.[14] The soft, delicate beauty of the apparition is then described in some detail and, arrested by the vision, Khemā reflects that she has never before seen such a woman as this. The commentaries, however, all have Khemā become self-effacing at this point. The *Therīgāthā* and *Aṅguttara Nikāya* commentaries, in an almost identical refrain, have her say:

> Women of such beauty, comparable to heavenly nymphs, stand near the Blessed One. I am not adequate even to be an attendant for her.[15]

The *Dhammapada* commentary has her state, 'I do not come within even a sixteenth part of her [beauty]'.[16] Regardless of the differences in describing her thought processes here, all texts then have the Buddha transform the woman, before Khemā's eyes, into a decrepit old woman—her hair gray and teeth all loose and broken. The *Apadāna*, again, is the most detailed in relating this:

> Then she was overcome by old age, wan, her mouth altered, teeth broken, with white hair, her speech trembling.
>
> Her ears were shriveled, her eyes white and her breasts were drooping and ugly, all her limbs were flabby and wrinkled and her body was covered with veins.[17]

14 *Ap.* 548. *nāyaṃ lūkho narāsabho.*

15 *Thī-a* (122). *Evārūpā nāma devaccharapaṭibhāgā itthiyo bhagavato avidūre tiṭṭhanti ahaṃ etāsaṃ paricārikatāya pi nappahomi ...*

16 *Dhp-a* IV.58. *ahaṃ imissā kalabhāgam pi na upemi.*

17 *Ap.* 548. *Tato jarābhibhūtā sā vivaṇṇā vikatānanā sīnadantā setasirā salālā vadanāsucī. Saṃkhittakaṇṇa setakkhī lambāsubhapayodharā, valīvitatasabbaṅgī sirāvitatadehinī.*

Khemā, upon seeing this shocking transformation, realized the truth of impermanence and, according to the *Apadāna* and the *Aṅguttara-nikāya* commentary, the Buddha then said to her:

> See the body, Khemā, diseased, impure, putrid, oozing, trickling, the delight of fools.[18]

Then comes the verse from the *Dhammapada*, which is now in all versions, even the *Apadāna*. This verse concerns lust and while it may not be immediately apparent why a story such as Khemā's exemplifies the problem of lust and carnal desire, such a concern is to some extent ameliorated by the discussion below about the intimate relationship between notions of beauty and sexuality in the early Indian context. The *Dhammapada* verse is:

> Those who are slaves to desire are caught in its current, like a spider in its self-made web. Those who have severed this go forth, free from longing, abandoning the pleasure of desire.[19]

What happens next varies considerably. In the end, in each narrative, Khemā attains arahantship, but how this comes about is different in each case. In the *Apadāna* there follow another twenty-three verses, the majority of which are essentially simply her description, rejoicing and acknowledgement of the progress she has made as a result of these events, and her attaining of Awakening. Complimenting this, interspersed through the verses, is ample praise of the Buddha and how he has trained her well, with the proper means. In verses 81–4, she converses with her husband, Bimbisāra, thanks him for bringing her into the presence of the Buddha, and asks him to permit her to go forth, which

[18] This verse appears in other places in the *Tha* and *Thī*. On its appearance in the verses of Nandā see Collett (2013b), and in *Tha* it is v. 394 (see later—attributed to the monk Kulla). *Ap*. 549. *Āturaṃ asuciṃ pūtiṃ passa kheme samussayaṃ, uggharantaṃ paggharantaṃ bālānaṃ abhinanditaṃ.*

[19] *Ap*. 70–1 (in the *Thī-a* recension, the *Dhammpada* verse is recorded as verse 70; however, in Lilley's PTS edition, the verse forms verses 70 and 71, thereby making the PTS version one verse longer than the *Thī-a* recension). *Ye rāgarattānupatanti sotaṃ, sayaṃkataṃ makkaṭako va jālaṃ, etam pi chetvāna paribbajanti, anapekkhino kāmasukkhaṃ pahāya.*

he does. Verse 91 records her conversation with the king of Kosala, which makes up the discourse in the *Saṃyutta-nikāya* (see later). In the penultimate verse, the Buddha proclaims her to be foremost of great wisdom. The *Aṅguttara-nikāya* commentary has her acquiring a specific type of realization and understanding at the end of the stanza, and attaining arahantship. The text then states than anyone who attains arahantship while still a lay disciple will either die that day or must ordain. She remonstrates to the king, who allows her to ordain, and she becomes well known for attaining this state while still a laywoman. Later, she is declared to be foremost in wisdom. The *Dhammapada* commentary has Khemā attain stream-entry after hearing the above verse on the decaying body, and then arahantship after the *Dhammapada* verse. In this version, it is the Buddha who makes the request to her husband that she should go forth. In fact, the words of the Buddha here are that Khemā should either go forth or pass into nibbāna, which here appears to equate with death. The king is horrified at the thought of her attaining nibbāna/dying and refuses to grant this. 'Never!' he says. However, he does permit her to go forth. The *Therīgāthā* commentary is the most convoluted in terms of what happens following the *Dhammapada* verse, but this looks to be due to some revision to enable the insertion of the *Apadāna* verses into the narrative. Following the *Dhammapada* verse the commentary states that Khemā attained arahantship, together with the realizations. And then says:

> But according to what has been handed down in the *Apadāna* when she heard the verse she was established in the fruit of stream-entry. Having obtained the permission of the king, she went forth. Then she attained arhantship.[20]

Then follows the text of the *Apadāna*. Following the *Apadāna* verse, Dhammapāla's commentary then continues as if from the first stating of her having attained arahantship. Following this attainment, she dwelt happily, and became renowned for her great wisdom. Later, the Buddha declared her to be so. Then, one day,

[20] *Thī-a* (123). *Apadāne pana imaṃ gāthaṃ sutvā sotāpattiphale patiṭṭhitā rājānaṃ anujānāpetvā pabbajitvā arahattaṃ pāpuṇī ti āgataṃ.*

as she was sitting at the foot of a tree, Māra approached her and the exchange which makes up the *Therīgāthā* verses is presented. Then follows the—exceedingly brief—commentarial exegesis on the *Therīgāthā* verses and thus the section concludes.

Khema in the Saṃyutta-nikāya

In this sutta, King Pasenadi, arriving at the village of Toraṇavatthu, asked one of his men to find out if there was a brahmin or ascetic in town whom he might visit. Khemā was in Toraṇavatthu at that time, and it was suggested to the king that he might want to visit her, as she was known to be 'wise, competent, intelligent, learned, a fluent speaker, a good debater'.[21] When the king visited Khemā he asked her questions concerning whether the Buddha exists after death or not, which are found as the topic of discussion in other places in the canon. Khemā answered these questions to the king's satisfaction, and he went away impressed by her. Later, when Pasenadi had an audience with the Buddha, he asked the Buddha the very same questions and was more impressed still by concord between the words of disciple and teacher. Overall, what the sutta reveals about the character of Khemā accords with what, in other texts of the canon, is deemed to be her most distinguished quality—her great wisdom. This is noted as her pre-eminence in the *Aṅguttara-nikāya* list of distinguished nuns, and all the biographical accounts of her life except the version in the *Dhammapada* commentary end with some comment on this characteristic of hers. The *Apadāna* also comments upon her proficiency as a debater and knowledge of *abhidhamma* method. The *Apadāna* also notes this conversation between Khemā and a king in Toraṇavatthu.

Khemā in the Jātakatthavaṇṇanā

There are five jātakas in the collection that feature an episode with a very similar story arc in which a Khemā features. On two

[21] *SN* IV.375. *Paṇḍitā viyattā medhāvinī bahussutā cittakathī kalyāṇapaṭibhānā.*

occasions, in the *Rohantamiga Jātaka* (501) and the *Mahāhaṃsa Jātaka* (534), the woman in the story of the past is identified as the nun Khemā, the present-day disciple. Each of the five narratives—the *Mora Jātaka* (159), the *Ruru Jātaka* (482), the *Mahāmora Jātaka* (491), the *Rohantamiga Jātaka* (501), and the *Mahāhaṃsa Jātaka* (534)—features a section in which a queen Khemā dreams of an animal or bird that proffers a teaching. This animal or bird, as it turns out, is the Buddha in a previous life. The form is variably a peacock, a golden deer, or a swan. In each case, the queen tells her king that she desires to hear the teaching of the golden animal or bird that has appeared in her sleep, and the king then attempts to find the extraordinary creature for her. What happens next differs in the various tales, as Khemā, although at times instrumental to how the narrative plot proceeds, functions more as a fairly peripheral character than a central protagonist. As the beautiful creature of whom Khemā dreams turns out to be the Buddha in a previous life, here again Khemā is portrayed as a perceptive—if not quite wise—person, who sees, realizes, and understands the true nature of the being that has arisen in her world. In some instances she realizes this prior to anyone else, on other occasions she is the only character with such insight.

Kṣemā in the Avadānaśataka

The story of Kṣemā in the *Avadānaśataka* is quite different from the biographical accounts in Pāli sources. In the *Avadānaśataka* account, Kṣemā is the daughter of King Prasenajit of Kosala, and so hails from a different region. At birth, she is betrothed to the son of King Brahmadatta who, as her suitor, is named Kṣemaṃkara. The narrative records that this potential marriage between the son and daughter of the kings of two regions will result in all enmity between the two being resolved and will engender a new peace between them. Therefore, there is a great deal resting on this union and so when Kṣemā decides she does not want to marry but would rather go forth, her decision could potentially have significant consequences. When Kṣemā tells her father of her desire he is displeased and refuses to allow it. He decides instead to bring the date of the marriage forward, and it is set for seven days hence.

When Kṣemā hears of this, she goes up onto a terrace and entreats the Buddha to help and guide her. On the day of the ceremony, as the preparations are being made Kṣemā performs a spectacular feat, rising up into the air, which convinces her father and Kṣemaṃkara that she is more suited to a life of renunciation than marriage. The one link between this narrative and the Pāli sources comes at the conclusion of the story, when Kṣemā is declared to be foremost of those with great wisdom (*mahāprajñā*). In this case she is also said to have the quality of *mahāpratibhāna*—that is, one who is skilled in debate, which is similar to one of her qualities stated in the *Apadāna*.

3

Kisāgotamī

Summary of Pāli sources

There are verses attributed to Kisāgotamī in the *Therīgāthā*, and therefore also a biography of her in the *Therīgāthā* commentary. There is also a biography of her in the *Apadāna*. She appears in the list of distinguished nuns in the *Aṅguttara-nikāya* (*AN* I.25), and therefore has a biographical account in the *Aṅguttara-nikāya* commentary. There is a short account of an incident between her and Māra in the *Aṅguttara-nikāya* commentary, and a longer story on this vignette in the *Saṃyutta-nikāya* commentary (I.149). Two Kisāgotamīs are mentioned in the *Buddhavaṃsa*, one being the wife of Buddha Phussa, the other one of the chief supporters of Buddha Tissa (vv. 23, 72 and vv. 16, 75). In the *Jātakatthavaṇṇanā*, a lizard in a past life account is said to be a former incarnation of Kisāgotamī (see *Tittira Jātaka* 438, III.536). She also appears in the *Nidānakathā*, in conversation with the Buddha (*JA* I.60), and the same story appears in the *Buddhavaṃsa* commentary (232). In the *Dhammapada* commentary (I.70) and the *Dhammasaṅgaṇī* commentary (34) she is said to be a cousin of Gotama—the daughter of Suddhodhana's brother Dhotodana. In the *Dhammapada* commentary, Kisāgotamī appears three times. The first two occurrences are occasions for her biography to be told, as it illustrates two different verses of the *Dhammapada*—114 and 287. In the second instance, only a small section of the biography is retold, and the reader is referred back to the initial telling of it. In the third mention of Kisāgotamī in the *Dhammapada* commentary, she is mentioned because of her distinguished ability, as listed in the *Aṅguttara-nikāya*, as a wearer of coarse robes. The *Dhammapada* verse that is related to this part of the commentary (395) could have been written for Kisāgotamī herself. This is discussed below.

Summary of other sources

The short discourse in the *Saṃyutta-nikāya* is also present in both the shorter and longer extant Chinese *Saṃyukta-āgamas*, in much the same form in both (see Anālayo 2013a, 123–4 and 133f.). As in the Pāli version, in both accounts Māra asks her if she has gone to the forest to look for a man (discussed in Chapter 9). In the Chinese *Ekottarika-āgama*, she appears on the list of distinguished nuns, but her distinguished quality is different. On this list she is said to be one who undertakes 'ascetic practice' (see Anālayo 2013a, 100). As noted by Anālayo, such practices would include wearing rag-robes, but would also include other practices such as begging for food, living at the root of a tree, and so on (see Anālayo [2013a 102n24] for a list of textual references to these practices). Kisāgotamī appears in the Mūlasarvāstivāda *Vinaya*, but here a different story of her life is told, which bears more similarity to the story of Paṭācārā in the Pāli texts (as noted by Finnegan 2009, 159n304). There is also a partial retelling of a story similar to that of Kisāgotamī in the Tamil *Maṇimēkalai*. While Richman (1988, 79–100) sees this story as a link between Pāli commentarial accounts and the Tamil epic, Schalk and Vēluppiḷḷai (2002, 391–3) is less convinced. Arguing on the basis of Tamil etymology and narrative content, Schalk considers it more likely that this version is based on the Sanskrit *Mahābhārata* version (XIII 1, 1–83). While linguistically the link may be stronger to the Sanskrit—which does not contain the Buddhist themes—it is difficult to deny, as Schalk attempts to do, critiquing Richman, that Buddhist themes are strong in the *Maṇimēkalai* version. A version of her biography is also told in the Sinhala *Saddharmaratnāvaliya* (Obeyesekere 2001, 134–7) which contains both the mustard seed aspect of the story, and the charcoal-to-gold alchemic episode that in the Pāli is found only in the *Dhammapada* commentary version of her biography, although a similar story occurs in the *Vimānavatthu* commentary as well.

Pāli accounts of Kisāgotamī

The verses attributed to Kisāgotamī in the *Therīgāthā* are as follows:

> 213. The state of having good friends has been praised by the sage with reference to the world; if he resorts to noble friends, even a fool would become wise.
>
> 214. Worthy ones are to be resorted to; in this way the wisdom of those who resort to them increases. Resorting to good men one would be released from all pains.
>
> 215. One should know *dukkha*, and the uprising of *dukkha*, and its cessation and the eightfold way, even the four noble truths.
>
> 216. The state of women has been said to be painful by the charioteer of men who are to be tamed; even the state of being a co-wife is painful; some, having given birth once,
>
> 217. even cut their throats; some tender ones take poisons; reborn as murderers in hell, both suffer misfortunes.
>
> 218. Going along, about to bring forth, I saw my husband dead; having given birth on the path, I had not yet arrived at my own house.
>
> 219. Two sons dead and a husband dead upon the path for miserable me; mother and father and brother were burning upon one pyre.
>
> 220. Miserable woman, with family annihilated, you have suffered immeasurable pain; and you have shed tears for many thousands of births.
>
> 221. Then I saw the flesh of my sons being eaten in the midst of the cemetery; with my family destroyed, despised by all, with husband dead, I attained the undying.

222. I have developed the noble eightfold path leading to the undying; I have realized nibbāna; I have looked at the doctrine as a mirror.

223. I have my dart cut out, my burden laid down; I have done that which was to be done. The therī Kisāgotamī, with mind completely released, has said this.[1]

Kisāgotamī's biography in the Pāli sources is probably one of the best known narratives about a female disciple. Its popularity appears to be borne from its poignancy; it is touching in its relating of the distress of a grieving mother, and vivid in its revealing of the truth of impermanence. This biography is told in the four texts—the *Apadāna*, the *Aṅguttara-nikāya* commentary, the *Dhammapada* commentary, and the *Therīgāthā* commentary.

The *Apadāna*, the *Aṅguttara-nikāya* commentary, and the *Therīgāthā* commentary all begin with accounts of her past lives, although the *Dhammapada* commentary only recounts her present life. According to the former three, in the time of Buddha Padumuttara she was born into a family in Haṃsavatī. Having heard the dhamma being taught by Padumuttara, she witnessed him place a nun as foremost of those who wear rough robes (*lūkhacīvara*) and aspired to that position herself. According to the *Apadāna* only, Padumuttara then predicted she would attain that position under Gotama Buddha. Similarly, only the *Apadāna* then offers detail of any other past lives, the *Therīgāthā* commentary and the *Aṅguttara-nikāya* commentary simply saying she journeyed on through other worlds of gods and men. The *Apadāna* reports that, following her birth during the era of Padumuttara,

[1] This is the only set of verses in the *Therīgāthā* which end with a statement asserting authorship. However, there are some verses in the *Theragāthā* which pronounce authorship in the same or a similar way. *Kalyāṇamittatā muninā lokaṃ ādissa vaṇṇitā, kalyāṇamitte bhajamāno api bālo paṇḍito assa. Bhajitabbā sappurisā paññā tathā pavaḍḍhati bhajantānaṃ, bhajamāno sappurise sabbehi pi dukkhehi mucceyye. Dukkhañ ca vijāneyya dukkhassa ca samudayaṃ, nirodhañ ca aṭṭhaṅgikaṃ maggaṃ cattāri ariyasaccāni. Dukkho itthibhāvo akkhāto purisadammasārathinā, sapattikaṃ pi dukkhaṃ appekaccā sakiṃ vijātāyo. Gale apakantanti sukhamāliniyo visāni khādanti, janamārakamajjhagatā ubho pi byasanāni anubhonti. Upavijaññā gacchantī addasāhaṃ patiṃ mataṃ panthe, vijāyitvāna appattāhaṃ sakaṃ*

she goes to the Tāvatiṃsa realm. She was then born during the era of Buddha Kassapa, and was one of seven sisters, followed by another birth in the Tāvatiṃsa realm. Then comes her last existence, and here all four versions pick up the story. According to all but the *Apadāna*, she was born into a family in Sāvatthī, a poor family by all accounts. The *Apadāna*, the *Aṅguttara-nikāya* commentary, and the *Therīgāthā* commentary recount the next events simply; she was married into a wealthy family, and was despised by them because of her background, until she gave birth to a son. This vanquished their contempt for her, and they instead honoured her as a mother. However, the *Dhammapada* commentary has a very different version of events here.[2] Prior to the death of her son, the *Dhammapada* commentary tells a story of a wealthy merchant—worth four hundred million—who suffers a great misfortune when all his wealth suddenly turns to charcoal. A friend tells him how he might overcome this present difficulty. He should continue to trade, setting out the charcoal as his goods in his shop. Then one day, a certain young man or woman will come along and ask him why he is selling yellow gold. He should ask that youth where the gold is, and once they pick up the charcoal and hand it to him he will experience an alchemical transformation of his goods. The friend says further that if the youth is female the merchant should marry her to his son, and turn over his (renewed) four million to her. In due course, Kisāgotamī comes along and asks the germane question. Having had his wealth reinstated as predicted, and seeing that Kisāgotamī is unmarried, the merchant marries her to his son,

---

geham. Dve puttā kālaṅkatā pati ca panthe mato kapaṇikāya, mātā pitā ca bhātā ca ḍayhanti ekacitakāyaṃ. Khīnakulikā kapaṇe anubhūtaṃ te dukkhaṃ aparimāṇaṃ, assu ca te pavattaṃ bahūni jātisahassāni. Passiṃ taṃ susānamajjhe atho pi khāditāni puttamaṃsāni, hatakulikā sabbagarahitā matapatikā amatam adhigacchiṃ. Bhāvito me maggo ariyo aṭṭhaṅgiko amatagāmī, nibbānaṃ sacchikataṃ dhammādāsaṃ apekkhi 'haṃ. Ahaṃ amhi kantasallā ohitabhārā kataṃ me karaṇīyaṃ, Kisāgotamī therī sivimuttacittā imaṃ bhaṇī ti (trans. Norman [Rhys Davids and Norman 1989, 195–6]).

[2] A similar story to this can be found in the *Vimānavatthu* commentary—see the account in Horner's translation of *Vimānavatthu*, with added commentarial excerpts ([1924] 2005, 71).

and gives her charge of the family fortune. In time, she becomes pregnant but, as in the other versions, her son dies at a young age.

In none of the versions of her biography does Kisāgotamī respond well to the death of her child. In the *Apadāna*, she is simply said to be overcome with grief, and in her pained state to have taken the corpse in her arms and wandered around lamenting. The *Therīgāthā* commentary and the *Aṅguttara-nikāya* commentary instead suggest that, due to the prior bad treatment of her husband's family, her unstable state is caused by her anxiety that the family will now cast her out. The *Dhammapada* commentary understands her overwhelming grief to be due to her never having seen death before. In all accounts but the *Apadāna*, she then goes around the town seeking medicine for her dead child. In the *Apadāna*, a friend responds to her grief by advising her to seek help from the best of physicians, that is, the Buddha. The friend becomes instead a certain wise man (*paṇḍitapuriso*) in the commentarial accounts, but in all versions she then approaches the Buddha and asks him for his help. In all accounts, she asks the Buddha to give her medicine for her son. In each instance, the Buddha then tells her to fetch a white mustard seed from each house in the town in which no death has occurred. In the *Therīgāthā* commentary and the *Aṅguttara-nikāya* commentary he does this because he sees that Kisāgotamī has the potential for significant religious attainment. Kisāgotamī obliges, and makes her way around Sāvatthī, going first to one house then the next. She fails in her quest, as she is told time and again that each family she meets has had to endure the death of loved ones. With this—and quite quickly, having only gone to three houses according to the *Aṅguttara-nikāya* commentary and the *Therīgāthā* commentary—she realizes that death is a reality of life and what she has found in these few houses will be the same throughout the city, and that in truth the dead are more numerous than the living. In the *Aṅguttara-nikāya* commentary and the *Therīgāthā* commentary versions, she understands this is a teaching from the Buddha, and in the *Aṅguttara-nikāya* commentary is deeply moved by this. She is finally able to lay the child to rest. In the *Apadāna* she rather brashly throws the corpse away, as she does also in the *Therīgāthā* commentary. In the other two accounts, she more gently lays the corpse down in either a forest or a graveyard. In all but the *Dhammapada* commentary version, there then follow two *Dhammapada* verses, each placed slightly differently in the narrative sequence. In the *Dhammapada* commentary, there is only one *Dhammapada* verse inserted at this juncture. In the *Apadāna*, after disposing of the corpse, she goes to see the Buddha, who, seeing her coming, recites *Dhammapada* verse 113:

> Whoever lives a hundred years not seeing arising and passing away, it is better to live one day seeing arising and passing away.[3]

The second *Dhammapada* verse, number 114, then follows immediately in the *Apadāna*. In the *Therīgāthā* commentary, after roughly throwing the corpse of her son away in the cemetery, she recited *Dhammapada* 114 herself:

> This is not the norm for a village, of a town, nor the norm of one family. This is the norm of the whole world of men and gods, that all of this is impermanent.[4]

Similarly, in the *Aṅguttara-nikāya* commentary, once having put the cadaver down, she utters verse 114. The *Dhammapada* commentary omits this verse, instead recounting that she goes straight to see the Buddha, which she does following her recitation in the other two. In all but the *Apadāna*, Kisāgotamī and the Buddha have an exchange in which he enquires as to whether she obtained a mustard seed, and she lets him know that she has had her realization. The Buddha then recites the second *Dhammapada* verse (114), after which, in all accounts, she has a religious experience. In the *Apadāna*, she 'purified the divine eye',[5] in the *Therīgāthā* commentary she established herself in stream-entry, in the *Aṅguttara-nikāya* commentary she reached the fruit of the path, and in the *Dhammapada* commentary she was established in the fruit of con-

3 *Ap.* 566.27, trans. Pruitt 1999, 231. *Yo ca vassasataṃ jive apassaṃ udayavyayaṃ ekāhaṃ jīvitaṃ seyyo passato udayavyayaṃ.*

4 *Ap.* 566.28. *Na gāmadhammo no nigamassa dhammo na cāpi yaṃ ekakulassa dhammo sabbassa lokassa sadevakassa eso va dhammo yad idaṃ aniccatā.*

5 *Ap.* 566.32, *dibbaṃ cakkhuṃ visodhayiṃ.*

version. She then either requested ordination from the Buddha or, in the *Apadāna*, simply went forth. In the three commentaries, she then went to the community of nuns and entered the Order. She quickly attained arahantship according to the *Apadāna*, although in the other three accounts this did not happen until the Buddha uttered verse 114, and in the *Dhammapada* commentary this is prefaced by a meditative reflection while watching a flame flicker. All but the *Dhammapada* commentary then mention that she became known as foremost of those who wear rough robes. In the *Apadāna*, this is prefigured by concurrent attainments, such as mastery of supernormal powers, divine eye and ear, destruction of all taints, together with the rooting out of continued existences. In the *Therīgāthā* commentary and the *Aṅguttara-nikāya* commentary it is accompanied by the preeminent use of the other monastic prerequisites, not just the robe. In the *Therīgāthā* commentary, she then recites her *Therīgāthā* verses.

Turning to the other account of Kisāgotamī in the *Dhammapada* commentary, the focus here shifts to her ascetic status. In this brief vignette, the god Sakka goes to visit the Buddha, and sits listening to his teaching. At that time, Kisāgotamī also decides to go and visit the Buddha, and she travels through the air to do so. However, seeing Sakka there she turns back. Sakka saw her and enquires as to who she is. The Buddha tells him that it was Kisāgotamī, foremost of nuns who wear rough robes. This incident is related as an illustration of the following *Dhammpada* verse, which sounds like it could have been uttered with Kisāgotamī in mind, given that leanness is mentioned and this is said to be the reason for her name (*kisa* meaning 'lean'):

> The person who wears rag-robes, is thin, whose veins stand out, who is alone in the forest in contemplation—that one I call a brahmin (395).[6]

[6] *Dhp-a* IV.157. *Paṃsukūladharaṃ jantuṃ kisaṃ dhamanisanthataṃ, ekaṃ vanasmiṃ jhāyantaṃ tam ahaṃ brumi brahmaṇan' ti.*

4

Paṭācārā

Summary of Pāli sources

Unlike many of the other nuns discussed in this volume, almost all of the evidence about Paṭācārā is sourced from Pāli literature. Of the six nuns whose biographies form this volume, she is the less well attested in the texts of other traditions. It is in the *Therīgāthā* that we find most evidence of Paṭācārā, as she is mentioned not only in verses attributed to her, but she also appears as an inspirational teacher and leader of other women. In the section of verses 112–32, which begin with five verses apparently uttered by her, we also have accounts of thirty nuns, one single nun and then five hundred women all of whom are taught, advised, or comforted by Paṭācārā. Following her appearance in the *Therīgāthā*, in the *Apadāna*, and the later commentarial works a biography of her life is recounted and this follows an identical story arc in each version. This account appears in the *Apadāna*, the *Therīgāthā* commentary, the *Aṅguttara-nikāya* commentary, and the *Dhammapada* commentary. There is also one very different story of a Paṭācārā in the *Cullakāliṅga Jātaka* of the

Jātakatthavaṇṇanā.[1] Paṭācārā appears in the canonical *Aṅguttara-nikāya* list, in which she is identified as one who is foremost of those who are *vinayadhārās*, that is, proficient in the discipline. She or her story is also mentioned in other commentarial literature, such as the *Dīgha-nikāya*, *Majjhima-nikāya*, and *Udāna* commentaries. In these cases either the entire story is recommended as one to be read as a demonstration of how one might overcome grief (*soka*) (such as in *DN-a* III.746–7), or a part of her story is used so as to exemplify a certain thing. In the *Udāna* commentary (*Ud-a* 127) part of her story is mentioned to highlight how a person's turmoil or difficulties might be assuaged by a few simple words from the Buddha.

Summary of other sources

Aside from the Pāli sources, Paṭācārā appears in the list of distinguished nuns in the Chinese *Ekottarika-āgama*, in which she is said to be notable as one who rigorously observes/recites the discipline (vinaya), thus to have the same eminent quality for which she is known in the Pāli sources (see Anālayo 2013a, 100). Elements of what look like Paṭācārā's biography are told in the Mūlasarvāstivāda *Vinaya*, however, the Mūlasarvāstivāda version is said to be the story of Kisāgotamī (see the introduction to Part I for more on the relationship between accounts of Paṭācārā and Kisāgotamī). Her biography is also told in the Sinhala *Saddharmaratnāvaliya* (trans. Obeyesekere 2001, 126–33).

[1] This story is so different that it appears to be a story of another Paṭācārā. The story takes place in the context, as the opening paragraph states, of a discussion of women joining the Order. In this story, Paṭācārā is one of five children born to a pair of Jains who are skilled in disputation. The Licchavis get these two Jains to marry, as they believe they will have clever children. Of the five children, four are daughters, but the other three daughters are not known of, or connected with any other women known of outside of this jātaka story. The male child, Saccaka, is either the same as or shares a name with a Saccaka known from the *MN*, who debates

Pāli accounts of Paṭācārā

Although the biographies of her in the *Apadāna* and later commentarial works largely concur, there is a potential discrepancy between the *Therīgāthā* verses and other accounts of her. The *Therīgāthā* verses attributed to her, while not antithetical to her later biographies, do not contain any content directly related to the story that comes to be associated with her. However, verses attributed to two other nuns in the *Therīgāthā* either appear to contain, in one case, or categorically contain, in another, verses pertaining to Paṭācārā's biography. These issues have been discussed in the introduction to Part I.

The *Apadāna* account, the *Therīgāthā* commentary, and the *Aṅguttara-nikāya* commentaries begin with previous lives of Paṭācārā. All three agree that she was born during the time of Buddha Padumuttara, in Haṃsavatī.[2] The *Apadāna* records her to have been born to a wealthy merchant, while the *Therīgāthā* commentary and the *Aṅguttara-nikāya* commentaries simply say she was born into a good family. All three versions agree that, having seen another nun declared to be foremost of those who know the vinaya, she herself aspired to that position, but in this first section it is only the *Apadāna* that recounts Padumuttara predicting that she will attain that position in the future, as a disciple of Gotama Buddha. Then, according to the *Apadāna*, she was reborn in the Tavatiṃsa heaven while the two commentaries note

with the Buddha in the *Cūlasaccakasutta* and the *Mahāsaccakasutta*. In the jātaka, the parents die and the five children carry on practising Jainism, Saccaka stays in Vesālī, but the women travel. Here we find the story of the *jambu* tree branch, which is part of Bhaddā Kuṇḍalakesā's life story and told in full in Chapter 5. The sisters challenge others to debate, and prove themselves skilled in the art of debate, until they meet Sāriputta, who triumphs over them in debate and so, on his advice, they ordain into the Order. The past life account tells of Sāriputta raising the women to the status of chief queens (*JA* 301).

[2] The *Dhp-a* notes her previous life under Buddha Padumuttara, but does this later on in the narrative.

she 'journeyed on through realms of gods and men'.[3] Following that, all three accounts record she was then born during the era of Buddha Kassapa, as one of the seven daughters of King Kikī. All three report that she lived a devoted life for 20,000 years, but only the *Apadāna* names her six siblings who did the same. The *Therīgāthā* commentary and the *Aṅguttara-nikāya* commentary report, in each separate narrative of each sibling, that each had a dwelling built for the Order, although it is unclear if this is something they did together.

Turning now to her present life in the time of Gotama Buddha, here the *Dhammapada* commentary picks up the story. All four texts recount that she was born in Sāvatthī, and all but the *Therīgāthā* commentary that she was born into the family of a wealthy merchant. When she grew up, she became attracted to an unsuitable man and, as the *Apadāna* reads, 'When, as a young woman, I saw a man from the country, under the influence of impetuous thoughts I went with him.'[4] This man was unsuitable for her, as what seems to be being indicated here is his low status. The low status is glossed in the commentaries by a change to his character. In the *Therīgāthā* commentary, the *Aṅguttara-nikāya* commentary, and the *Dhammapada* commentary, his lack of suitability comes from him having been a servant in her father's household.[5] The commentaries then narrate that when she learned she was to be married off to a suitable match, she ran off with the servant. The *Aṅguttara-nikāya* commentary has Paṭācārā say to her lover, 'After tomorrow you will be kept from seeing me by a hundred warders. If you are able, go now and take me with you!'[6] In a vignette of its own, the *Aṅguttara-nikāya* commentary then imagines Paṭācārā's life with this man of little means:

3 *devamanussesu saṃsaritvā.*

4 *Yadā ca yobbanūpetā vitakkavasagā ahaṃ naraṃ janapadaṃ disvā tena saddhiṃ agañch' ahaṃ* (*Ap.* 558) Emended *jārapatiṃ* to *janapadaṃ*—see the discussion on *jārapati* on page 175n18.

5 The term used for the servant is *kammakāra* in the *Thī-a* (106) and the *AN-a* (I.357) but *cūḷūpaṭṭhāka* in the *Dhp-a* (II.260).

6 *Tvaṃ sve paṭṭāya maṃ pāṭihārasatena pi daṭṭhuṃ na labhissasi, sace te kammaṃ atthi idānim eva maṃ gaṇhitvā gacchāti* (*AN-a* I.357).

> The husband sowed the field in the forest, bringing collected sticks and wood etc. The woman fetched water with the water-pot and with her own hand pounded the rice, did the cooking and other domestic chores. Thus she experienced the consequences of her wrongdoing.[7]

After some time with her husband, Paṭācārā became pregnant and, according to the commentaries, wished to go home to see her parents. However, the *Apadāna* narrates that it was not until pregnant with her second child that the desire arose. When she discusses this wish with her husband, the *Dhammapada* commentary presents him as fearful of torture at the hands of her parents were they to return home. The remaining two commentaries, in a tone less favourably disposed to the husband, recount that Paṭācārā tried to persuade him to take her, but upon umpteen prevarications of '... we'll go tomorrow...', she realized 'this fool will never take me',[8] and so she set out alone. Her husband caught up with her on the road, just as labour pains began. She gave birth on the road, and he persuaded her to go back home with him.[9] All this was repeated with the pregnancy of the second child, but with different consequences. This time, labour pains began just at the moment a storm broke. Then, in a gathering storm of her own, all manner of misfortunes began to befall Paṭācārā and her family. First, her husband was killed by a snake, his body turning blue as the poison engulfed him, according to one commentary (*Dhp-a* II.263). Then,

7 *So taṃ ... araññe khettaṃ kasitvā dārupaṇṇādīni āharati itarā kuṭena udakaṃ haritvā sahatthā koṭṭanapacanādīni karontī attano pāpassa phalaṃ anubhoti* (*Dhp-a* II.261). See pages 171–2, on Paṭācārā's performance of such menial tasks as these.

8 *...sve gacchāma... nāyaṃ bālo maṃ nessatī ti* (*AN-a* I.357 and *Thī-a* 106).

9 The *Dhp-a* and the *JA* both record a similar opening paragraph to this for the stories of Cūḷapanthaka and his brother, Mahāpanthaka, both named as such because they were born 'on the road'. In these stories, an unnamed woman runs off with a servant, and, as above, when she is about to give birth decides to go back to her parents' home. Her husband catches up with her on the road and she gives birth. In these instances, the children live and are the protagonists in the stories, the mother being rather incidental (*Dhp-a* I.239ff. and *JA Cullakaseṭṭhijātaka* 4).

trying to cross a flooded river, she lost first one child, then the other. This occurred, according to the *Dhammapada* commentary, because of her slow intellect, to which the *Therīgāthā* commentary adds also a physical weakness, which in part is the result of having spent all night crouched on the ground with her child and newborn trying to shield them from the torrid storm. She took one child and crossed, but as she was returning for the other a bird of prey swooped down and took the first.[10] While she is waving her hands around in anguish mid-stream, her other child saw her and attempted to go to her, but was instead carried off by the current.

Finally, bereft and distraught at her loss, she made her way to Sāvatthī only to discover that her mother, father, and brother were all also deceased. The *Therīgāthā* and *Dhammapada* commentaries recount that she met a man on the road coming from Sāvatthī, and the *Aṅguttara-nikāya* commentary that she asked once she reached the city, but either way the answer was the same: her family home had been destroyed by the storm that night, killing all within, and now the bodies of the three occupants—her mother, father, and brother—were burning upon one funeral pyre. In each of the three commentarial versions, her interlocutor then informed her that the pyre was still burning and pointed out that 'its billow of smoke can be clearly seen'.[11] Paṭācārā's grief reached its climax at this point, which is dramatized in the commentaries in an unusual way. According to the commentaries, at this moment, overwhelmed with the grief of losing so many loved ones, her clothes fell off. According to the *Aṅguttara-nikāya* commentary she became at that moment 'unable to bear the oppression of clothes', while the *Therīgāthā* commentary states that she 'did not notice that the cloth that was covering her was falling off', given that she was out of her mind with grief.[12] The *Dhammapada* commentary recounts that

[10] The bird is an osprey according to the *Thī-a*, and a hawk according to the other commentaries.

[11] *...esā dhūmavaṭṭī paññāyīti* (*Mp* I.359). The two other versions vary slightly.

[12] *Attano nivatthasāṭakaṃ sandhāretuṃ asakkontī* (Mp I.359, trans. Bode [1894, 558]) and *nivatthavattham pi patamānaṃ na sañjāni* (*Thī-a* 108).

the devastating grief made her instantly mad, and then, in this newly disturbed state of mind she did not realize her clothing had fallen from her body. In the *Apadāna*, there is no mention of Paṭācārā ever being naked, the text simply saying that, overwhelmed with grief, she uttered the following verse:

> Both my sons are dead, my husband is dead on the road. My mother, father and brother are being burnt upon one pyre.[13]

This verse from the *Apadāna* is repeated in each of the commentaries, and it is one of only two verses of Paṭācārā's story that they repeat more or less verbatim from the *Apadāna* account. However, in the commentaries, unlike her grief-stricken but still rational state in the *Apadāna*, she is now crazed and/or naked.

This naked and crazed state engenders a period of vagrant wandering according to the *Therīgāthā* and *Dhammapada* commentaries, although the *Aṅguttara-nikāya* commentary never mentions that she has lost her senses to any mental derangement. Emphasizing her mental instability, the *Therīgāthā* and *Dhammapada* commentaries recount that when other people saw her they threw rubbish and earth at her, shouting at the crazy woman to go away. Then one day, Paṭācārā met the Buddha, according to the *Therīgāthā* commentary, because she went inside the monastery in which he was teaching, but according to the other accounts simply because either she saw him or he saw her from afar. The *Dhammapada* commentary then has recourse to the Buddha's omniscience, revealing that he 'sees' Paṭācārā as one who has made an aspiration during the time of Padumuttara Buddha and it is here, rather than at the beginning of the narrative, that the *Dhammapada* commentary digresses into her

[13] *Ubho puttā kālakatā panthe pati mama mato, mātā pitā ca bhātā ca ekacitamhi ḍayhare* (*Ap*. 559). Lilley notes that two of her four manuscripts include *mayhaṃ* in the second *pāda* ([1925] 2006, 559n8). This concurs with the verse as it appears in the commentaries: *Ubho puttā kālaṅkatā panthe mayhaṃ pati mato, mātā pitā ca bhātā ca ekacitamhi ḍayhare ti* (*Thī-a* 108), *ubho puttā kālakatā panthe mayhaṃ pati mato, mātā pitā ca bhātā ca ekacitake ḍayhare ti* (*Mp* I.359), *ubho puttā kālakatā panthe mayhaṃ patī mato, mātā pitā ca bhātā ca ekacitakasmiṃ ḍayhare ti* (*Dhp-a* II.266).

previous encounter with Padumuttara.[14] The *Therīgāthā* and *Dhammapada* commentaries then record that the Buddha's disciples, seeing this crazed woman approaching, try to shield the Buddha from her, but he allowed her through. The Buddha then speaks to Paṭācārā, and each account has him saying different things, all of which are both comforting and didactic. According to the *Aṅguttara-nikāya* commentary, the Buddha simply says a few words to our protagonist, 'Sister, regain your senses',[15] and at this she is instantly revived from her grief-stricken, vagabond, deranged state. She becomes aware of her nudity at this moment, is embarrassed, and then quickly thrown a garment by a bystander. The *Apadāna*, instead, has the Buddha say to her at this point, '... Daughter, do not mourn: be confident, seek yourself. Why do you grieve uselessly?'[16] The verse immediately following this is the second verse from the *Apadāna* repeated in commentaries:

> Neither children nor a father nor any relatives are a shelter. Relatives are no protection for one who is affected by death.[17]

This verse proves crucial in each account, as this, plus a second verse added in the commentaries, is the catalyst by which Paṭācārā attains stream-entry.[18] According to the commentaries, she then requested ordination, and the Buddha either took her or sent her to the nuns. According to all four versions, she subsequently attains the state of an arahant, although exactly how this occurs is different in each case. In the *Apadāna* she attains arahant status

[14] The *Dhammapada* commentary includes in this section reference to Buddha Padumuttara's prediction of Paṭācārā's future discipleship with Gotama, a section it shares only with the *Apādana*.

[15] *Satiṃ paṭilabha bhaginī* (*AN-a* I.359).

[16] *Putte mā soci assasa attānaṃ te gavesassu; kiṃ niratthaṃ vihaññasi?* (*Ap.* 559)

[17] *Na santi puttā tāṇāya na pitā na pi bandhavā antakenādhipannassa n'atthi ñātīsu tāṇatā* (*Ap.* 559; *AN-a* I.360; *Thī-a* 109; *Dhp-a* II.268).

[18] The second verse is: 'Knowing this matter, a wise person, restrained by morality, would quickly purify the path leading to nibbāna', *etam atthavasaṃ ñatvā paṇḍito sīlasaṃvuto nibbānagamanaṃ maggaṃ khippam eva visodhaye ti* (*AN-a* I.360; *Thī-a* 109; *Dhp-a* II.268).

very quickly. She mastered supernormal powers, including the divine eye and divine ear. In her own words, she then 'learned all the discipline in presence of the All-seeing One, all the detail, and I recited it as it was'.[19] With this, the Buddha placed her as foremost of *vinayadhārīs* and said, 'Paṭācārā is unique.'[20] The *Apadāna* account ends with some of the popular stock verses found in the *Apadāna* and the *Thera-Therīgāthā* about completion of the Buddha's teaching and the attainment of the highest state. The *Aṅguttara-nikāya* commentary is the briefest of all following her gaining of stream-entry. This text simply states that she soon after attained the status of arahant, and became well versed in the vinaya, which was acknowledged by the Buddha. The *Therīgāthā* and the *Dhammapada* commentaries add more, seemingly in an attempt to explain the verses attributed to her in the *Therīgāthā*, which is perfectly understandable for a text that is a commentary on the *Therīgāthā*, but less obviously so for the *Dhammapada* commentary. In her *Therīgāthā* verses, she appears to have an important realization while washing her feet, and this is accordingly taken up and expounded in the two commentaries. The two are almost identical here. They both describe her one day taking her water-pot and washing her feet, and watching the water as it pours out. Some water goes only a short distance, some further, and some further still. She recognizes this as a metaphor for the coming into being and passing away for beings during different stages of their lives:

> Just as the water poured out at first by me, beings die in youth. Just as the water that was poured out the second time went further, beings die in middle age. Just as the water poured out the third time went further still, beings die in old age.[21]

[19] *Tato 'haṃ vinayaṃ sabbaṃ santike sabbadassino uggahiṃ sabbavitthāraṃ vyāhariñ ca yathātathaṃ* (*Ap.* 560).

[20] *Paṭācārā ca ekikā* (*Ap.* 560).

[21] *... mayā paṭhamaṃ āsitta-udakaṃ viya ime sattā paṭhamavaye pi maranti, tato dūraṃ gataṃ dutiyavāraṃ āsittaṃ udakaṃ viya majjhimavaye pi, tato dūrataraṃ gataṃ tatiyavāraṃ āsittaṃ udakaṃ viya pacchimavaye pi maranti yevā ti ...* (*Thī-a* 109).

Both texts then say that the Buddha, seated in his perfumed hut, sent out his radiance as if to stand face-to-face with her and he explained to her the meaning more fully of what she had realized:

> Paṭācārā, all beings are subject to death. Therefore, it is better to live for just one moment of one day seeing this [than] to live a hundred years not seeing the arising and passing away of the five aggregates.[22]

According to both accounts, he then utters the *Dhammapada* verse (113) that this narrative serves as an illustration of in its commentary. The verse sagely proclaims that it is better to live one day seeing the true nature of arising and passing, than to live a hundred years in ignorance of it.

[22] *Paṭācāre sabbe p' ime maraṇadhammā tasmā pañcannaṃ khandhānaṃ udayabbayaṃ apassantassa vassasataṃ jīvato taṃ passantassa ekāham pi ekakkhaṇam pi jīvataṃ seyyo* (*Thī-a* 109).

5

Bhaddā Kuṇḍalakesā

Summary of Pāli sources

There are verses attributed to Bhaddā Kuṇḍalakesā in the *Therīgāthā and* her story is told in the *Therīgāthā* commentary. She is mentioned in the list of distinguished nuns in the *Aṅguttara-nikāya,* on which she is listed as distinguished for her quick realization (*khippābhiññā*). Based upon this listing, her biography appears in the commentary on the *Aṅguttara-nikāya*. There is also an apadāna on Kuṇḍalakesā and her story is told, in part, in two jātakas in the *Jātakatthavaṇṇanā,* and themes from the story reoccur in a number of other jātakas as well. The *Sulasā Jātaka* (419) tells a similar story to Bhaddā's biography, but is said to be a previous life story of a servant of Anāthapiṇḍika and a robber. This jātaka has elements in common with a story in the *Petavatthu* commentary, although the version concerning *petas* (ghouls) is far removed from the biography of Bhaddā. A version of her biography also appears in the *Dhammapada* commentary, although this one is less comprehensive.

Summary of other sources

Bhaddā Kuṇḍalakesā appears on the list of distinguished nuns in the *Ekottarika-āgama*. In this case, her distinguished ability is said to be that she is foremost of those who 'attain final liberation'. Bhaddā Kuṇḍalakesā is the last nun on the *Ekottarika-āgama* list, number 51 of 51. She does not appear in the first or second decade of the list, in which are found listed most of the other prominent nuns from the Pāli canon, nor is she listed with the same or similar qualities as in the Pāli. As noted by Anālayo, the passage in which she appears, 'appears to have suffered a textual loss' (2013a, 111n56). He further notes that a nun named Bhaddā, noted as outstanding for 'quick realization', appears in a different place in the *Ekottarika-āgama* (2013a, 111n58). It would appear that there was also, at one time, a Tamil Buddhist text on the story of Bhaddā, the *Kuṇṭalakēci*. However, this text is now lost, although parts of it are recounted and retold in the Jain rejoinder to the text, the *Nīlakēci*, and there are about a hundred verses of it in various Tamil commentaries (Anne Monius, email 2011). The story of Bhaddā also appears in the Sinhala *Saddharmaratnāvaliya* (Obeyesekere 2001, 117–25).

Pāli accounts of Bhaddā Kuṇḍalakesā

The *Therīgāthā* verses attributed to Bhaddā Kuṇḍalakesā set the scene for one of the mainstay features of her biographical accounts—her previous status as a Jain practitioner. Although her conversion is mentioned in all accounts that follow below, how her conversion came about is recorded differently in the various biographies, and the difference in this case is striking. The variation between conversion accounts, between the canon and commentarial accounts, is one of the most major discrepancies found in all the accounts examined in this volume. Her *Therīgāthā* verses, which begin with reference to her Jain status, are as follows:

> Hair cut, wearing dirt, with one robe, I wandered previously, thinking there was fault where there was no fault, and that there was no fault where there was fault.
>
> Leaving from my daytime dwelling on Mount Gijjhakūṭa, I saw the stainless Buddha, attended by his community of monks.

Having bent my knee, having paid homage, I stood face-to-face with him, hands in the gesture of respect. 'Come, Bhaddā,' he said, that was my ordination.

I travelled over Aṅga and Magadha, Vajjī, Kāsi, and Kosala. Free from debt, for 50 years I enjoyed the alms of the kingdoms.

Indeed, that lay disciple is wise and has produced much merit, that one who gave a robe to Bhaddā who is now free from all bonds.[1]

The texts that record her biography are the *Apadāna*, the *Therīgāthā* commentary, the *Aṅguttara-nikāya* commentary, and the *Dhammapada* commentary. The *Sulasā Jātaka* (419) also contains a story that is very similar to Bhaddā's biography (see pages 64–5). The *Dhammapada* commentary only relates her present life, excluding any mention of past existences. The other three, however, begin with Bhaddā's life during the time of Buddha Padumuttara. The *Apadāna* tells us she was born into the family of a wealthy merchant in Haṃsavatī, while the *Aṅguttara-nikāya* commentary and the *Therīgāthā* commentary simply record that she was born into a good family, but again in Haṃsavatī. All three have her make an aspiration to become one of quick realization, when she sees another being accorded this accolade, and the *Apadāna* has Padumuttara predict she will attain that position during the time of Gotama Buddha.[2] Following her birth under Padumuttara Buddha

[1] *Thī* (vv. 107–11). *Lūnakesī paṅkadharī ekasāṭī pure cariṃ, avajje vajjamatinī vajje cāvajjadassinī. Divāvihārā nikkhamma gijjhakūṭamhi pabbate, addasaṃ virajaṃ buddhaṃ bhikkhusaṅghapurakkhataṃ. Nihacca jānuṃ vanditvā sammukhā pañjali ahaṃ, ehi bhadde ti avaca sā me ās' ūpasampadā. Ciṇṇā aṅga ca magadhā vajjī kāsī ca kosalā, anaṇā paṇṇāsavassāni raṭṭhapiṇḍaṃ abhuñji 'haṃ. Puññaṃ ca pasaviṃ bahuṃ sappañño vat' āyam upāsako, yo bhaddāya cīvaram adāsi muttāya sabbagandhehi.*

[2] It is difficult to decide upon how best to translate khippābhiññā. As this is the distinguished quality she is declared to have in the *AN* list, perhaps it is best to translate it as 'quick realization'. Corroborating this, in some of the commentarial accounts it is also noted at the conclusion that she attained to high states of religious experience quickly. However, there is also a more mundane sense in which the quality is attributed to her. In the *Apadāna, khippa* is used adverbially in three verses, in which

the *Aṅguttara-nikāya* commentary and the *Therīgāthā* commentary say that she journeyed on in worlds of gods and men for a hundred thousand aeons, while the *Apadāna* is more specific and records that she went first to the Tavatiṃsa realm, and then several other of the heavenly realms. All three then give detail of her birth under Buddha Kassapa, as one of the seven daughters of King Kikī. All then agree that in the era of Gotama Buddha she was born in Rājagaha, and this time all concur that she was the daughter of a wealthy merchant (seṭṭhikula). At this point, the *Aṅguttara-nikāya* commentary digresses into a narrative about Bhaddā's husband-to-be. In a unique vignette, the *Aṅguttara-nikāya* commentary tells us that on the very same day that Bhaddā was born, in the same city a son was born to the king's first brahmin priest (*purohita*). At the moment of his birth, all the weapons in the city, including those in the royal palace began to glow. This alarmed the king, who discovered the next day the cause was the birth of this boy born under the robber's star. The purohita advised the king that there was no particular harm foretold for the king due to the birth of this boy, but that he could send the boy away if the king so wished it. The king did not, so the boy grew up in the purohita's house, while Bhaddā grew up in the wealthy merchant's house. As soon as this boy, Sattuka, could walk, he took up the art of stealing, always bringing things back from wherever he went until his parent's home was full.[3] Once he grew up, his father, seeing that there was no way to keep him from his destiny, provided him with suitable attire and tools for housebreaking and sent him on his way! Soon, there was no house in the city that had not been penetrated by him, and when this came to the king's attention, he demanded the thief be caught. It is here that the other texts pick up the story, introducing Sattuka only as an adult.

---

she narrates how she quickly understood that Sattuka was intending to rob her, and then acts quickly in her own defence. Thus, in this account, the first one of the biography, she demonstrates a life-saving quick-wit.

3 Sattuka means 'enemy'. He is considered an enemy of the king because his actions create disharmony in relation to the smooth running of the king's sovereignty.

The *Dhammapada* commentary also picks up the story at this point, beginning its account with a rich merchant of Rājagaha, who had a sixteen-year-old daughter. As, according to the *Dhammapada* commentary, women of this age 'burn and long for men',[4] Bhaddā's father confines her to the top storey of the house. All versions recount Bhaddā's first sight of Sattuka similarly. The *Apadāna* is briefest on it, simply saying Bhaddā saw him as he was being led away to execution, and immediately become infatuated. All versions talk of her infatuation, but the other three situate her first sight of Sattuka as a glimpse out of a (latticed) window. The commentaries each repeat a similar refrain, communicating the grip of her obsession. 'If I have him I will live, if not I will die.'[5] All four versions agree that Bhaddā's father paid a thousand coins to have the thief released. After Bhaddā and Sattuka were married, he soon connived to steal her jewellery and ornaments. All four versions essentially relate this section the same, and it is very similar in the *Sulasā Jātaka*. Sattuka persuaded Bhaddā to go to a mountain, known as the 'thief's precipice', apparently to make an offering (to the goddess dwelling there according to the commentaries), but in reality to steal her jewels. The *Apadāna* tells us of his intention only briefly, while the commentaries provide details of the conniving dialogue by which he persuades her to accompany him. According to the commentaries, when they had arrived at the foot of the mountain, Sattuka realized he must stop their entourage going up with them, in order to successfully accomplish his task. The *Therīgāthā* commentary and the *Aṅguttara-nikāya* commentaries then narrate that on their walk up the mountain Sattuka uttered no loving word to Bhaddā, and because of this she understood his intention. In the *Dhammapada* commentary account she does not realize his intention so early, not until he tells her once they reach the summit. Sattuka demands she take off her jewels, and she appears to acquiesce, but does this while plotting herself now. In all but the *Dhammapada* commentary account, she then

4 *purisajjhāsaya honti purisalolā.*

5 *Thī-a* (97) *sace taṃ labhāmi jīvissāmi no ce marissāmī.* This same refrain is repeated in other stories of infatuation.

asked if he might allow her one final embrace, before killing her. He agrees to this fatal deed, and as she goes to embrace him—either for the first or second time—she instead pushed him over the cliff, and he falls to his death. In the commentaries, the goddess dwelling on the cliff then recites two verses from the *Apadāna* (now well known in relation to Bhaddā's story) on how a woman can be wise in some situations. The commentaries then tell us that, having done this deed, she realizes she cannot go home, so goes forth amongst the Jains, or female renouncers according to the *Dhammapada* commentary. All but the *Dhammapada* commentary detail that her new community pulls out her hair, as part of their highest ordination ceremony according to the *Aṅguttara-nikāya* commentary. The *Aṅguttara-nikāya* commentary and the *Therīgāthā* commentary also note that when her hair grew back it grew curly, and this is why she was called *kuṇḍalakesā* ('curly hair').

At this point the *Apadāna* and the commentaries part ways, and each continue to a different conversion narrative. The *Apadāna* then recounts that she learnt the Jain doctrine and lived alone. Then, in a somewhat ambiguous verse, narrates that she one day saw the error of her ways:

> Dogs seized a human hand that had been cut off, dropped it close to me and went away. Seeing the sign, I received the hand that was full of maggots.[6]

Then, stirred up by her experience, it was recommended to her that she go to the disciples of the Buddha. The disciples took her into the presence of the Buddha, who taught her the dhamma. She requested ordination, and was ordained by the Buddha with the words 'Come Bhaddā'.[7] The Buddha proclaims her as foremost of those with quick realization, and then, in the concluding verses, she voices all her attainments won through religious insight.

6 *Ap.* 563 (vv. 38–9) ... *samayaṃ taṃ vicintemi suvāṇā mānusaṃ karaṃ. Chinnaṃ gayha samīpe me pātayitvā apakkami disvā nimittaṃ alabhiṃ hatthaṃ taṃ puḷavākulaṃ.*

7 This phrase in Bhaddā Kuṇḍalakesā's verses is repeated in the monks' *Theragāthā* for the male Bhadda (v. 478): *ehi bhadda 'ti maṃ āha sā me ās' ūpasampadā.*

The commentaries begin with this same point of departure: Bhaddā learns and masters the doctrines of her (Jain) renouncer community. In the *Dhammapada* commentary, she is instructed to learn a thousand doctrines, but this is a preface for the *Dhammapada* verse to come. Following this, she takes up wandering from village to town, seeking to debate. Each commentary relates that she would place a rose-apple branch in a pile of sand near the gate to the town or village, and make it known that anyone who wished to challenge her in debate should trample down the branch. Each account indicates that she became an adept debater, and soon found none that could match her. The *Dhammapada* commentary goes so far as to say that whenever men knew she was in town, fearful of being drawn into a debate with her, they would run away. Each account tells us that a time comes when she arrives at Sāvatthī, that Sāriputta sees the rose-apple branch she has set up, has it trampled down, and thus sets up a contest between them. Learning of Sāriputta's challenge, Bhaddā went to meet with him, accompanied by a large crowd from the town. The two began to debate, with Bhaddā questioning Sāriputta on all questions and doctrine in which she had expertise. He could answer them all. When she had exhausted her best efforts and not defeated her interlocutor, it was then Sāriputta's turn to question her. He asked her one question, 'What is just one?' She could not answer. She was defeated in debate and so, according to the *Therīgāthā* commentary and the *Aṅguttara-nikāya* commentary, requested to go forth with Sāriputta as her teacher. He advised her to become a disciple of the Buddha, which she did, and according to all three accounts, very soon after that attained arahant status. This happens as a result of the *Dhammapada* verse according to the *Therīgāthā* commentary and the *Aṅguttara-nikāya* commentary, but the *Dhammapada* commentary itself has the verse come after the event, when the monks discuss Bhaddā's story and express surprise that she was admitted to the Order when she knew little dhamma. The *Therīgāthā* commentary and the *Aṅguttara-nikāya* commentary agree that *Dhammapada* verse 101 belongs in Bhaddā's biography, but in the *Dhammapada* commentary itself, Bhaddā's story is told to exemplify verses 102 and 103. In reality the verses are quite similar, with the first two each expressing how one word with poignancy and meaning is better than a thousand meaningless words. In each case, the Buddha tells the monks something akin to:

> Better than a thousand verses of meaningless words is one word of a verse that brings peace.[8]

In each of the accounts, Bhaddā is ordained as a follower of the Buddha.

Bhaddā Kuṇḍalakesā in the Jātakas

Unlike some of the other nuns whose biographies are told in this volume, there are no instances in the *Jātakatthavaṇṇanā* in which a character is said to be a previous incarnation of Bhaddā. However, elements of her story turn up in several of the jātakas, and two tales bear strong resemblances to her biography. The *Sulāsa Jātaka* (419, III.435–9) begins with a present-life account of a female servant of Anāthapiṇḍika. The servant asks to borrow a piece of jewellery to wear on a trip to the park from Anāthapiṇḍika's wife, Paṇṇalakkhaṇadevī. When she is at the park with her friends, a thief connived to steal her jewellery, and so began talking with her and offering her fine food to eat. She assumed his behaviour was borne from a sexual interest, so that night she went to him. He drew her out to a private place, but she became aware of his intention to kill her and steal the ornament, so she threw him down a well, and to ensure death occurs, also threw a brick at him. He died, and she recounted the story to Paṇṇalakkhaṇadevī. The Buddha told the story of the past as an example of how this same girl had been quick-witted in the past, killing the same man before. In the story of the past, the woman is the town courtesan, Sulasā by name. Sattuka in this version has the same name. As he was being lead off for execution, Sulasā, standing at a window saw him. She

[8] *Dhp* (vv. 101–3). *Sahassam api ce gāthā anatthapadasaṃhitā, ekaṃ gāthāpadaṃ seyyo yaṃ sutvā upasammatī. Yo ca gāthā sataṃ bhāse anatthapadasaṃhitā, ekaṃ dhammapadaṃ seyyo yaṃ sutvā upasammati. Yo sahassaṃ sahassena sāngāme mānuse june, ekañ ca jeyya-m-attānaṃ sa ve saṅgāmajuttamo ti.*

gained his release by offering a thousand pieces. But after Sattuka had spent three or four months with her, he decided to leave, but not without killing her first and taking her ornaments and other possessions. He deceives her again on the pretext he wants to make an offering to a—this time—tree-goddess who dwells on a mountain. He declares his intention to kill her once they reach the summit, but once again she outwits him with her request for one final embrace. This is essentially the end of the story, with the goddess recounting the verse on how women can be wise.

The story in the *Kaṇavera Jātaka* (*Jātakatthavaṇṇanā*, 318, III.58–63) is quite different, although it has many similar elements. This time, the *bodhisatta* (the Buddha in a previous life) is the robber. Following his apprehension, as he was being led away for execution, a courtesan named Sāmā was standing at an open window on an upper floor and saw him. She desired him, and eventually secured his release for the price of a thousand pieces, but this time it was more tricky. This time she had to lie, and say the robber was her brother, and she also had to coerce a client, a young man who was in love with her, to do her bidding for her. Besotted, he agreed and this unfortunate decision led to his untimely demise. The thief, now with Sāmā, again acted in an unsavoury manner, but through different intentions this time. He was concerned that Sāmā, once she was bored of him, might have him executed. So, he connived to take her out into the garden, and pretending to embrace her, squeezed so hard he made her unconscious. From this point, the story contains no more similarity to Bhaddā's.

6

Uppalavaṇṇā

Summary of Pāli sources

The idea of the historical figure of Uppalavaṇṇā has captured the hearts and minds of Buddhist authors and composers of narrative more so than any of the other nuns who are the subject of chapters in this volume. She is mentioned more in both the Pāli texts and texts of other traditions. This popularity is counterpoised with her biography being the most unpredictable of those studied in this volume. The three versions of the biography in Pāli do appear to be sourced from, or be attempts at relating, the same story, but the variation in this case is much greater. Uppalavaṇṇā also features much more in the *Jātakatthavaṇṇanā* than do the other nuns studied in this volume. Both in the many births recounted in the various versions of her biography and in the *Jātakatthavaṇṇanā* there are lovely, even poetic, vignettes relating to her name—'(blue) lotus-coloured one'. In one episode, she offers alms covered with lotus flowers, in various births lotus flowers spring up on the ground in the wake of her step (mirroring the episode in the legendary accounts of the life of the Buddha), and in a *Jātakatthavaṇṇanā* story she is a goddess who accuses the bodhisatta of stealing the smell of lotus flowers.

Uppalavaṇṇā and Khemā are identified as the two chief female monastics of the Buddha in the *Aṅguttara-nikāya* (twice, *AN* I.88, II.164), the *Saṃyutta-nikāya* (*SN* II.236), and the *Buddhavaṃsa* (v19, 98), and this is repeated in the *Dhammapada* commentary. In alignment with this, in the *Jātakatthavaṇṇanā*, she is one of the company who are often reborn alongside the bodhisatta. This group includes not only his blood relatives and sometimes wife, but also the two chief monks—Sāriputta and Moggallāna—and Ānanda, both a blood relative and his attendant.

Uppalavaṇṇā has *Therīgāthā* verses dedicated to her, and so also a biography in the *Therīgāthā* commentary; she is listed as foremost in supernormal powers (*iddhi*) in the *Aṅguttara-nikāya*, so also appears in its commentary. Some of the verses that form part of the extant *Therīgāthā* section attributed to her are also in the section on her in the chapter on nuns in the *Saṃyutta-nikāya*. She is also mentioned several times in the *Vinaya*, once in relation to a (female) disciple of hers, who is said to have followed the Buddha for several years learning the *Vinaya* (*Vin.* II.261). She is also mentioned in connection with the very first rule, the first *pārājikā*, which is to do with abstention from sexual intercourse (*Vin.* III.35). In this passage, Uppalavaṇṇā is said to have been raped. This sexual assault forms the largest part of the narrative account of her in the *Dhammapada* commentary.

The two versions of Uppalavaṇṇā's biography in the two *Apadāna* recensions differ. These two also differ from the account of her in the *Therīgāthā* commentary and the *Aṅguttara-nikāya* commentary. The account in the *Dhammapada* commentary does not accord with the other accounts in large part, in that here the focus is the incident of sexual assault. There are also many *Jātakatthavaṇṇanā* tales in which she features, and in which she has various roles (see pages 81–7).

Summary of other sources

A question has been raised –but not answered—as to whether Uppalavaṇṇā is depicted in early Buddhist art. She may be depicted in several versions of a scene of the Buddha's descent from the world of the gods. There are several stone reliefs which depict this scene, dating from potentially the third century BCE to the third century CE. A central feature of these scenes is the stairway upon which the Buddha descends. At the bottom of the stairway, in some of the images, is a bowing figure waiting to greet him. It is this figure that is suggested to be Uppalavaṇṇā.[1] This episode is recounted in Pāli texts, but in the Pāli versions, Uppalavaṇṇā does not feature in this episode, and instead it is Sāriputta who is the first to greet the Buddha as he makes his descent (*Dhp-a* III.199 and *JA* 1990–1, 483). The figure on the sculptures is a small, shaven-headed, robe-clad figure, and as Young points out, it 'could be either a monk or a nun' (2004, 194). Due to the ambiguity of the figure, and the various versions of the episode, there has been some debate as to whether the figure is indeed Uppalavaṇṇā.

The above episode is often part of a longer, well-known story of the performance of a miracle—or twin-miracle—by the Buddha. There are various versions of the story both in Pāli and in texts of other traditions. The episode is also recorded by Fǎxiǎn, a Chinese pilgrim who travelled in South Asia during the fifth century. In Fǎxiǎn's account, Uppalavaṇṇā is the first to meet the Buddha on his descent (Legge [1886] 1965, 49). The miracle story also appears in the *Divyāvadāna*, but the section on the descent is separate from it. Uppalavaṇṇā appears in the episode of the descent (Cowell and Neil 1886, 401) and she also features in the miracle story, as she does in the *Dhammapada* commentary version. In these two Sanskrit and Pāli cases, she is one of several disciples who offer to perform miracles for the Buddha, essentially to teach his detractors a lesson. The story further appears in the *Ekottarika-āgama* and its commentary (Anālayo 2013a, 102) and in certain other various southeast and east Asian versions, some of which feature Uppalavaṇṇā and some do not (see Young 2004, 192–4 and 2007).

[1] On the various reliefs, there are scenes that have no figure at the bottom of the stairs, some that have one, one that is damaged and can be seen to have had a figure in that place, and one with two women (but not monastics) kneeling and awaiting the Buddha (see Fabri [1930] and Young [2007, 17]). Neither Fabri nor Young mention the version of the image from Nāgārjunakoṇḍa, now in the Metropolitan Museum of Art, New York, dated to the third century CE, which is the image with two women at the bottom of the staircase.

Uppalavaṇṇā's popularity within other Buddhist traditions is unparalleled. For example, she is listed as a chief disciple in the Sanskrit Gilgit *Ekottarikā-āgama* (Okubo 1982, 21–2 as cited in Skilling 2001a, 248) and the Chinese *Ekottarikā-āgama* (see Anālayo 2013a, 100), as well as in the *Mahāvastu* (Senart 1882, 251). She also appears in the list of distinguished nuns in the Chinese *Ekottarikā-āgama*, listed with the same quality as in the Pāli one. Her short account in the *Saṃyutta-nikāya* is repeated in both versions of the Chinese *Saṃyukta-āgama*, she features is various tales in the Mūlasarvāstivāda *Vinaya* (see for example Silk 2009, 137–63 and Finnegan 2009, 227–9), is mentioned in the Sanskrit Mahāsaṃghika-Lokottaravāda *Vinaya* and its Chinese counterpart (see, for example, *saṅghātiśeṣa* 6), and in various other East Asian sources. For example, the Japanese Zen master Dōgen tells a story of her.[2] Further to this, there is a long account of her in the Mūlasarvāstivāda *Vinaya*, translated by Silk, which is a long tale of multiple acts of incest. Silk's argument on the relationship between the Mūlasarvāstivāda *Vinaya* account and that in the *Therīgāthā* commentary is that the Mūlasarvāstivāda *Vinaya* account and that in Dhammapāla's commentary are essentially the same story, and that the Mūlasarvāstivāda *Vinaya* version is an expanded version of the *Therīgāthā* commentary account. However, he does not mention—neither did Horner ([1930] 1990, 37)—that the account in the *Therīgāthā* commentary is claimed to be an account of the mother and daughter of Gangātīrya, not of Uppalavaṇṇā herself. Just prior to the beginning of the exegesis proper, the commentary records that Uppalavaṇṇā repeated the verses 'relating to the mother and daughter of the Elder Gaṅgātīriya, who lived as co-wives'.[3] The story is also mentioned, although fleetingly,

[2] Bingenheimer notes that her name is translated in the shorter *SA* while in the longer *SA* has a combination of translation and transliteration (2008, 8). See Young (2007, 26–9) for a survey of some East Asian sources on Uppalavaṇṇā.

[3] *Thī-a* (188) ... *gaṅgātīriyattherassa mātuyā dhītāya saddhiṃ sapattivāsaṃ uddissa.*

in the *Theragāthā* commentary's biography of Gangātīrya, as noted by C.A.F. Rhys-Davids ([1909] 2000, 112n3).

A biography of Uppalavaṇṇā also appears in the Sinhala *Saddharmaratnāvaliya* which, as to be expected, does mirror the *Dhammapada* commentarial account (trans. Obeyesekere 2001, 109–12).

Pāli accounts of Uppalavaṇṇā

As accounts of Uppalavaṇṇā in the Pāli sources are multifarious, I have divided this first part of the chapter into sections which tell the varying accounts of her biography. In addition, as she figures so prominently in the *Jātakatthavaṇṇanā*, I have included a section detailing these stories. Uppalavaṇṇā as an 'idea' seems to have penetrated the minds of the composers and compilers of these texts more so than the historical memory of the other nuns. But the ways in which she is remembered or 'constructed' vary considerably, ranging from being cited as an exemplary disciple, through depictions as a victim of rape to those as a benevolent goddess who teaches and comes to the aid of the bodhisatta. The verses attributed to Uppalavaṇṇā in the *Therīgāthā* are as follows:

> The two of us, mother and daughter, were co-wives; I experienced religious excitement, amazing, hair-rising.
>
> Woe upon sensual pleasures, impure, evil-smelling, with many troubles, wherein we, mother and daughter, were co-wives.
>
> I saw the danger in sensual pleasures and I saw renunciation of the world as firm security; I went forth at Rājagaha from home to the homeless state.
>
> I know I have lived before; I have purified the divine eye; and there is knowledge of the state of mind of others; I have purified the ear element;
>
> I have realised supernormal power too; I have attained the annihilation of the *āsavas*: I have realised the six supernormal knowledges; I have done the Buddha's teaching.
>
> I fashioned a four-horsed chariot by supernormal power, paid homage to the Buddha's feet, the glorious protector of the world, and I stood to one side.

'Going up to a tree with a well-flowered top, you stand there alone at the foot of the tree, you do not even have a companion; child, are you not afraid of rogues?'

Even if 100,000 rogues like you were to come together, I shall not move a hair's breadth, I should not even shake. What will you alone do to me, Māra?

'I shall disappear, or I shall enter into your belly; I shall stand between your eyebrows; you will not see me standing there.'

I have mastery over my mind; I have developed the bases of supernormal powers well; I have realised the six supernormal knowledges; I have done the Buddha's teaching.

Sensual pleasures are like sword stakes, the elements of existence the executioner's block; what you call 'delight in sensual pleasures' is now non-delight for me.

Everywhere enjoyment of pleasure is defeated; the mass of darkness (of ignorance) is torn asunder, in this way, evil one, you are defeated, death.[4]

As mentioned, Dhammapāla glosses the first two of these—on the status of co-wife—as the verses of one of the former wives of Gaṅgātīriya but, as with other instances in which Dhammapāla glosses speech in the first person as recitation of the verses of another, there is little reason to assume this was actually the intention. If it were the case, as would seem so, that at the time Dhammapāla composed his commentary, the idea of a story of a

[4] Thī (vv. 224–35). This is essentially Norman's revised translation (Rhys Davids and Norman 1989, 197), but with one or two changes. *Ubho mātā ca dhītā ca mayaṃ āsuṃ sapattiyo, tassā me ahu saṃvego abbhuto lomahaṃsano. Dhiratthu kāmā asucī duggandhā bahukaṇṭakā, yattha mātā ca dhītā ca sabhariyā mayaṃ ahuṃ. Kāmesv ādīnavaṃ disvā nekkhammaṃ daḷhakhemato, sā pabbujiṃ rājagahe agārasmā anagāriyaṃ. Pubbenivāsaṃ jānāmi dibbacakkhuṃ visodhitaṃ, ceto paricca ñāṇañ ca sotadhātu visodhitā. Iddhi pi me sacchikatā patto me āsavakkhayo, cha me abhiññā sacchikatā kataṃ buddhassa sāsanaṃ. Iddhiyā abhinimmitvā caturassuṃ rathaṃ ahaṃ, buddhassa pāde vanditvā lokanāthassa sirīmato. Supupphitaggaṃ upagamma pādapaṃ ekā tuvaṃ tiṭṭhasi rukkhamūle, na cāpi te dutiyo atthi koci na tvaṃ bale bhāyasi dhuttakānaṃ. Sataṃ sahassānaṃ pi dhuttakānaṃ*

co-wife was more closely associated with the life of Gaṅgātīriya, and by then not recorded in other accounts of Uppalavaṇṇā, then this is likely his motive. Whether these *Therīgāthā* verses were originally intended to be attributed to Uppalavaṇṇā is now difficult to say. Dhammpāla re-tells this story as part of the commentarial exegesis on Uppalavaṇṇā, going against his more usual format. A reason for Dhammapāla's problem with attributing these verses to Uppalavaṇṇā may have been her association with the Buddha's family of origin. The verses 230–2 correspond to some of the verses attributed to her in the bhikkhuṇisaṃyutta in the *Saṃyutta-nikāya*, and represent part of her conversation with Māra.[5] As with the other short stories in the bhikkhuṇisaṃyutta, Māra approaches her and tries to outwit her to stop her from continuing to follow the Buddha's path.

Uppalavaṇṇā in Apadāna I

In the European edition, the first verses, 1–22, involve Uppalavaṇṇā relating the virtues of her discipleship, including her realized supernormal powers (iddhi), making obeisance to the Buddha, acknowledging her skin that is the colour of the blue lotus (*uppala*), and distinguishing herself as the daughter of the Buddha and sister to Rāhula. Many women in this biographical genre speak of themselves as, or are spoken of as, daughters of the Buddha, just as males are similarly sons, but these are more often than not

---

samāgatā edisakā bhaveyyuṃ, lomaṃ na iñje na pi sampavedhe kiṃ me tuvaṃ māra karissas' eko. Esā antaradhāyāmi kucchiṃ vā pavisāmi te, bhamukantare tiṭṭhāmi tiṭṭhantiṃ maṃ na dakkhisi. Cittamhi vasībūtāhaṃ iddhipādā subhāvitā, cha me abhiññā sacchikatā kataṃ buddhassa sāsanaṃ. Sattisūlūpamā kāmā khandhānaṃ adhikuṭṭanā, yaṃ tvaṃ kāmaratiṃ brūsi arati dāni sā mama. Sabbattha vihatā nandi tamokkhandho padālito, evaṃ jānāhi pāpima nihato tvam asi antakā ti. Norman notes that verse 229 has no finite verb and adds *ekamantaraṃ aṭṭhāsiṃ* on the basis of the commentary ([1969/1971] 2007 124n229). I have added quotation marks for verse 232. See Anālayo (2013a, 124–5 and 133f.) for a discussion on whether this verse is spoken by Uppalavaṇṇā or Māra.

5 These also appear in the *Ap*. I recension.

a reference to discipleship conceived as a metaphorical familial relationship, rather than an assertion of bloodline. Uppalavaṇṇā's case, however, is less straightforward, as it is much less common to find mention of blood relation to the monk known to be the Buddha's son, Rāhula. The next set of verses, 23–39, recount her 100,000 *kalpas* living as a *nāga* girl named Vimalā. At this time, Padumuttara Buddha visits the nāga world and takes a meal offering from the nāga king. Having finished his meal and washed his bowl, Padumuttara points out to the nāga girl a nun who possesses the sorts of supernormal powers she desires, and predicts she will herself attain them.

The remainder of the verses, with the exception of 71–6, appear in the recension in the *Therīgāthā* commentary.[6] The remainder of the narrative recounts her various lives. Upon death in her last existence, she is reborn in the Tāvatiṃsa realm. Following that, she was born into the world of men, and offered alms covered with blue lotus flowers. Then she is reborn in the era of Buddha Vipassī into a merchant family in Vārāṇasī. She made an offering of lotuses to Buddha Vipassī and—in her mind–wished to be reborn with a beautiful complexion.[7] Next she is born during the era of Kassapa, as one of the seven sisters. Following this is another existence in the Tāvatiṃsa, then several human and non-human births before her final birth at the time of Gotama Buddha. In the second of these human births she is said have been born in the town of Āriṭṭha into a brahmin family and is their captivating daughter named Ummadantī (see page 85, jātaka number 527). In her next birth she was born in the country into a family that was not wealthy, and her role was to guard their rice fields. One day, she

6 Verses 71–6 are essentially a repeat of Uppalavaṇṇā's *Therīgāthā* verses. Verses 71–4 are also Uppalavaṇṇā's verses in the *SN* to Māra (the same as the *Therīgāthā*). Verses 75–6 are common verses, one appearing in full in the *SN* attributed to Āḷavika, and half of the other in Kisāgotamī's verses, but both occur often in the *Therīgāthā*.

7 *...cetasā va vaṇṇasobhaṃ apatthayiṃ*. Lilley emended from *ca teh' eva vaṇṇassetaṃ apatthayiṃ*, following Pruitt's emendation in *Ap* II. Lilley's manuscript G. has *vaṇṇasobhaṃ*. For more on the wish to be reborn beautiful also see *JA* no. 527 and Anālayo (2014a, 108–41).

offered to a paccekabuddha[8] five hundred grains of parched rice, covered with lotus flowers (but this time the word is *paduma*) and made a request for five hundred sons. In her next birth, she was then born in a forest inside a lotus. She became the chief queen of the king of Kāsi, and gave birth to exactly five hundred sons. While playing when young, her sons saw a leafless lotus and became paccekabuddhas.[9] Experiencing grief at the loss of her sons, she died and took another human rebirth in a village on the slopes of Mount Isigili. In this birth she saw other paccekabuddhas who reminded her of her sons, and she made an offering to them. Passing on from this existence, she was reborn in a beautiful park in Tāvatiṃsa, then journeyed on through several more births until her final birth during the era of the historical Buddha.

She was born into a family of merchants in Sāvatthī. She was sought after by many suitable and handsome men, but had no interest in household life; so she went forth and before half a month had passed she attained realization of the four noble truths. Then follow the inserted verses (71–6), with no attempt to relate them to the narrative, and the account ends with some of the typical final *Apadāna* verses, with the Buddha placing Uppalavaṇṇā as foremost of those with supernormal powers, and Uppalavaṇṇā saying she has done the Buddha's teaching, and destroyed all bonds.

Uppalavaṇṇā in Apadāna II

The first verses in this recension, 1–13, are absent in the European edition. This account begins with her birth at the time of Padumuttara Buddha, but this time she is not a female nāga; instead, she is born as a human, into a merchant's family in Haṃsavatī. She became a disciple, and seeing the Buddha praise

8 A paccekabuddha is a type of Buddha, a single or solitary Buddha, one who attains Awakening but does not proclaim his truth to others.

9 Although they are called *pacceka*-leaders in the text (*paccekanāyakā*) the implication here seems to be that they became paccekabuddhas, as this is what happens in the other versions, and buddhas are often referred to as leaders (*nāyaka*) in the *Apadāna*, such as in the often repeated epithet *lokanāyaka* ('leader of the world').

a nun as foremost of those with supernormal powers (iddhi), she wished for that position. She invited the Buddha and his community and fed them for seven days, also making offerings of robes and garlands, and she declared her aspiration to the Buddha. He predicted that she would attain the position during the era of Gotama Buddha, as a disciple named Uppalavaṇṇā, famed for her beauty. The remainder of this account mirrors that above. In her next birth she went to the Tāvatiṃsa realm, and then had three successive human births. In the first she gave alms covered with lotus flowers to a paccekabuddha. Then, during the era of Vipassī she was born into another merchant family in Vārāṇasī. Again, she made offering of lotus flowers to Buddha Vipassī and wishes to be born with a beautiful complexion. Next she is reborn as one of the seven daughters of King of Kāsi during the time of Buddha Kassapa. Following this is another visit to Tāvatiṃsa, and another human birth into an important family during which she makes an offering of a yellow cloth to an arahant. After this comes the life as Ummādantī, then the birth into a poor working family and the story of the paccekabuddha to whom she offers rice and makes a request for five hundred sons. Next is the life during which she is chief queen to the king of Kāsi, has five hundred sons who become paccekabuddhas after seeing a lotus without leaves and all depart, then the life-episode in which she sees eight paccekabuddhas, followed by rebirth in the beautiful park in Tāvatiṃsa, some unspecified journeying on, and finally her last existence in Sāvatthī.

Uppalavaṇṇā in the Therīgāthā *and* Aṅguttara-nikāya *commentaries*

The biographical account in these two texts, as Pruitt (1999, 232n1) notes, is almost word-for-word, thus suggesting one may have been copied from the other. As the *Aṅguttara-nikāya* commentary is attributed to Buddhaghosa and the *Therīgāthā* commentary to Dhammapāla, it is most likely the *Aṅguttara-nikāya* commentary is the earlier one.[10] This account begins at the time of Padumuttara

10 As this account is more like the narrative in *Ap.* II, it may suggest that this recension was the one Buddhaghosa knew.

Buddha, and as per the *Apadāna* II version, she is born into a good family in Haṃsavatī. Again, she was a disciple and seeing the Buddha place a nun as foremost of those with supernormal powers she aspired to that position herself. As in *Apadāna* II, she makes an offering for seven days, but this time the saṅgha is conceptualized as 'the community of monks with the Buddha at its head', rather than simply the community (saṅgha) as in *Apadāna* II.[11] She then journeyed on through worlds of gods and men and was reborn during the era of Kassapa as one of the seven sisters. Following this, she took another birth in a *deva* (god) realm, then another human one. This human birth is the one that appears in both *Apadāna* recensions, but here the detail is slightly different. She is born into a life in which she must work for a living, but in this case her job is not specified to be in the rice fields. Here, her offering of five hundred grains of parched rice is inspired by a lotus flower she sees blooming in a pond. She takes the flower and a leaf in order to make a parcel to offer, goes home, and cooks the rice and waits. Then a paccekabuddha arrives and she makes the offering but quickly regrets it, thinking, 'Those who have gone forth have no use for flowers. I'll take back the flower and adorn myself.'[12] So she took the flower from the paccekabhuddha's hand, then had a second change of heart, realizing this was a mistake, and gave it back again. She requested from the paccekabuddha that as a result of the offering she has 'sons equalling the grains of rice in number'[13] and also that in every place that she is born, lotus flowers appear at each footstep. The paccekabuddha took her flower and placed in upon a staircase used by other paccekabuddhas, and as a result of this she was reborn into a deva realm and in the wake of every one of her footsteps, a lotus flower would blossom.

[11] ... *buddhapamukhassa bhikkhusaṅghassa*. See Strauch (2013) for a discussion of the phrase 'the community of monks with the Buddha at its head' and a Gāndhārī version of a sutta which includes the otherwise little-known phrase 'the community of nuns with the Buddha at its head'.

[12] *Pabbajitā nāma pupphena anathikā, ahaṃ pupphaṃ gahetvā pilandhissāmī AN-a* I.346.

[13] ... *lājagaṇanāya puttā*.

In her next birth she was born inside a lotus flower, on a lake at the foot of a mountain. An ascetic, going to the lake, saw the lotus flower and picked it; the flower opened to reveal the baby girl. The ascetic took her in as his daughter (milk coming to his thumb to feed her), and once again, when the toddler began to run around, lotus flowers would spring up in her step. In this life, she was known as Padumavatī. When she was older, a forester saw her and did not imagine one so beautiful could be human. However, when he saw her preparing food for her 'father' the hermit, he became convinced she was indeed human. The forester took some food with the ascetic, and then went to Vārāṇasī to inform the king of this jewel of a woman he had met. The king wanted her for himself and so persuaded the ascetic to let him take her as his chief queen. Once he was with her, he did not pay attention to his other wives. The wives became jealous of her, desiring to create disharmony between her and the king. They spoke to the king, asking how such a woman, who has lotus flowers appear where she walks, could be human. 'Surely she is a demon,' they said. When she was pregnant and near to giving birth, the king was called away to battle at the border. The jealous wives took this as an opportunity and formulated a plot against her. They bribed an attendant to take her child away when it was born. Although she only had one child, four hundred and ninety-nine more were born from the moisture of her womb.[14] At this, each of the jealous women, of whom there were also conveniently five hundred, took a child away, while the attendant smeared a log of wood with blood and placed it near Padumavatī, who had not yet come round from the birth. When she did come round, the attendant scolded her, thrusting the log of wood in front of her and telling her this was what she had given birth to. Ashamed, she got the attendant to dispose of the log. Meanwhile, the five hundred wives had a box

14 Within the Pāli canon, four different types of possible births are listed, including this type—moisture-born (*saṃsedajā*). (See, for example, *MN* I.73, D III.230; *Mil.* vv. 128–9.) However, moisture-born is often used as a description of the rise of (what we would call) bacterial growth from rotting substances, such as rotting food or flesh, rather than the way it is used here.

made for each child and kept them quiet in the boxes. When the king returned they told him to question the attendant, and that his beloved had given birth to a log of wood. Hearing the account the jealous wives wanted him to hear of what has transpired, the king realized Padumavatī must be descended from non-humans and threw her out of the house.

She was taken in by an old woman, and meanwhile the jealous wives carried on scheming to dispose of the bodies of the children. They requested the king take them to the Ganges to make an offering, and each was able to conceal their box containing one child under their garments. At the river, they went in and released the boxes. However, the boxes were caught in a net not far off and the king, emerging from the Ganges, saw them. He had them opened, and Sakka had caused an inscription to be written in one of the boxes so that the king would know these were his five hundred sons, born of Padumavatī. Feeling remorseful at having not believed her, he sent out a search party, offering a thousand coins for anyone who knew where she was. She was found and the pair reunited. The king made the five hundred women her slaves, but after it was made known they were her slaves, she had them released and each of them (except one) was given a son to rear. She kept her womb-born child for herself.

When they were older, the young princes all played together in the royal garden, with its ponds covered with lotus flowers. They saw young lotuses in bloom and old ones dying. At this sight they had a collective realization of impermanence and at that all rose up and sat cross-legged on top of the lotus flowers. They became paccekabuddhas and disappeared into the sky. Padumavatī was broken-hearted and soon died from the grief of losing her sons.

The subsequent birth is the story of the eight paccekabuddhas, as in the other two versions. Again, in this account there is more detail, and in this case she is born in a different place—in Rājagaha, and born into a working life. She marries into a good family, and this time is said to see eight of the paccekabuddhas who are her sons, rather than simply some who remind her of them. She invited the eight to a meal at her house the next day, and prepared seating and food for eight, but they bought their brothers along with them, so all five hundred turned up. But she was not perturbed by this. As they sat down more seats than the eight prepared manifested and the house grew bigger. She offered the food prepared for eight but it was enough to feed the five hundred. She then brought eight handfuls of blue lotus flowers and offered them asking that in subsequent births her body's complexion be the colour of the hearts of these dark lotuses.

Next, she was born again in a deva realm and then finally reached her last birth during the era of Gotama Buddha. Here, as in all versions, she is born into a merchant family in Sāvatthī. She was so beautiful that many men desired her but her father, fearing he could upset some, asked her to go forth instead.[15] She agreed and, again, as in all versions, very quickly made good progress to arahantship.

Uppalavaṇṇā in the Dhammapada *commentary*

There is essentially only one account of Uppalavaṇṇā in the *Dhammapada* commentary, but the second part of it appears in two places. The account appears initially as an exegesis for a verse on the ripening of kamma (verse 69). The second part of it also appears later on as an exposition of a *Dhammapada* verse in the chapter on the true nature of a brahmin. The account of Uppalavaṇṇā includes a summary biography of various births and this takes up the first third of it. We are told that Uppalavaṇṇā made an aspiration at the time of Buddha Padumuttara. Then instead of going into the detail of her various lives, the text simply tells us that 'performing meritorious deeds for a hundred thousand aeons, she journeyed on through worlds of *devas* and men'.[16] The text also repeats that during the era of Gotama, she was born in Sāvatthī, as the daughter of a rich merchant, and that her complexion resembled a blue lotus flower, so she was named Uppalavaṇṇā. Further, it tells the story of the present life as above, that she was desired by many but her father, not wanting to offend any, asked her to go forth which she did happily. There is also a passage here

[15] Note that in the *Ap.* accounts Uppalavaṇṇā decides for herself to go forth, while in the commentaries it is her father who desires it.

[16] ... *kappasatasahassaṃ puññaṃ kurumānā devesu ca manussesu ca saṃsarantī*..., *Dhp-a* II.48.

on how she comes to attain arahantship—through contemplating the flame of a lamp, which is also found in the *Therīgāthā* and *Aṅguttara-nikāya* commentaries.

The remainder of the story does not appear in any of the above accounts, although it obviously relates to a passage in the Pāli *Vinaya*, in the monks' section, on the first pārājika about abstaining from sexual intercourse. This *Vinaya* passage tells how Uppalavaṇṇā was raped, and advises that this is not to be deemed a breach of the first pārājikā, as she was not willing. The account in the *Dhammapada* commentary looks to be based upon the *Vinaya* passage as features of the two accounts overlap. In this commentarial version, Uppalavaṇṇā resides in a hut in the forest.[17] One day, a young brahmin named Ānanda, her cousin, steals into her hut and hides. When she returns he obstructs her, overcomes her, does what he intended to do, and leaves. As a result of his action the earth burst open, swallowed him up, and he was reborn into a terrible hell-world. This matter was told to the Buddha who explains it by saying that anyone who commits such a nefarious act may well experience it as pleasurable at the time but—as the *Dhammapada* verse recited here makes clear—this is because they are unaware of the consequences.

Next in the text comes the commentarial exegesis, which is usually the end of a section, but following this is a further narrative section, which may well have been added in here, as this is the section repeated later on, in Book 26, in relation to *Dhammapada* verse 401. In its latter appearance in Book 26, it is in its correct sequential place, coming between the exegesis of verses 400 and 402. The two versions of it are identical. Both say: Some time later, the community (a community of followers we assume) assembled in the dhamma-hall and began to discuss the incident. They raised questions as to whether someone such as Uppalavaṇṇā, who had destroyed the defilements and thus was advanced on the path, would enjoy a sexual encounter, given that she was after all simply a human being 'of moist flesh'[18] and not an inanimate object, like a tree or

[17] See the discussion in Chapter 9 on nuns and their (lack of) use of huts (*kuṭi*).

[18] *allamaṃsasarīrā*.

ant-hill. When the Buddha arrived, he instructed them that this would not have been the case—not because it was a sexual assault—but because those who have destroyed the defilements do not enjoy pleasures of the senses nor need to gratify their passions (see Chapter 9 for a discussion for sexual assault, and especially page 153 on this incident). The Buddha then pronounces the *Dhammapada* verse on how a true brahmin does not cling to the pleasures of the senses. Finally, the narrative concludes by indicating that this incident was the cause for the prohibition, as stated in the Pāli *Vinaya* (II.278), that nuns should not stay alone in the forest due to the possibility of sexual assault. The Kosalan king, Pasenadi, is summoned and agrees to build a residence for nuns so that they can live together in safety.[19]

Uppalavaṇṇā in the Jātakatthavaṇṇanā

Uppalavaṇṇā appears in many *Jātakatthavaṇṇanā* stories, in various roles. In some, she is listed in the end section but her character is named only in passing, and has no role in the story. In others her character plays a central role, sometimes as a loving mother, a benevolent goddess, or a captivating beauty.

Kharādiya Jātaka (15, I.159). In this jātaka Uppalavaṇṇā was a deer, the sister of the bodhisatta, and a mother, who asked the bodhisatta to instruct her son, but the unruly boy would take no heed of his teacher.

Tipallatthamiga Jātaka (16, I.160). In this jātaka she was the mother of Rāhula, then born as a stag and is again depicted as a caring mother, hoping her son will learn the ways of the deer, and this time her ambitions for her son are rewarded, as this child learns how to successfully escape a hunter's trap.

Kaṇha Jātaka (29, I.193). In this jātaka, Uppalavaṇṇā is an old woman, and the bodhisatta is a bull. She reared the bullock as if he was her own child, and because of her care and nurturance, the bodhisatta

19 As noted in Chapter 9, this account, as it now stands, gives a clear picture of the range of views on sexual assault found in the Pāli corpus, ranging from assumptions that a woman might enjoy it, to inspiring an edict that nuns must be protected from potential assailants.

sought to earn money to repay her. But he exhausted himself and for that she was annoyed with him, as a mother would be to a misguided child. Here again she epitomizes a loving mother, as she bathes him and settles him after his arduous day.

Mudulakkhanā Jātaka (66, I.302). The bodhisatta is a sage living a solitary life and goes for alms to a beautiful queen, whom he catches sight of bathed, perfumed, adorned, and with her soft, fine clothing falling off. At this ravishing sight, he is overcome with lust. This altruistic woman goes out of her way to help him to forget his infatuation by being very demanding and, essentially, because of her constant demands he loses interest in her. Uppalavaṇṇā was this woman who, in this instance, seems to have been the more robust of the two, driven as she was to motivate the sage to lose his worldly infatuation.

Sārambha Jātaka (88, I.374). In this jātaka, Uppalavaṇṇā is said to have been the wife of a brahmin, and although he is a key character, his wife has no role in the story. The story here is almost identical to the *Nandivisāla Jātaka* (28), and so not repeated in the text. Only the details that change are mentioned, but while Uppalavaṇṇā is mentioned in the set of details that change, in the telling of the story there is no wife. Both of these are similar to the *Kaṇha Jātaka*, although, in this instance it is a brahmin, rather than an old woman, who rears the bull. The moral of this tale and the *Nandivisāla Jātaka* differ from the *Kaṇha Jātaka* as they are both told as a warning against speaking harshly, with the bodhisatta as a bull here refusing to perform a task for the brahmin when he is addressed harshly.

Kurudhamma Jātaka (276, II.365). In this jātaka, Uppalavaṇṇā is a courtesan who keeps the five moral precepts.[20] This narrative is structured around some pithy questioning of five different people as to whether they keep to the Buddha's precepts, as they are purported to do. The courtesan is questioned as to whether she does indeed adhere to following the precepts, as others who are virtuous, and it transpires that she does. As mentioned in Chapter 9, in this story there is no moral

[20] The word used is either 'gaṇikā' or '*nagarasobhaṇā*'.

indignation expressed against the lifestyle or role of the courtesan—she is moral as any other, and her lifestyle appears to have had no bearing on that.

Uraga Jātaka (354, III.162). The preface to this jātaka situates it as told to a man who is grieving for his dead son. The Buddha tells him that all things are subject to dissolution, and that previously, the learned ones of the past did not weep when they lost a son. In this jātaka, Uppalavaṇṇā is the brahmin's daughter, sister of the deceased son.[21] None of the family grieves when the son dies, so Sakka asks them why they were not grieving, and each relates their view as to why weeping is pointless. Uppalavaṇṇā's verses are as follows:

> If I were to weep I would become thin; what would be the fruit for me? My relatives and friends would not be happier.
>
> He who burns does not know his friends lament. Because of this I do not grieve, he has gone where he has gone.[22]

In the story, Khujjuttarā is said to have been the slave, Uppalavaṇṇā the daughter, Rāhula the son, Khemā the wife, and the bodhisatta the brahmin. These together then, the lay disciple Khujjuttarā, the two nuns, a monk, and the Buddha, are collectively the learned ones of the past—three women and two males.

Sirikālakaṇṇi Jātaka (382, III.257). In this jātaka, Uppalavaṇṇā is the goddess Sirī, daughter of Dhataraṭṭha, one of the four heavenly kings.[23] In this tale, Sirī and another goddess, a daughter of another of the kings, disagree over which of them should be allowed to bathe first. Their fathers, the other two kings, and Sakka cannot settle this disagreement, so they send the two goddesses to the bodhisatta, an honest and pure

[21] Malasekhere notes this jātaka as the *Dhonasākha Jātaka* 353, but it is the next one, 354.

[22] *Sace rode kisī assaṃ, tassā me kiṃ phalaṃ siyā, ñātimittāsuhajjānaṃ bhiyyo no aratī siyā. Ḍayhamāno na jānāti ñātinaṃ paridevitaṃ, tasmā etaṃ na socāmi gato so tassa yā gatīti* (*JA* III.165–6).

[23] Dhataraṭṭha is traditionally one of the four kings of Buddhist cosmology.

householder, who keeps a clean, unused bed and couch for whenever a good and righteous person should call. Sirī is offered the home comforts in the end, as she proves herself to be the good and righteous goddess. She does this by recounting, when questioned by the bodhisatta, that she associates only with those who are kind, friendly, honest, and righteous and that if a fool were to become infatuated with her loveliness, she would avoid him.

Bhisapuppha Jātaka (392, III.307). In this enchanting jātaka, Uppalavaṇṇā is a goddess who accuses the bodhisatta, then a sage, of stealing the smell of lotus flowers. The bodhisatta protests to her that he has not picked nor damaged the flower, and that it is with other men who destroy flowers that she should take umbrage. The goddess explained to him that such men are not worthy of her attention; she chooses to speak only to unblemished men who seek purity, and for whom any whisper of iniquity displays itself like a dark cloud in the clear sky. The bodhisatta, comprehending her insightfulness, asks her to tell him if she sees him do ill again. But she replies that she is not there to serve him, and that he needs to find the path for himself.

Manoja Jātaka (397, III.321). In this jātaka, the bodhisatta is a lion, and Uppalavaṇṇā his daughter, but here she has no part in the extant story.

Kumbhakāra Jātaka (408, III.375). Uppalavaṇṇā is the bodhisatta's daughter, although she barely figures in the narrative at all. The bodhisatta is born as a potter; he hears a discourse of some paccekabuddhas and becomes disinclined to household life, seeking to leave the world. His wife has a similar desire, deceives him, renounces the world, and goes forth before him, leaving him to care for the son and daughter. He brings them up, until they are old enough to cook rice for themselves, and then leaves to go forth himself. One day, he sees his former wife, who accuses him of having killed the children, but he denies it, asserting that he taught them how to take care of themselves before he left.

Jāgara Jātaka (414, III.403). In this jātaka, Uppalavaṇṇā is a tree-spirit from whom the bodhisatta gains merit.

Saṅkha Jātaka (442, IV.15). In this jātaka, Uppalavaṇṇā is a compassionate goddess of the sea, called Maṇimekhalā.

Bhisa Jātaka (488, IV.304). Uppalavaṇṇā is the bodhisatta's sister, but her role is minimal; she is one of a group of siblings who renounce instead of marrying.

Rohantamiga Jātaka (501 IV.413). In this jātaka, Uppalavaṇṇā is again sister to the bodhisatta. In this tale, the bodhisatta is a deer, who gets caught in trap. Ensnared and with his life at risk, Sutanā, his sister, will not leave him, and neither will his brother. However, when Sutanā sees the hunter coming, she is afraid and runs away a little on impulse. However, in an act of altruism, she comes back, ready to die rather than abandon her brother. In so doing, she helped to win his freedom.

Kiñchanda Jātaka (511, V.7). In this jātaka, Uppalavaṇṇā is a benevolent goddess of the river, who saves the bodhisatta, an ascetic, from hunger.

Jayaddisa Jātaka (513, V.21). Uppalavaṇṇā is a younger sister of the bodhisatta, who, although mentioned in passing, has no role in the narrative.

Tesakuṇa Jātaka (521, V.109). In this jātaka, Uppalavaṇṇā is a Kuṇḍalinī, a mynah bird the king takes as his own child, along with an owl and a parrot. Sāriputta was the owl and the bodhisatta the parrot. The king assembles a multitude of people, to make known the wisdom of his 'children'; he goes first to see the owl and questions him, then the mynah bird, and then the parrot. When he goes to visit the 'daughter', she thinks to herself that she is being tested because she is a woman and that the king is questioning what a woman would be able to teach him. The answer to that question is that she can offer a great deal, as it turns out, as she matches the owl in his exposition of righteous kingship, although, of course, the parrot (bodhisatta) gives the best discourse of the three.

Ummadantī Jātaka (527, V.209). Uppalavaṇṇā is Ummadantī, a woman who was so beautiful that men could not control themselves in her presence.[24] The extant text tells us that she had asked

24 The words *ummāda* and *ummādanā* mean something that maddens or is a distraction, thus Ummadantī's name indicates she is one who is distracting or maddens (with desire).

for this privilege to be hers in a past life, and it was granted due to her offering a scarlet robe. The king (the bodhisatta), being told of her beauty, sent men to see her on his behalf, but taking an audience with her they were overcome with infatuation and so she, disgusted with them, had them thrown out. Angered by the actions of Ummadantī, they told the king she was a witch and that he should not marry her. At being spurned she bore a grudge against the king, and instead married his commander-in-chief (Sāriputta). Up until this point, the king has never seen her and so she conspires for him to glance upon her, so that he will become consumed with desire for her. This transpires, and thus she has her revenge. Then her husband decides he should offer Ummadantī to the king. He does so but after an exchange of stanzas in which he teaches the king about righteousness, the king forgets about his infatuation.

Sudhābhojana Jātaka (535, V.382). In this jātaka, Uppalavaṇṇā is one of Sakka's four daughters. They see a flower which they each desire, and ask their father to decide who should have it—he cannot choose one of them over the other, so sends them to a sage whom he charges with the decision. The daughter that is Uppalavaṇṇā is chosen, as she is the most noble and honourable of the daughters.

Mūgapakkha Jātaka (538, VI.1). King Kāsirājā had 16,000 wives but no children. His chief queen, Candādevī, who was virtuous, after undertaking some religious practice, desired a son. Sakka had the bodhisatta become her son. The bodhisatta, as an infant, had no desire to grow up to succeed his father as king. One day when he was laying under a white umbrella, the goddess of the umbrella (Uppalavaṇṇā), who had been his mother in a past life, instructed him to pretend to be disabled, deaf, and dumb. He did as she instructed, and as a disabled deaf-mute was considered to be bad luck. He was sent to be murdered and buried but managed to escape alive and lead a renunciate life. His mother and father, on hearing of his escape, set out to visit him. When they do, he gives a discourse and as a result the king and queen and 16,000 wives all desire to go forth.

Mahājanaka Jātaka (539, VI.30). Uppalavaṇṇā is a goddess of sea called Maṇimekhalā. The episode in the narrative in which she features is very similar to the *Saṅkha Jātaka*. Appointed to watch over the sea, she saved the bodhisatta when his ship sank and took him to Mithilā, as if he was her own beloved child.

Sāma Jātaka (540, VI.68). Uppalavaṇṇā is a goddess again, called Bahusodarī, but this time has a larger part to play in the overall narrative plot. The bodhisatta lives with his parents in a hermitage, but one day they are blinded by a viperous snake. He cares for them, but is one day shot by a poisonous arrow at the hands of the king, which is to prove fatal. The king, in his guilt, offers to look after the bodhisatta's parents. Now the goddess, who had formerly been a mother to the bodhisatta, intervenes. She takes the poison from the bodhisatta's body, and restores the parents' sight.

Khaṇḍahāla Jātaka (542, VI.129). In this jātaka, Uppalavaṇṇā is Selā, one of many daughters of the king, but she is mentioned only fleetingly, as the king has many wives and children, some of whom have more prominent roles.

Bhūridatta Jātaka (543, VI.157). Uppalavaṇṇā is Accimukhī, the bodhisatta's sister, born of another mother. In seeking to come to his aid, she becomes a frog to accompany another brother to rescue the bodhisatta. As the frog, she emits three drops of poison which are spectacularly dangerous, as they have the power to scorch the earth and poison all the water. Her actions helped the bodhisatta to be freed.

Mahā-ummagga Jātaka (546, VI.329). Uppalavaṇṇā is Bherī, a wise woman who has gone forth. She becomes embroiled in a plot involving the king, but in questioning her, the king takes her counsel and is admiring of her wisdom.

Vessantara Jātaka (547, VI.479). In this well-known jātaka, Uppalavaṇṇā is Kaṇhajinā, the daughter of Vessantara, whom he gives away.

Part two

Themes and issues

7

Female teachers

DHAMMADINNĀ

Themes in the Pāli accounts

Dhammadinnā is best known for her role as a teacher, or dhammakathikā, in the Pāli literature, so in this chapter I will discuss the roles of the female teacher and the pupil. Surveying the textual and epigraphic evidence, two threads seem to run through the early tradition with regard to women as teachers and pupils. First, we find examples of women like Dhammadinnā—both named and unnamed—who are recognized and esteemed as teachers. Second, in the inscriptional evidence, we find closer male–female teacher–disciple relations recorded than are suggested by the extant texts, particularly the Pāli texts. On the contrary, in the extant formalized canon, and repeated in the commentaries, we find a more institutional, distant, and formal male–female teacher–pupil relationship defining the parameters of nuns' routines. So, on the one hand, nuns are exemplary teachers of groups and individuals, teachers of men and women, and monks and nuns can be close disciples of one another, but on the other hand, in the formalized schema nuns are given sanctioned instruction every fortnight by the monk whose turn it is to act as advisor to them.

Female teachers in the early canon

Dhammadinnā is known as a dhammakathikā, and as can be seen of the distinguished qualities afforded to nuns on the *Aṅguttara-nikāya* list, this one is closest to a teaching role. On the longer list of monks, there are other roles that indicate a potential talent for teaching. These can also be found on the longer list of distinguished nuns in the *Ekottarika-āgama*. On the longer *Aṅguttara-nikāya* list of monks we also find Soṇa Kuṭikaṇṇa, who is foremost of 'excellent speakers'; Mahākaccāna, who can 'explain in detail'; Mahākaṭṭhita who is foremost of those with analytical knowledge; and Ānanda, who is learned.[1] In addition to these is Dhammadinnā's counterpart, Puṇṇa Mantāṇiputta. On the *Ekottarika-āgama* list, as well as wise and learned nuns with incisive, analytic minds, there are others who are specifically said to be competent in debate (Danti[kā]—18), good at teaching in a proselytizing context (Soṇā—13), 'teaching and transforming others' (Suyamā—43), and teaching widely, explaining and expounding (Padumarañjana—7, Samantapabhāsā—41) (Anālayo 2013a, 114–15). Each of these roles suggests some ability for teaching, as each is concerned with either depth of comprehension, proficiency in exposition, or both.

Of all the above roles, dhammakathikā appears to be best known, as it occurs on inscriptions as well as in the texts. From the stūpa at Amarāvatī, Burgess records an inscription made by a dhammakathikā:

> *sidha oḍiparivenene vāsika dhamakathikasa budhi...*[2]
>
> Success, [gift of] Budhi... a *dhamakathika* dwelling in Oḍiparivenena

[1] There are also three others who possess characteristics that could be useful in teaching—Piṇḍola Bhāradvāja is said to have a lion's roar, Vangīsa to compose inspired verse and Kumāra Kassapa to exhibit variegated speech.

[2] Burgess ([1886] 1996, 94).

Also, on the Sāñcī stūpa, we find:

aya-cuḍasa dhamakathikasa atevāsino balamitrasa dānaṃ[3]

Gift of Balamitra, pupil of Reverend Cuḍa, the *dhamakathika*.

If we assess the Pāli suttas on Dhammadinnā and Puṇṇa Mantāṇiputta respectively, we can garner something of the parameters of the role of dhammakathikā in the Pāli canon. As described in Part I, Dhammadinnā's ability to 'speak well on dhamma' is illuminated through a question-and-answer debate. In the sutta on Puṇṇa Mantāṇiputta, the *Rathavinita-sutta* of the *Majjhima-nikāya* (*MN* 24), his ability is demarcated somewhat differently, but also through him proving his mettle in his answers to questions, this time those of Sāriputta. Putting the two examples together, the qualities of a dhammakathikā appear to be, first, the ability to understand the dhamma in relation to one's own experience and, second, the ability to communicate that to others effectively—whether through giving talks or though debate.

Khemā, the subject of Chapters 2 and 8 of this volume, is another firm example of an esteemed female teacher. As noted in Part I, in the *Saṃyutta-nikāya* (IV 34) King Pasenadi arrives in the village of Toraṇavatthu and asks one of his men to find him a brahmin or ascetic to visit, and thus ensues his dialogue with Khemā, from which he departs impressed. A third interesting example is of a much less well-known figure, Kajañgalā. From the one mention of her in the Pāli canon, it is clear Kajañgalā is a good teacher, authorized by the Buddha, and skilled at teaching others. Given this, it is strange that we know so little of her.

Although Kajañgalā is noted in the text of another tradition—in the *Avadānaśataka*—to be foremost in an attribute that might warrant inclusion on the *Aṅguttara-nikāya* list of distinguished nuns, she does not feature on it. In the Pāli *Aṅguttara-nikāya* there are only thirteen nuns listed with distinguished qualities, but in the Chinese *Ekottarika-āgama* parallel list, a grand number of fifty-one nuns are enumerated overall, each being said to have an eminent quality (see Anālayo 2013a, 97–115). The *Aṅguttara-nikāya*/*Ekottarika-āgama* is a composite text and it has been estab-

3 Majumdar in Marshall and Foucher, Vol. I ([1939] 1983, 342).

lished for some time that there are several redactions of the text (see Waldschmidt 1980, 169–74). As noted by scholars previously, the extant Chinese *Ekottarika-āgama* shows evidence of Mahāyāna influence and includes longer *sūtra*s as well as sūtras of a composite nature.[4] Given this difference, it does beg the question as to whether the *Aṅguttara-nikāya* list may have been longer at some point. A few clues do suggest this may have been the case. Skilling (2001a) has already noted some of these. He listed the four nuns said to have foremost qualities in the *Avadānaśataka*—Khemā/Kṣemā, Kajaṅgalā/Kacaṅgalā, Somā, and Surpiyā—and notes that only one of these, Khemā, appears on the Pāli list. Of these four, Khemā and Somā appear on the *Ekottarika-āgama* list, but the other two do not, Khemā with the quality she usually has (see Chapter 8) and Somā with a different quality to that ascribed to her in the *Avadānaśataka*. Taking Skilling's initial observation further, if we look at the quality ascribed to Kacaṅgalā, and how she is presented in different sources, the situation becomes still more noteworthy. The nun Kajaṅgalā/Kacaṅgalā is mentioned in various instances in Pāli, Sanskrit, Tibetan, and Chinese sources. In the story of her given in the *Avadānaśataka* she takes the place of the Buddha when he retires to meditate, and she expands on the teaching he has given to the nuns:

> When the Blessed One, having taught the nuns briefly, entered into seclusion for meditation, Kacaṅgalā explained [the teaching] to them.[5]

Following this, she is said to be foremost of nuns who are *sūtrāntavibhāgakartrī*—that is, someone who can explain and analyse the teachings/suttas. Although Kajangalā does not appear on the list of distinguished nuns in the *Aṅguttara-nikāya*, there is another story of her in the Pāli in which she quite clearly and categorically exhibits this very same distinguished quality.

4 See Allon (2001, 9–22) for a detailed study of extant *Aṅguttara-nikāya/Ekottarika-āgama* texts and fragments. For Mahāyāna influence, see Anālayo (2013c).

5 *Yadā bhagavān bhikṣuṇīnāṃ saṃkṣepeṇoddiśya pratisaṃlayanāya praviśati tadā kacaṅgalā bhikśunīnāṃ vyākaroti* (AŚ 78).

Kajangalā is mentioned nowhere else in the Pāli canon apart from in this one *sutta* in the *Aṅguttaranikāya* (AN V 54–9)—which caused Caroline Rhys Davids to ask, in her introduction to Woodward's translation, who is this 'mysterious woman-teacher' Kajangalā (*AN* [1936] 2003, V.vii). The *Aṅguttara-nikāya* is, of course, the set of numerical sayings, grouped by number, although, as has been previously noted (Allon 2001, 14) not all of the suttas in each section are concerned directly with one number, although most are. In the sutta prior to that which features Kajangalā, the Buddha enumerates and then explains the ten great questions. In the next sutta, Kajangalā is asked by her group of lay disciples to expand the Buddha's teaching and explain the ten questions to them 'in full' (*vitthārena*), although in the extant text her explanation is about the same length as that of the Buddha. But certainly the idea here is that she is expanding on a brief saying/teaching of the Buddha known to her group of lay disciples, and she is providing the detail for them, which, although not identical to how the Buddha has discussed it in the previous sutta, is endorsed by the Buddha at the end of the section on her exposition. This raises the question as to why Kajangalā is not included on the *Aṅguttara-nikāya* list for her distinguished quality, as she appears in the *Aṅguttara-nikāya* later on, exhibiting the quality for which she is said to be distinguished in the *Avadānaśataka*.

As with each of the qualities that are noted on the *Aṅguttara-nikāya/Ekottarika-āgama* list, Dhammadinnā is said to be *foremost* of the nuns who are dhammakathikās. Hence she is not the only one with such skills, as this implies there were others. And others are mentioned in the textual record. In the *Therīgāthā*, we find references to unnamed female teachers being approached by other women for instruction. Twice this appears in an identical verse, said to have been spoken by Uttamā (v. 43) and an unknown nun (v. 69):

> I went up to a bhikkhunī who was fit to be trusted by me. She taught me the doctrine, the elements of existence, the sense bases, the elements.
>
> I heard the doctrine for her as she instructed me; for seven days I sat in one and the same cross-legged position, consigned to joy and

> happiness. On the eighth day I stretched forth my feet, having torn asunder the mass of darkness (of ignorance).[6]
>
> I went up to a bhikkhunī who was fit to be trusted by me. She taught me the doctrine, the elements of existence, the sense bases, the elements.
>
> I heard the doctrine for her and sat on one side. I know that I have lived before; I have purified the divine eye; and there is knowledge of the state of mind of others; I have purified the ear-element; I have realised supernormal power too; I have attained the annihilation of the *āsavas*; I have realised these six supernormal knowledges; I have done the Buddha's teaching.[7]

Other examples of women approaching other women for teaching and guidance in the *Therīgāthā* are in Soṇā's verses (vv. 102–4), Candā (vv. 124 and 126), and Vijayā's (vv. 170–2), as follows:

> Soṇā
>
> I bore ten sons in this material body, and then being weak and aged I approached a bhikkhunī.
>
> She taught me the doctrine, the elements of existence, the sense-bases, and the elements. When I heard the doctrine from her, I cut off my hair, and went forth.[8]

6 *Thī* vv. 43–4, trans. Norman (Rhys Davids and Norman 1989, 173). *Sā bhikkunim upāgacchiṃ yā me saddhāyikā ahu, sā me dhammaṃ adesesi khandhāyatanadhātuyo. Tassā dhammaṃ suṇtivāna yathā maṃ anusāsi sā, satthāhaṃ ekapallaṅke nisīdiṃ pītisukhasamappitā, aṭṭhamiyā pāde pasāresiṃ tamokkhandhaṃ padāliya.*

7 *Thī* vv. 69–71, trans. Norman (Rhys Davids and Norman 1989, 178). *Sā bhikkunim upāgacchiṃ yā me saddhāyikā ahu, sā me dhammaṃ adesesi khandhāyatanadhātuyo. Tassā dhammaṃ suṇitvāna ekamante upāvisiṃ, pubbenivāsaṃ jānāmi dibbacakkhuṃ visodhitaṃ. Ceto paricca ñāṇañ ca sotadhātu visodhitā, iddhi pi me sacchikatā patto me āsavakkhayo, cha me 'bhiññā sacchikatā kataṃ buddhassa sāsanaṃ.*

8 *Thī* vv. 102–4, trans. Norman (Rhys Davids and Norman 1989, 181). *Dasa putte vijāyitvā asmiṃ rūpasamussaye, tato 'haṃ dubbalā jiṇṇā bhikkhuniṃ upasaṅkamiṃ. Sā me dhammam adesesi khandhāyatanadhātuyo, tassā dhammaṃ suṇitvāna kese chetvāna pabbajaṃ. Tassā me sikkhamānāya dibbacakkhuṃ visodhitaṃ, pubbenivāsaṃ jānāmi yattha me vusitaṃ pure.*

Candā

> But then I saw a bhikkhunī who had obtained food and drink, and approaching her I said 'Send me forth into the homeless state'...
>
> I heard her utterance and took her advice. The noble lady's exhortation was not in vein; I have the triple knowledge; I am without *āsavas*.[9]

Vijayā

> I approached a bhikkhunī, honoured her, and questioned (her). She taught me the doctrine, and the elements, and sense-bases, the four noble truths, the faculties and the powers, the constituents of awakening and the eight-fold way for the attainment of the supreme goal.
>
> I heard her utterance, took her advice, and in the first watch of the night I recollected that I had been born before.[10]

There are also other instances in which nuns describe or are described to have been instructed by another woman. These can be found in, for example, the verses attributed to five hundred women, who say that Paṭācārā 'plucked out the dart' (*abbūḷhasalla*) in their hearts. Also, Uttarā (v. 178) is said to have acted on the advice of Paṭācārā, and Subhā (v. 363) is said to have been instructed by Uppalavaṇṇā.

That nuns taught at the time of the Buddha has been examined previously by various scholars. For example, Horner notes that '... although they were under no formal obligation to preach, there were among them some who were born teachers...' ([1930] 1990, 251), and more recently Krey, in an article that looks in some detail at the two suttas in which Dhammadinnā and Khemā teach, notes that

9 *Thī* vv. 124 and 126, trans. Norman (Rhys Davids and Norman 1989, 184). *Bhikkhuniṃ puna disvāna annapānassa lābhiniṃ, upasaṃkamma avocaṃ pabbajiṃ anagāriyaṃ... Tassāhaṃ vacanaṃ sutvā akāsiṃ anusāsaniṃ, amogho ayyāya ovādo tevijja mhi anāsavā.*

10 *Thī* vv. 170–2, trans. Norman (Rhys Davids and Norman 1989, 189). *Bhikkhuniṃ upasaṅkamma sakkaccaṃ paripucch' ahuṃ, sā me dham mam adesesi dhātu-āyatanāni ca. Cattāri ariyasaccāni indriyāni balāni ca, bojjhaṅgaṭṭhaṅgikaṃ maggaṃ uttamatthassa pattiyā. Tassāhaṃ vacanaṃ sutvā karontī anusāsaniṃ, rattiyā purime yāme pubbajātim anussariṃ.*

'these *suttas* point to the high intelligence and competence of the two nuns ... by explicitly giving evidence of the acknowledgment of their wisdom' (2010, 18). And Anālayo (2011a, 5) notes the 'profundity' and 'great variety of themes' that Dhammadinnā expounds in the *Cūḷavedalla-sutta* and its parallels.

In the monks' *Theragāthā* we do not find as much emphasis on receiving teachings from a more experienced teacher as we see in the *Therīgāthā*, although, as Kathryn Blackstone (2000) has noted previously—as part of her convincing argument for female authorship of the *Therīgāthā*—the *Therīgāthā* contains accounts of more personal experience than does the counterpart, the *Theragāthā* (Blackstone 2000, 40).[11] That both nuns and laywomen have the ability to teach on a par with their male counterparts is further reinforced by a section in the *Iddhipādasaṃyutta* of the *Saṃyutta-nikāya.* In these passages, the Buddha, in conversation with Māra, talks about how he wants his community to be at his death, or 'final *nibbāna*':

> I will not attain final Nibbāna, Evil One, until I have monk disciples who are wise, disciplined, confident, secure from bondage, learned, upholders of the Dhamma, practising in the proper way, conducting themselves accordingly; who have learned their own teacher's doctrine and can explain it, teach it, proclaim it, establish it, disclose it, analyse it and elucidate it; who can refute thoroughly with reasons the prevalent tenets of others and can teach the efficacious Dhamma. (trans. Bodhi 2000, 1724, with one change)[12]

This passage is then repeated verbatim three times with 'monk disciples' replaced first with 'nun disciples' (*bhikkhuniyo sāvikā*),

[11] While 34.2 per cent of nuns include some kind of history of themselves, only 9.5 per cent of monks do the same, and of the monks 'almost all the descriptions are oblique or extremely brief'.

[12] *SN* V.260–1. *Na tāvāham pāpima parinibbāyissāmi yāva me bhikkhū na sāvakā bhavissanti viyattā vinītā visāradā pattayogakkhemā bahussutā dhammadharā dhammānudhammapaṭipannā sāmīcipaṭipannā anudhammacārino sakam ācariyakam uggahetvā ācikkhissanti desissanti paññāpessanti paṭṭhapessanti vivarissanti vibhajissanti uttanīkarissanti uppannam parappavādaṃ sahadhammena suniggahītaṃ niggahetvā sappāṭihāriyaṃ dhammaṃ desissanti ti.* [I have changed Bodhi's 'bhikkhu disciples' to 'monk disciples'.]

then 'male lay disciples' (*upāsakā sāvakā*), and then 'female lay disciples' (*upāsikā sāvikā*). Thus, each of these four groups of people should be able to thoroughly, properly, and fully teach the Buddha's dhamma. What this passage tells us is that not only should nuns be capable and proficient teachers, but this is also something of an expectation for laywomen.[13] Dhammadinnā, then, although signalled as exceptional in this regard, was far from being the only woman esteemed as a teacher of the Buddha's dhamma.

Female teachers in the Apadāna

Given that Dhammadinnā seems to have gained some renown as a teacher, it is noteworthy then that, in her apadāna, while she is described as a teacher in the present, it is not past deeds as a teacher or a wise or skilled person that got her to that position. Her apadāna tells us instead that what gave rise to this acclaimed ability and position are, first, the usual and standard vow, that is, she sees another who has this position in the saṅgha under a former Buddha, and vows to attain it herself, then second, it is a simple act of giving—the offering to Sujāta, the disciple of Padumuttara—that affords these grand consequences.

The thrust of Dhammadinnā's kammic trajectory in the *Apadāna* is not underpinned by former teaching roles, although interestingly for another female teacher, Sukkā, things are quite different. In the case of Sukkā's apadāna, in contrast to that of Dhammadinnā, what we do find is some acknowledgement of the occupation of female teacher in the past. In this case, Sukkā is said to have been a teacher in the past, and it is her past deeds in this very role that give rise to her accomplished status in the present. In no less than five previous existences, each a time of a previous Buddha, Sukkā was an eloquent and accomplished teacher of the Buddha's

[13] This apparent aspiration of the Buddha can be set alongside Schopen's evidence (2010) from the Mūlasarvāstivāda *Vinaya*, on how lacking some monks may have been in aptitude and ability (see pages 107–8).

dhamma. During the era of Vipassī Buddha she was 'learned, an upholder of the *dhamma*, possessed of intelligence' (*bahussutā dhammadharā paṭibhānavatī*, *Ap.* 605). Under Sikhī she was 'expert in the teachings of the Buddha, elucidating the sayings of the conqueror' (*buddhasāsanakovidā jotetvā jinavākyāni*, *Ap.* 606). When Vessabhū Buddha arose in the world, she was an 'upholder of the *dhamma*, illuminated the teachings of the conqueror' (*dhammadharā jotayiṃ jinasāsanaṃ*, *Ap.* 606). The name Kakusandha is missing from the next set of verses, but perhaps this Buddha is being referred to here, as this is the correct place on this list. Under this unnamed 'best of conquerors', Sukkā 'made clear the thought of the sage with ease' (*munimataṃ jotayitvā yathāsukhaṃ*, *Ap.* 606). During the era of Koṇāgamana she was also 'learned, an upholder of the *dhamma* and illuminated the teaching of the conqueror' (*bahussutā dhammadharā jotayiṃ jinasāsanaṃ*, *Ap.* 606). Under Kassapa it was the same—she was 'learned in the true *dhamma* and skilled in questioning' (*pariyāputasaddhamma paripucchāvisāradā*, *Ap.* 606), and she also gave many talks on dhamma. As a result of all of this, alongside her resolve, she is reborn in the time of the historical Buddha, and taught the dhamma to a 'great assembly of people' (*mahājanasamāgame*, *Ap.* 607).

Sukkā's apadāna, then, is quite different to that of Dhammadinnā in terms of the apparent cause of her present status as teacher of others. What this suggests is perhaps the lack of a clearly defined (mytho-)historical path that can lead to a woman gaining the status of teacher. The text suggests this can come about as a result of a variety of good deeds done in the past. And while it is possible to gain the status of female teacher according to the *Apadāna*, and it is confirmed that women were teachers under past Buddhas, there is no special focus or emphasis on women seeking or setting out to achieve this role. This could be grounded in a historical reality that nuns were no longer teachers by the time of the *Apadāna* or else, conversely, that many nuns would be expected to be teachers such that there was no need or desire to emphasize teaching roles, as they had become standard. It is the latter of these possibilities that is borne out by the evidence of inscriptions.

Inscriptional evidence

Further to the above, inscriptional evidence demonstrates that Buddhist women were teachers of other women.[14] Three inscriptions from Sāñcī are donor inscriptions made by female pupils (*antevāsinī*) of female teachers:

> *yasilaya atevasini-sagharakhitāye dānaṃ*[15]
>
> The gift of Sagharakhitā, female pupil of Yasilā.
>
> *mulāyā dāna thabho gaḍāya atevāsiniyā*[16]
>
> The pillar is the gift of Mulā, female pupil of Gaḍā.
>
> *[dha]madevaya dānaṃ mitasiriya atevasiniyā*[17]
>
> The gift of Dhamadevā, female pupil of Mitasiri.

There are also two from Mathurā district, the first a fragmentary inscription on the pedestal of a seated Buddha, from a mound of Rāl-Bhaḍār, now in the Mathurā Museum, and the second originally believed to be from the village of Pālīkheṛā, inscribed on the pedestal of a bodhisattva figure.

> *Huviṣkasya[s](am) 30 1 [he 4] d(i) 20 dana bh(i)k(ṣu)ṅiy(e) Dinnaye ant(e)vāsinī[aṃ] khuḍaye [gra]...*
>
> In the year 31 of Huviṣka, in the 4th month of winter(?), on the 20th day, the gift of Khuḍā (and) ... the female pupils of the nun Dinnā[18]
>
> *(mahārājasya) [d](e)vaputrasa huv[i]ṣkasya sa[ṃ] 30 9 va 3 di 5 etasya[ṃ] purva[y](aṃ) bh[i]khuṅiye Puśaha[th]iniye [a](ṃtevāsi)ni[y](e) bh[i]khuṅiye Budhadevāye bodhisatvo pratithāpito sahā mātāpitīhi sarvasat[v]ahitasukh[a]*
>
> In the year 39 of *mahārāja devaputra* Huviṣka, in the 3rd (month) of the rainy season, on the 5th day, on this date, the bodhisattva was set

[14] Schopen has made use of epigraphic evidence in numerous publications on, or including, the study of Buddhist nuns, and others have studied some of these inscriptions as well, including Kumkum Roy (1988) and Nancy Barnes (2000).

[15] Majumdar in Marshall and Foucher, Vol. I ([1939] 1983, 311).

[16] Majumdar in Marshall and Foucher, Vol. I ([1939] 1983, 367).

[17] Majumdar in Marshall and Foucher, Vol. I ([1939] 1983, 363).

[18] Translated by Lüders (1961, 149–50).

up by the nun Budhadevā, the female pupil of the nun Puśahathini, together with her parents from the welfare and happiness of all beings.[19]

Burgess also records similar at Amarāvatī, in Andhra Pradesh:

aya-retiyā atevāsiniya aya-dhamāya dānaṃ[20]

Gift of Venerable Dhamā, female pupil of Venerable Retī.

This last one is from a cave site near Kuḍā, a small village on the banks of the Rajapuri creek, in the western region:

Siddhaṃ therāṇaṃ bhadata pātimitana bhadaṃta āgimita[na] ca bhāgiṇeyiya pāvayitikāya nāganikāya duhutaya pavayitikāya padumaṃntikāya dhaṃmaṃ leṇaṃ poḍhī ca sahā ātevāsiniya bodhiya saha ca ativāsiniya asālhamitāya[21]

Success, a cave and cistern the gift of the renouncer Padumantikā, daughter of the renouncer Nāganikā, sister's daughter of the Elder Reverend Āgimita and the Elder Reverend Pātimita, and of her pupil Bodhi and her pupil Asālhamitā.

Other Indian inscriptions go further than providing evidence of female Buddhist teachers; they detail a type of teacher–pupil relationship not recorded in the Pāli texts. In these inscriptions, nuns are recorded to be direct disciples of monks. The following four are from Amarāvatī:

sidhaṃ kudūranivāsika bhaya-nāgasa atavāsikasa daharabhikusa vidhikasa atevāsiniya cha budharakhitāya natiya cha chūlabudharakhitāya cha utarāyake paṭo dāna

Success, the tablet at the northern gate, the gift of the young monk Vidhika, pupil of Reverend Nāga, who resides at Kudūra, and of [his] pupil Budharakhitā, and of [her] granddaughter, and of the younger Budharakhitā.[22]

[r]āyaselanivāsino vasibhūtasa (ma)hatherasa ayira-bhūtarakhitasa (a)(te)vāsikasa chula-ay(i)rasa ara[ha]-[ta]sa ayira-budharakhitasa atev(ā)s(i)niya bhikhuniyā nadāya thaṃbho dā(na)[23]

19 Translated by Lüders (1961, 166).

20 Burgess ([1886] 1996, 82).

21 Burgess and Pandit (1881, 7).

22 Translated by Hultzsch in Burgess ([1886] 1996, 93).

23 Burgess ([1886] 1996, 104).

The pillar is the gift of the Venerable Chula, pupil of the great Elder, of self-controlled mind, Venerable Bhūtarakhita, resident of [R]āyasela—and of the nun Nadā, pupil of the Arhat, Venerable Budharakhita.

vinayadhirasa aya-punavasusa atevāsiniya uvajhāyinī samuḍiyāya atevāsiniya malaṃyā pāḍakā dāna[ṃ][24]

Gift of footprints by Malā, pupil of the female teacher Samuḍiyā, pupil of Venerable Punavasu, a *vinayadhāra*.

Lüders also notes a further similar inscription from Amarāvāti, of the nun (*bhikhunī*) Budharakhitā, who is the female pupil (*atēvāsi*[*nī*]) of the elder Budharakhitā, the overseer of works of the Chētikas who lived at Rāgagiri (Lüders' list of Brāhmī inscriptions 1912, 148, no. 1,250). In the first example above, the male teacher is the venerable Nāga, and his female pupil is Budharakhitā. Two other women are mentioned, but their relationship to Nāga is unclear. In the second inscription, a male and a female disciple of two different teachers donate a pillar together. The nun is Nadā, and her male teacher is Budharakhita, which as we can see is a popular name. The third inscription is another case of a female pupil with a male teacher, as well as a female pupil with a female teacher. In this example, Samuḍiyā is both teacher and pupil, both teacher of Malā, the donor, and pupil of Punavasu, who is a vinayadhāra. This inscription with Punavasu as vinayadhāra was misread by Nalinaksha Dutt (1931, 640), and is the basis for a notion that has been etched into the modern scholarly discourse on women in early Indian Buddhism, the idea that there exists an inscription that records a female vinayadhārā/ī. Unfortunately, this is not the case.

There are also other examples of male–female teacher–disciple relations from western India, which demonstrate that this practice was not region specific. The Shelarwadi caves are situated 24 kilometres from Pune. When Das Gupta visited, in 1940, he found the following inscription in cave number 2, almost entirely covered by mud:

24 Burgess ([1886] 1996, 37). Burgess notes a lacuna for a 'mutilated word preceding the name' Samuḍiyā ([1886] 1996, 37 n4), although this is not clear on the photograph, and Lüders translates it without lacuna.

Sidha || therāṇaṃ bhayata-sihāṇa ateāsiṇiya pāvaīti[k]āya ghapa[rā]ya bālikää saghāya budha(dhā)-a cha chetiya-gharo deya-dharma...[25]

Success, the meritorious gift of a *chaitya* hall is made by Budhā and Saghā the daughter(s) of the renouncer Ghaparā, pupil of the Elder, Venerable Siha...

The male teacher's name, Siha, and his titles appear in the genitive plural, and this is not uncommon on inscriptions from the west. Schopen has discussed this previously as it appears on other inscriptions, as *pluralis majestatis* for deceased persons, a gesture of respect (2004, 176–7). Another inscription, from Kuḍā, with the male teacher's name in this same form, is detailed by Burgess:

Sidhaṃ theraṇa bhayata vijayāṇa ativāsiṇiya pava[yi]tikāya sapilāya deyadhamaṃ leṇaṃ saha sā lohitahi veṇhuyāhi saha ca ativāsiṇiya bodhiya...[26]

Success, the meritorious gift of a cave by renouncer Sapilā, pupil of the Elder, Venerable Vijaya, with Lohitā and Veṇhuyā, and her pupil Bodhī...

Similarly, Senart notes an inscription from the Nāsik caves:

bhayaṃta-savasānaṃ aṃlevāsiniya pavayitāya tāpasiniya cha deyadhama [leṇa] chātudisasa bhikhusaghasa dataṃ[27]

Given to the community of monks in the four directions, the meritorious gift [of a cave] by the renouncer Tāpasinī, female pupil of Reverend Savasa.

Lüders, on his list of Brāhmī inscriptions, also notes two further examples, both from cave sites in the west, at Kaṇhēri. The first (1,006) is a donative inscription by an elder renouncer (*pavaïtikā thērī*) Poṇkīasaṇā, who is the pupil of the male Elder (*thēra*) Ghōsa, and the second (1,020) is the gift of the renouncer (*pavaïtikā*) Sāpā, pupil of the male Elder (*thēra*) Bōdhika.

25 The inscription concludes—*māta-pita udisa saha [cha] sa-vehi bhikhā[khu] –kulehi sahā cha āchari[ye]hi bhata-vireyeho sa-māpito* (Das Gupta 1949–50, 77–8).

26 Burgess and Pandit (1881, 18). Burgess also notes that the instrumental for the two fellow disciples is plural.

27 Senart (1905–6, 76).

These examples of Indian inscriptions clearly demonstrate that not only did nuns have pupils (*antevāsinī*), and so would have occupied the role of teachers, but, equally importantly, there were male–female teacher–pupil arrangements within the Buddhist communities of the time. Further, the inscriptions that record this phenomenon are not confined to one place, thus suggesting that this was a feature of saṅghas within a variety of regions. These direct teacher–disciple relations between monks and nuns are not in evidence in the textual tradition. Instead, the texts prescribe more formal teaching relations, as exemplified by the role of monk advisor to nuns (see the following section). Some of the mentioned inscriptions can be dated, and some date to prior to the Common Era, to potentially a similar time as the *Apadāna* (Collett 2015). Those from Sāñcī and potentially some of the western cave inscriptions are the earliest. The Mathurā and Amarāvatī ones are later, dating to the centuries following the Common Era. Thus, potentially both the phenomena of female teachers and male–female teacher disciple relations existed for a period of some four hundred years (200 BCE to 200 CE).[28]

Monk advisor to nuns

The role of monk advisor to nuns is well documented in both Pāli and other sources. The notion of a male monastic advisor to the nuns is something we see in the list of *garudhammas*, or eight chief rules, for nuns. Number three of these in the Pāli specifies that nuns should seek advice/teaching from monks every fortnight. This is a rotational role—monks take it in turns—and open only to certain monks, who possess certain qualities.[29] The *Aṅguttara-nikāya* lists eight qualities a monk should possess in order to become an advisor to the nuns. These include that he must be virtuous, learned, know the discipline well, be a good

[28] Some of the dating is done on palaeographic grounds, with an awareness of the incumbent problems of doing so. Others include dates, or can be linked to similar ones with dates (Collett 2015).

[29] Although it was a rotational role, certain monks performed the duty on a regular basis. Kieffer-Pülz notes a monk regularly agreed upon to be an advisor is called *sammata* (2013, 37).

speaker, be capable of inspiring, be agreeable, not have committed any serious offenses against any nuns, and have seniority of twenty years' standing or more. Bhikkhu Bodhi, in his translation of the text, notes that this sutta is 'evidently referring to the third *garudhamma*' (2012, 1805n1748). Kieffer-Pülz notes that the role of advisor to nuns appears to have become a key role by the time of early Pāli commentaries, as criteria and the process of installing a monk to such office was simplified, presumably making it a role more monks could be easily promoted to (2013, 37–8).

While it is certainly possible to imagine a scenario in which nuns have monk advisors despite the fact that there existed illustrious and esteemed female monastic teachers, the two notions do not sit comfortably alongside one another. The institutional and temporary role of monk advisor concurs still less with the evidence of epigraphy. Moreover, there are other problems with the design of this role. First, as discussed, a monk must be at least of twenty years' standing before he can be considered for the role, so it is difficult to see how this could have come into effect at the advent of the nuns' Order, which, it could be argued, might have been the time it was most necessary. Second, the role is inscribed as part of the eight rules that, as is now generally accepted, are an interpolation. Third, there are some interesting discrepancies in parallel versions of a sutta on a monk who takes this role (Anālayo 2010a).[30]

We find the male advisor to nuns discussed much more often in the canon than the counterpart male advisor to monks. Sometimes, in cases found in the Pāli *Vinaya*, the reason for this is that the office was not carried out well. In other instances, the role is brought up because, apparently, monks took advantage of it, and used it as an opportunity to cavort with women. *Pācittiya* rules 21–4 in the monks' section of the *Vinaya* are concerned with advisors to nuns. Each rule is said to have been made for a different reason. First, in pācittiya 21, a group of six monks decide

30 In non-Pāli versions, the sutta begins with the Buddha instructing a large group of nuns, but the Pāli version begins differently, with no such instruction taking place. According to the *Saṃyukta-āgama* version, the large group of nuns included Khemā, Kisāgotamī, Paṭācārā, and Uppalavaṇṇā (Anālayo 2010a, 334).

that they will appoint themselves as advisors to the nuns so that they can spend the day enjoying the company of women, and engaging in 'worldly-talk' (*tiracchānakathā*).[31] As they provide the nuns with substandard teaching, not fitting of those in an advisory role, the nuns complain about them to the Buddha.[32] Pācittiya 22 involves the monk Cūḷapanthaka. Knowing it is Cūḷapanthaka's turn to advise the nuns, the nuns approach him reluctantly, having discussed amongst themselves the outcome—they know he will do as he usually does, and offer them the exact same teaching as he has done before. The nuns complained about this to Cūḷapanthaka, and so he enacted a magical display for them. Although the nuns enjoyed it, unfortunately, it went on past sunset, so that the nuns could not re-enter the town as the town gate had been locked. When people saw them return in the morning, they criticized the nuns, assuming they had inappropriately spent the night in the monastery with the monks. In pācittiya 23, the group of six monks again attempt a ruse and go to the nuns' dwelling, apparently in order to advise the nuns. As the monks' venture to the dwelling of the nuns is seen and criticized, the rule is made that monks must not go to the dwellings of nuns in order to advise them. This prefigures the final of this set of rules—Mahāpajāpatī Gotamī is ill, and because this rule has been made, no monks will come to advise her. Therefore, an addendum is added, that monks may go for these purposes to the nuns' quarters if a nun is ill.

In part then, the reason for the more common appearance of advisor to nuns is because, when the monk or monks in the role do not do a good job, the nuns sometimes complain about them. In a comparative study of the (Mūla-)sarvāstivāda *Vinaya* ruling about the qualities of a monk qualified to be advisors to nuns, Schopen (2010) notes that while a monk is required to be an urbane speaker, the level of learning and knowledge required for monks to take up the role is surprisingly low. To be a *bahuśruta*, to 'have great learning', in the texts Schopen examines appears to require only that

[31] As Horner notes, what is included in this type of frivolous talk is, for example, talk of kings or talk of robbers (Horner *Vin.* trans. II.263n3).

[32] This is one instance in which the nuns do talk directly to the Buddha.

one either knows the *Pratimokṣa-sūtra* (that is, 'one short *vinaya* text' [Schopen 2010, 112]) or should at least have heard and understood it. Thus, with some nuns—and Dhammadinnā is the exemplar here—more able and accomplished on the finer points of dhamma than their 'advisors', who could potentially be of rather more limited aptitude, complaints could easily have been commonplace.

Female teachers in the commentaries

In general, the commentaries do not include narrative accounts of female teachers other than those found in the canon. There are a few exceptions to this, and some examples of wise, skilled, and learned women, some of whom figure centrally in narrative plots, and others of whom are mentioned in passing. There is, for instance, Queen Mallikā (mentioned in Chapter 12) who is portrayed as wiser and more insightful than her husband, the king, or Lakhumā in the *Vimānavatthu* commentary, who is said to be 'endowed with intelligence' and progresses quickly on the path. One woman whose teaching credentials are more fully endorsed in the commentaries is Khujjuttarā, a laywoman. She is noted on the *Aṅguttara-nikāya* list of laywomen as foremost of those who are learned (*bahussuta AN* I.26) but there are no canonical narratives in which she features. There is an account of her in several of the commentaries, in which she teaches Queen Sāmāvatī and her female attendants, and all these women make good progress under her instruction (see, for example, *Dh-a* I.208 or *AN-a* I.418).

The nuns who are the subject of this volume, and other prominent nuns, become close to what we might term 'canonized saints' in the commentaries. They are exemplars of the path, and of the teachings, and their biographies can be noted as examples of the expression of particular doctrine or teaching. As seen in Part I, in their biographies they are women who overcome struggle to succeed in following the path set out by the Buddha. They are capable and competent, wise and skilled, intelligent, compassionate, zealous, and insightful. The most pronounced exception to this are depictions of Dhammadinnā in the later commentaries, in which—in some accounts more than others—she is portrayed as particularly subservient to her husband.

In these later biographies, unlike in the *Apadāna*, Visākha, Dhammadinnā's husband, is the first to follow the Buddha and attain great religious insight. In all four commentarial versions, upon hearing a discourse by the Buddha, Visākha becomes a non-returner. Then, having attained this high state, on returning home to Dhammadinnā, Visākha shuns her. She is portrayed as a woman rejected by her husband, not comprehending what she might have done wrong. It is Visākha's role to explain the situation to her—in a thorough-going reversal of fortune to the *Cūḷavedalla-sutta*—he is the one with knowledge and understanding here, and Dhammadinnā the one needing to be enlightened. Once informed, Dhammadinnā understands the situation, but in the *Majjhima-nikāya* commentary she asks another question, as to whether the Buddha's dhamma is open to women as well, further showing deference and a reversed hierarchy in terms of knower/questioner. Once she decides for herself to go forth, the texts record that Visākha *took her* to the nuns, sometimes ceremonially, as noted in Part I in the description from the *Majjhima-nikāya* commentary of him seating her upon a golden chariot. In this case, Visākha is very much the agent; he bathes and dresses her in her finery, and brings together friends/relatives for the ceremonial journey. It is only once ordained, and when the commentarial biographies begin to mirror the canonical text, that Dhammadinnā regains full agency. And this only in some instances, as, also noted in Part I, in the *Therīgāthā* commentary it is the Buddha's omniscience, rather than her own female intellect, that causes her insightful answers to Visākha's questions.

It is unclear why Dhammadinnā is presented in this way in the commentarial accounts, but one possible reason is her recorded status as dhammakathikā. By the time of the commentaries, the position of dhammakathikā may have become a more formal, official role of high office, and perhaps one open only to monks. Thus Dhammadinnā being portrayed as exemplary in this role could have begun to prove problematic for the tradition.[33]

[33] Mahinda Deegalle begins a discussion of the history of dhammakathikas in Sri Lanka (2006, 37f.), but a more thorough study of the topic remains to be done.

***

The conclusion to this assessment of female teachers and pupils in the Pāli canon suggests several things. First, there is evidently a layer in the canon within which female teachers and others with distinguished roles are revered and esteemed. Dhammadinnā herself is the best example of this, and the canonical *Cūḷavedalla-sutta* the best evidence. But many others follow closely in her footsteps—Khemā, the subject of the next chapter, in a canonical narrative of her dialogue with a king proves herself to be a teacher of note; then we have also briefer examples of other nuns such as Sukkā, or the brief but significant mention of Kajaṅgalā. Second, the texts suggest that a formalized, institutional teaching relationship developed in the settled communities, whereby a monk advisor would be charged with giving instruction to nuns at scheduled times each month. This formalized role jars not only with the recorded instances of exemplary female teachers, but also with the epigraphic evidence which attests to both (likely) esteemed and influential female teachers, as well as nuns who considered themselves direct disciples of monks. Juxtaposing these different factors alongside one another raises questions as to the extent to which the role of monk advisor to nuns was enacted. The inscriptions that record female teachers and nuns within a relational saṅgha network, as teachers and pupils, potentially date to a broad time frame, some four hundred years, and the geographical spread of the inscriptions studied in this article seems to demonstrate that neither the phenomena of nuns with female teachers nor that of those who considered themselves direct disciples of monks were region specific aspects of early Buddhist communities. This combined with the fact that much of what is included in the Pāli *Vinaya* about monk advisors to nuns entails criticism or complaint of those in the role—or acting as such—suggests that attempts to comprehensively employ the role may not have been wholly successful.

8

Female beauty

KHEMĀ

Ornamentation and adornment

A central theme in Khemā's biography is her obsession with her own beauty. As mentioned in Chapter 2, this is a popular theme in the biographical accounts of early Buddhist nuns. Standards of both male and female beauty are culture-specific, and in this chapter I will examine the vicissitudes of notions of beauty in the Indian milieu. I will argue that the Buddhist texts demonstrate—as does other corroborating evidence—that it is the adorned and ornamented body that is considered beautiful and desirable, rather than the simple naked body. In order to assert this, I will have recourse to contemporaneous Brahmanical texts, studies of courtly culture from Indian history, assessments of art historical evidence, and archaeology. Setting these alongside the Buddhist texts, I will present a model for female (and male) beauty—with the adorned and ornamented body as the site of desire—and conclude with a reassessment of images of the decaying and decomposing body as an anathema to and antithesis of the cultural artifice of beauty.

In his book, Daud Ali paints a convincing picture of life at court in early medieval India. Although the focus of his work is later than the time period under scrutiny here, some of the sources he has recourse to are earlier, such as the *Nāṭyaśāstra* and *Arthaśāstra*. In his survey of the royal court as a social and cultural institution during the Gupta period, he demonstrates the importance of key features of courtly life such as manners, ethics, disposition, courtship and love, and, at the centre of this, the pre-occupation with beauty and refinement. After a discussion of some other aspects of beauty, in commenting upon the importance of adornment within this context he writes:

> Though the accounts of anatomical perfection and bodily grace outlined above suggest the extent to which courtly notions of beauty were mannered and stylized, neither formed the first and foremost *principle* of beauty prevalent among men and women of the court. This place was occupied by the idea of 'ornamentation'—a cultural figuration of practices and ideas so vast and significant as to subsume within it both anatomical and gestural beauty (both of which were ornaments of the self).... (Ali 2004, 162–3)

This idea of the 'principle' of beauty as adornment appears to have had leverage in earlier times as well. In a more recent book, Dehejia (2009) has surveyed representations of the body in Indian art and finds adornment of the body to have been central in representations of both the male and female body from the time of the earliest stone sculptures and, without exception, throughout Indian history. Like Ali, Dehejia's focus is not the centuries prior to the Common Era, although she does begin her survey by assessing the earliest representations of the body in Indian art, which do date back to this period.

Some of the earliest representations of the human body in Indian art are found on the artwork at Buddhist stūpa sites. Frederick Asher (2006) has challenged past assumptions about the dates of Buddhist stūpas and their railings and presented a fresh model for their chronology, dating them from approximately the second or first centuries BCE onwards. His work is, in part, based on a reconsideration of the possibility that artists in the same period used different styles but, he stresses, although there does appear to have been different regional styles, this does not detract from the very obvious pan-Indian style, which may have 'made the process of long-distance pilgrimage less daunting' (2006, 62). In accordance with this pan-Indian style but also showing some regional differences, the stone sculptures and carved narrative scenes at stūpa sites depict both humans and non-human beings as ornamented and adorned. The only exceptions to this are figures within crowd scenes, or those which are too small to afford detail to their representations. Some figures, usually the more prominent ones, are more fully adorned than others, but overall the types of adornment found on the various figures who make up narrative scenes or themselves adorn gateways and pillars are consistent. Typical of these, Dehejia describes the figure of the *devatā* Sirimā, carved in sandstone at the Bhārhut stūpa, Madhya Pradesh, and dateable to c. 100 BCE:

> Standing firm on both feet and directly facing the viewer, Sirima is portrayed with a typical hourglass figure, with large rounded breasts, a narrow waist, and smooth, broad hips. Slung below her navel and held in place with a jeweled *mekhala* is a long skirt, with its elaborately arranged pleats hanging between her legs. Cloth bands wrap around her head, a pendant adorns her forehead, and completing her adornment are heavy ear ornaments, three sets of necklaces, armlets, and a row of bangles and anklets. (Dehejia 2009, 79)

If Hiltebeitel is correct in his dating of the unified core of the *Mahābhārata* to 150–0 BCE (2001, 20–1), then the depictions of beauty and use of ornamentation within the *Mahābhārata* may have been written at a similar time to when the railing and pillars of the stūpa sites were constructed. The depictions of humans and non-human beings in the *Mahābhārata* are replete with the mention of adornment and ornamentation. For example, in the long and elaborate descriptions of the great hall in Book 2, men wear 'colorful bracelets and garlands' (*citrāṅgdāś citramālyāḥ*), and have 'earrings glowing like fire' (*jvalitakuṇḍalāḥ* 2.8.37). Also, gods, such as Vāruna, for example, sit 'adorned with celestial jewellery, garments and ornaments' (*divyaratnāmbaradharo divyābharaṇabhūṣitaḥ* 2.9.6). Vāruna is also said to be '[c]overed in fragrant garlands and heavenly ointments and perfumes' (*divyagandhāś ca divyagandhānulepanāḥ* 2.9.7). Vaiśravana, also, is 'covered in colorful robes and ornaments' (*vicitrābharaṇāmbaraḥ*

2.10.6), and the host of demons are described having 'gleaming earrings, garlanded, diademed, and also celestial clothes' (*rucirakuṇḍalāḥ sragviṇo maulinaś caiva tathā divyaparicchadāḥ* 2.9.15–16). Much later in the epic, women go to the scene of the battle, in its aftermath, to see their men, once adorned and beautiful, now fallen. Some of the men are described to have been 'with beautiful face and lovely earrings' (*suvaktraṃ cārukuṇḍalam* 11.25.25), or with 'amulets gleaming' (*rucirāṅgadāḥ* 11.25.13 and 15). A king's wife 'saw his two arms once adorned with sandal paste now smeared with his blood' (*yasya kṣatajasaṃdigdhau bāhū candanabhūṣitau avekṣya* 11.25.2).

Also in the *Mahābhārata*, in an episode prior to the great war, during the period in which the Pandavas are in exile and living in disguise, a military man sees Draupadī, the shared wife of the brothers, who is living as a hairdresser, and he becomes enamored with her. He describes her bedazzling beauty at some length:

> Your beauty, loveliness, and delicacy are exceptional, and your face shines with its allure like the dazzling moon. Fair-browed girl, you have large, beautiful eyes, like lotus petals and your speech is like that cry of a cuckoo, entirely beautiful-limbed girl.[1]

However, interestingly, it is not until his mind turns to thoughts of lovemaking that he begins to include mention of adornment.[2] When he propositions Draupadī, he says:

> O black-eyed girl ... Decked in brightly colored ornaments and garlands, embellished with every ornament, enjoy love with me willingly, radiant girl.[3]

[1] *MBh* 4.14.14, trans. Garbutt (2006, 107). *Rūpam agryaṃ tathā kāntiḥ saukumāryam anuttamam kāntyā vibhāti vaktraṃ te śaśāṅka iva nirmalam. Netre suvipule subhru padmapatranibhe śubhe vākyaṃ te cārusarvāṅgi parapuṣṭarutopamam.*

[2] There is just one exception to this in his long protestations of paramour when he says, 'Your breasts are both gorgeous and deserve pearl necklace ornaments' (*MBh* 4.14.20, trans. Garbutt 2006, 107). *Hārālaṅkārayogyau tu sthanau c' obhau suśobhanau.*

[3] *MBh* 4.14.27–8, trans. Garbutt (2006, 109). *Asitāpāṅgi...citramālyā mbaradharā sarvābharaṇabhūṣitā kāmaṃ prakāmaṃ seva tvaṃ mayā saha vilāsini.*

Although unwilling, Draupadī is forced to go to meet him on his request. When she arrives he says:

> Let golden garlands, conch shells, beautiful golden earrings, fashioned in varied cities, a splendid jewel, silk clothes and antelope skins be brought for you. My divine bed has also been made ready for you.[4]

Later, to protect her honour, Draupadī plots to have the man killed, convincing one of her husbands, Bhima, to do the deed. They hatch a plot whereby she will appear to acquiesce to the man's advances, then lure him to his execution. As he prepares to go:

> Made foolish with desire, he was intently engaged in hurriedly attaching garlands, ornaments and fragrances to himself, and while he was doing this he was thinking of the large-eyed lady...[5]

In this episode, it is not only the case that beauty equates with adornment, but that bodily adornment and ornamentation is part of the preparation for lovemaking. This is further confirmed by an episode from the Ramāyāṇa, discussed below, and, as we shall see, by the evidence of early Buddhist texts.[6]

Further to the above, the last pieces of evidence to note before turning to the Buddhist texts are evidence from archaeology. Although there is much work still to be done in excavating the sites of early Buddhism in north India, findings to date demonstrate an extensive use of jewellery and an advanced level of

4 *MBh* 4.16.3, trans. Garbutt 2006, 119. *Suvarṇamālāḥ kambūś ca kuṇḍale parihāṭake nānāpattanaje śubhre maṇiratnaṃ ca śobhanaṃ āharantu ca vastrāṇi kauśikāny ajināni ca. Asti me śayanaṃ divyaṃ tvadartham upakalpitam.*

5 *Mbh* 4.22.20, trans. Garbutt 2006, 163. *Gandhābharaṇamālyeṣu vyāsaktaḥ sa viśeṣataḥ alañcakre tadātmānaṃ satvaraḥ kāmamohitaḥ tasya tat kurvataḥ karma...anucintayataś capi tām evāyatalocanām.*

6 Roswell, in his study of Indian music, notes that the etymology of *alaṅkāra* is 'to make sufficient'. With regard to the art of music-making, he says that, therefore, 'the obvious implication is that decoration is an essential aspect of structure and is a necessary condition if music is to give pleasure' (1992, 165). In the (early) Indian milieu, music, as with the other arts, was thought to be improved with 'ornamentation' (see Roswell 1992, 162ff.).

manufacturing of ornaments at the major town and cities of the ancient *mahājanapadas*, or city-state principalities. As noted by Allchin, the larger settlements in the Gangetic plain show signs of manufacturing, from perhaps the fifth century onwards. Findings at these sites include copper used in ornaments, and beads made from a range of semi-precious stones such as agate, amethyst, carnelian, garnet, lapis, onyx, quartz, and rock crystal. There is also evidence of gold, coral, ivory, glass, and shell, and, at one site, even a unique set of jeweller's moulds were found (1995, 112). Generally, as noted by several archaeologists, jewellery-making appeared to have been a fine craft in early historic India, and migrating groups even brought with them their own lines in jewellery and other crafts (see Neelis 2007). This accords with the evidence of the *Arthaśāstra*, which goes into some detail when noting jewellery and gems that should be received by the treasury (2.11.1–42). This section of the *Arthaśāstra* details some of these above items, as well as pearls, rubies, and diamonds, and there are also two further chapters (2.13 and 14) in the text which contain details about the art of the goldsmith and jeweller. In an article on jewellery, Bérénice Bellina surveys the use of beads made of agate and carnelian across India and south-east Asia during the first millennium BCE. As she finds evidence for beads made by Indian methods of manufacture in the 'local styles' of south-east Asia, she concludes that these were likely 'made to order', thus showing that Indian manufacturers and their methods were highly regarded. As she concludes, 'Imported artifacts, which included agate and cornelian ornaments were status markers, representing more advanced technology and sophistication of the time' (2003, 295). While this does not help to establish the relationship between beauty and adornment under discussion, it does demonstrate that jewellery was popular in India in the centuries prior to the Common Era and that its methods of production were advanced.

Thus there is evidence that this focus on ornamentation and adornment as the 'foremost principle of beauty' has its antecedents in earlier phases of Indian history than those that are the focus for Ali's study. Early Indian art, contemporaneous texts, and the evidence of archaeology demonstrate that ornamentation and bodily adornment were important aspects of social life in India prior to the Common Era. This is confirmed by early Buddhist texts. In the *Thera-Therīgāthā*, verses of both monks and nuns describe how they, as householders, were obsessed by and addicted to ornamentation. In the *Therīgāthā*, there are eight instances of women talking about themselves in relation to their beauty, and in all except three of these cases—in which beauty is mentioned only fleetingly—it is adorned beauty that is highlighted.[7] The first instance is of a former prostitute, Vimalā. She describes how she would conduct herself in her former life of prostitution, when, intoxicated with her own good looks and '... having decorated this body' (*vibhūsetvā imaṃ kāyaṃ*) and adorning herself with her ornaments (*pilandhanaṃ*), she was like a hunter who had laid a trap (vv. 72–5). As part of a rather composite set of verses, Nanduttarā notes how, previously:

> Delighting in finery and adornments and bathing and anointing I tended to this body afflicted by desire for sensual pleasure.[8]

Sujata, describing her life prior to her ordination, describes how she was:

> Ornamented, well-dressed, wearing a garland smeared with sandal-wood paste, covered with all my ornaments, attended by a crowd of slave-women.[9]

In a verse which is, in the extant text, attributed to Cāpā (but is in reality more about her former husband) she seeks to understand why her husband is abandoning her when her body is smeared with sandal paste and she is wearing the best muslin garments (v. 298). Ambapāli, in reflecting upon the deterioration of her body in old age, remembers its former glory:

7 The three cases are, first, one of Khemā's own verses, the very first one, in which Māra tells her she is young and beautiful. In the second case of unadorned beauty, Anopamā recounts how she 'endowed with a beautiful form' (*vaṇṇarūpena sampannā* v. 151). Aḍḍakāsī simply states that she became disgusted with her beauty (*nibbind' ahaṃ rūpe* v. 26).

8 *Thī* v. 89. *Vibhūsamaṇḍanaratā nhāpanucchādanehi ca, upakāsiṃ imaṃ kāyaṃ kāmarāgena additā.*

9 *Thī* v. 145, trans. Norman (Rhys Davids and Norman 1989, 187). *Alaṃkatā suvasanā mālinī candanokkhitā, sabbābharaṇasañchannā dāsīgaṇapurakkhatā.*

> Covered with flowers my head was fragrant like a perfumed box; now because of old age it smells like a dog's fur.... (v. 253)
>
> Possessing fine pins, decorated with gold, adorned with plaits, it looked beautiful.... (v. 255)
>
> Formerly my eyebrows looked beautiful, like crescents well-painted by artists.... (v. 256)
>
> My earlobes looked beautiful, like well-fashioned and well-finished bracelets.... (v. 259)
>
> Formerly my hands looked beautiful, with delicate signet rings, decorated with gold.... (v. 264)
>
> Formerly my calves looked beautiful, possessing delicate anklets, decorated with gold... (v. 268)[10]

Lastly, the philanderer who accosts the nun Subhā Jīvakambavanikā desires to engage in lovemaking with her. He tells her:

> If you will do my bidding, be happy, come, live in my house. Living in the calm of the palace, let women make you ready.
>
> Wear fine muslin, and put on garlands and rouge. I shall make many varied ornaments for you, of gold, jewels, and pearls.
>
> With a cover well-washed of dirt, beautiful, spread with a woolen quilt, new, climb upon the bed, very costly, decorated with sandalwood, having an excellent smell.[11]

[10] *Thī* vv. 253–68, trans. Norman (Rhys Davids and Norman 1989, 201–2). *Vāsito va surabhikaraṇḍako pupphapūraṃ mama uttamaṅgabhu, taṃ jarāya sasalomagandhikaṃ...* (v. 253). *Saṇhagandhakasuvaṇṇamaṇḍitaṃ sobhate su veṇihi alaṅkataṃ...* (v. 255). *Cittakārasukatā va lekhitā sobhate su bhamukā pure mama...* (v. 256). *Kaṅkaṇaṃ va sukataṃ suniṭṭhitaṃ sobhate su mama kaṇṇapāḷiyo pure...* (v. 259). *Saṅhamuddikāsuvaṇṇamaṇḍitā sobhate su hatthā pure mama...* (v. 264). *Saṅhanūpurasuvaṇṇamaṇḍitā sobhate su jaṅghā pure mama...* (v. 268).

[11] *Thī* vv. 376–8. *Yadi me vacanaṃ karissasi sukhitā ehi agāraṃ āvasa, pāsādanivātavāsinī parikamman te karontu nāriyo. Kāsikasukhumāni dhāraya abhiropehi ca mālavaṇṇakaṃ, kañcanamaṇimuttakaṃ bahuṃ vividhaṃ ābharaṇaṃ karomi te. Sudhotarajopacchadaṃ subhaṃ gonakatūlikasantataṃ navaṃ, abhirūha sayanaṃ mahārahaṃ candanamaṇḍitaṃ sāragandhikaṃ.*

Also in the nuns' verses, mirroring the *Mahābhārata* depictions and those on early art discussed earlier, there are two suggestions of male adornment. First, in the verses of Isidāsī, in performing her duties for her husband, she says: 'taking a comb, an ornament, collyrium and a mirror, I myself adorned my husband, like a servant-girl'.[12] Second, in the verses of Sumedhā, her suitor, Anīkaratta, is ornamented (as he approaches her with union in mind). In the verse, he is described with 'his body adorned with jewels and gold' (*maṇikanakabhūsitaṅgo* v. 482).

In the *Theragāthā*, there is also evidence of male adornment, in verses associated with four separate monks. Probably the best known of these is Nanda, a (half-) brother of the Buddha, who is best known for his attachment to the sensual world, but who is also in the *Saṃyutta-Nikāya* admonished for his concern to have nice robes and for wearing eye makeup (*akkhīni añjetvā SN* II.281).[13] In his *Theragāthā* verse, Nanda confesses:

> Distracted by my addiction to ornamentation, I was conceited, vain and afflicted by desire for pleasures.[14]

In the second set of verses attributed to a monk called Pārāpariya, he laments how monks have fallen since the time of the Buddha, noting they are now quarrelsome, overcome by defilement and cheats and fraudsters. In noting their appearance he remarks that they adorn themselves like courtesans (*gaṇikā va vibhūsāyaṃ* v. 939). The other two instances of male adornment are less obvious in terms of their overall meaning within the context of the text, but nevertheless are entirely clear in their depiction of male beautification. In verses attributed to a monk known as Jambugāmika's son, there is a question, as if posed to him, about his interest in

[12] *Thī* v. 411. *Kocchaṃ pasādaṃ añjanañ ca ādāsakañ ca gaṇhitvā, parikammakārikā viya sayam eva patiṃ vibhūsemi.*

[13] In the Chinese shorter *Saṃyukta Āgama* version, there is no mention of eye make-up (*SĀ* 3.3.5, trans. Bingenheimer 2011, 65–6). Also, elsewhere in the Pāli canon, some Licchavi males are said to wear make-up (see Chapter 9, pages 140–2), as are some male gods.

[14] *Thā* v. 157. *Ayonisomanasīkārā maṇḍanaṃ anuyuñjisaṃ, uddhato capalo cāsiṃ kāmārāgena aṭṭito.*

aspects of his appearance. The question 'Do you not delight in adornments?' (*kacci no bhūsanārato* v. 28) follows a similar question about clothes. The commentary attributes these questions to his father, the layman Jambugāmika, who is concerned as to whether his son is truly committed to his life of discipleship. The commentarial exegesis on the line expresses the only possible meaning of the question—that it refers to 'delighting in adorning one's own body' (*attabhāvavibhūsanāya rato abhirato, Tha-a* I.92). The third reference to male adornment in the *Theragāthā* is in the verse of Yasa:

> Well-anointed, well-dressed, adorned with my ornaments, I have attained the three knowledges. The Buddha's teaching has been done.[15]

Turning now to assess how men describe women in relation to ornamentation and their beauty (and sexuality) in the *Theragāthā*, the references to this are particularly noteworthy. Previously, Karen Lang (1986) surveys many of these references and concluded that women are seen as a 'snare of Māra' (*maccupāsa*) for the monks in the *Theragāthā*. However, what Lang failed to notice was that on all occasions except one in which these monks represent the body as the snare of Māra, it is the ornamented body, not the unadorned female form that is conceptualized as enticing. This is most often expressed in the last two pādas of a verse. The pādas are identical in each case, but the first two pādas of the verse are different. There are three incidents of it:

Candana

> Covered in gold, attended by a crowd of servant women, taking her child on her hip, my wife approached me.
>
> And seeing her coming, the mother of my child, *adorned, well-dressed, like a snare of Māra laid out.*[16]

[15] *Tha* v. 117, trans. Norman (Rhys Davids and Norman 1989, 17). *Suvilitto suvasano sabbābharaṇabhūsito, tisso vijjā ajjhagamiṃ kataṃ buddhassa sāsanan ti.*

[16] *Tha* vv. 299–300. *Jātarūpena pacchannā dāsīgaṇapurakkhatā, aṅkena puttam ādāya bhariyā maṃ upāgami. Tañ ca disvāna āyantiṃ sakaputtassa mātaraṃ, alaṃkataṃ suvasanaṃ maccupāsaṃ oḍḍitaṃ.*

Nāgasamāla

Adorned, well-dressed, wearing a garland, anointed with sandal, in the middle of the main road a female dancer dances to music.

I entered for alms. As I was going along I saw her *adorned, well-dressed, like a snare of Māra laid out.*[17]

Sundarasamudda

Adorned, well-dressed, carrying a garland, decorated, with her feet reddened with lac, having put on slippers, a courtesan.

Removing her slippers, (standing) before me with cupped hands, she spoke to me, softly and tenderly, with a smile.

'You are young to have gone forth. Abide in my (lovemaking) charter, enjoy human sensual pleasures. I will make you happy, I promise you truly, indeed I bring fire.

When we are both old, supported by sticks, we can both go forth, being lucky in both worlds'.

And I saw that courtesan beseeching me with cupped hands, *adorned, well-dressed, like a snare of Māra laid out.*[18]

Also, similarly, in a variation on this, Raṭṭhapāla's verses avow that the adorned and ornamented form of a woman is the problem:

See the painted puppet, a mass of sores, a corporeal body, diseased, with many (bad) intentions, for which there is no permanent stability.

See the painted form with jewels and earrings, covered with skin and bones, made beautiful with clothes.

[17] *Tha* vv. 267–8. *Alaṃkatā suvasanā mālinī candanussadā, majjhe mahāpathe nārī turiye naccati naṭṭakī. Piṇḍikāya paviṭṭho 'haṃ gacchanto naṃ udikkhisaṃ, alaṃkataṃ suvasanaṃ maccupāsaṃ va oḍḍitaṃ.*

[18] *Tha* vv. 459–63. *Alaṃkatā suvasanā māladhārī vibhūsitā, alattakakatāpādā pādukāruyha vesikā. Pādukā oruhitvāna purato pañjalīkatā, sā maṃ saṇhena mudunā mhitapubbaṃ abhāsatha. Yuvāsi tvaṃ pabbajito, tiṭṭhāhi mama sāsane, bhuñja mānusake kāme ahaṃ vittaṃ dadāmi te, saccan te paṭijānāmi aggiṃ vā te harām' ahaṃ. Yadā jiṇṇā bhavissāma ubho daṇḍaparāyanā, ubho pi pabbajissāma ubhayatha kaṭaggaho. Tañ ca disvāna yācantiṃ vesikaṃ pañjalīkataṃ, alaṃkataṃ suvasanaṃ maccupāsaṃ va oḍḍitaṃ.*

The feet are reddened with lac, the face is smeared with powder, enough to delude a fool, but not for one who seeks the far shore.

Hair braided eightfold, eyes smeared with collyrium, enough to delude a fool, but not for one who seeks the far shore.

The adorned putrid body is like a newly painted collyrium-box, enough to delude a fool, but not for one who seeks the far shore.[19]

Here, Raṭṭhapāla's verses are cleverly making an analogy between the usual 'covering' of the human body with the artificial 'covering' of make-up, jewellery, and other adornments. In the second of these verses, the artifice of beauty through adornment with jewellery and clothes is likened to nature's 'artifice'—covering the corporal body with skin. The reader/listener is taken from the painted and adorned form, to the gross internal reality of the body. And this technique, used to attempt to dissolve desire, will be discussed in more detail below.

It is easy to see, from the above examples, that within the articulated world of the composers of the *Thera-Therīgāthā*, the notion of the adorned body as the most beautiful and sexually inviting is as prevalent as it is in the art of early India and in the *Mahābhārata*. The *Thera-Therīgāthā* verses do not match the sophisticated and refined procedures of Indian court as illuminated by Ali, but they do attest to similar ideas about adorned beauty.

Moving on to look at a text from the Mauryan period, the *Apadāna*, we find less evidence of this preoccupation. If we begin with the story of Khemā, we will see that in the *Apadāna* there is less emphasis on ornamentation than found in the *Thera-Therīgāthā* descriptions of beauty but more than there are in the later texts, written in the cloistered Buddhist monasteries of South India or Sri Lanka. In the first biography of Khemā, from the

19 Tha vv. 769–73. *Passa cittakataṃ bimbaṃ arukāyaṃ samussitaṃ, āturaṃ bahusaṃkappaṃ yassa n' atthi dhuvaṃ ṭhiti. Passa cittakataṃ rūpaṃ maṇinā kuṇḍalena ca, aṭṭhitacena onaddhaṃ saha vatthehi sobhati. Alattakakatā pādā mukhaṃ cuṇṇakamakkhitaṃ, alaṃ bālassa mohāya no ca pāragavesino. Aṭṭhāpadakatā kesā nettā añjanamakkhitā, alaṃ bālassa mohāya no ca pāragavesino. Añjanī 'va navā cittā pūtikāyo alamkato, alaṃ bālassa mohāya no ca pāragavesino.* Oldenberg and Pischel ([1883] 1999), emended as per the note in their edition. *pāpā* > *pādā*.

Apadāna, ornamentation is mentioned in both the descriptions of Khemā's own physical beauty and that of the apparition. In the description of Khemā's own beauty, a term for ornamentation is used idiomatically, which, as it is contained in an idiom, suggests a strong relationship between beauty and ornamentation, but does not otherwise invoke it. The verse is as follows:

> When I was a young woman, adorned with beauty, my father gave me to King Bimbisāra.[20]

Here, *rūpalāvaññabhūsitā* ('adorned with beauty') stands as the sole descriptor of the protagonist's loveliness. Next, when the beautiful female apparition is described, in a eulogy to her stunning beauty, she is said to be adorned with beautiful ornaments and garments, but this is not quite as lavish as in the *Thera-Therīgāthā* examples above:

> Her ears were like golden swings, her breasts hung down like jars, she had a slender waist, superb hips, thighs like a banana tree and beautiful ornaments.
>
> She was dressed in a red garment and a pure blue one, possessing a form of which one can never get enough, and she was endowed with a joyful nature.[21]

Further, if we look at the other versions of this beauty story in the *Apadāna*, we find other instances of beauty being defined in relation to ornamentation. Abhirūpanandā is also said to be 'adorned with beauty' with the use of the same term, and when Nandā Janapadakalyāṇī's mother is attempting to persuade her to go forth, she tells her that her beauty will

[20] *Yadā 'haṃ yobbanaṃ pattā rūpalāvaññabhūsitā, tadā adāsi maṃ tāto bimbisārassa rājino* (v. 38, II.546). Emended Lilley from *rūpavant' āvibhūsitā* to *rūpalāvaññabhūsitā*, following Pruitt's emendation in the *Thī-a* edition (*Therīgāthā-aṭṭhakathā*, 38, 126), Lilley's variations in her manuscripts and the similar compound in the Abhirūpanandā biography (*Ap.*, v. 9, II.608) for which Lilley has in the text *rūpavaṇṇavibhusitā*, but also has a variation of *rūpalānañ ca bhusitā* from her Burmese manuscript.

[21] *Ap.* 548. *Hemadolā va savanā kalasākārasutthanī, vedimajjhā varassoṇī rammorū cārubhūsanā. Rattaṃsukasusaṃvitā nīlā maṭṭhanivāsanā, atappaneyyarūpena hāsabhāvasamanvitā.* Emended *aṃsaka* > *aṃsuka*.

not last long. She warns that 'the youthful body is powerless to old age' (*jarāvasānaṃ yobbaññaṃ rūpaṃ*), and in commenting on her daughter's good looks she says:

> Look at this splendid form, lovely, charming, ornamented and adorned resembling a mass of beauty. Honoured like the best in the world, an elixir for the eye, praised in the community for its merit, bring joy to the family of Okkāka.[22]

If all these excerpts are compared with the depictions in the later commentaries, a difference can be noted, in that the commentaries less frequently envision a beautiful woman as ornamented. Khemā, in her biography in the *Therīgāthā* commentary is simply said to have a golden complexion. The apparition here is said to resemble a heavenly nymph (*devacchara*). In the *Aṅguttara-nikāya* commentary Khemā is said to have beautifully hued skin, and the apparition is simply described again as a devacchara. The *Dhammapada* commentary also simply describes the apparition as just this, an apparition (*itthiṃ nimmiṇi*), with no mention of ornaments. The only mention of ornaments in relation to the various versions of the beauty story in all three commentaries is in the version associated with Nandā, in the *Dhammapada* commentary, where the apparition 'wore crimson garments and was decorated with all her ornaments' (*rattavatthanivatthaṃ sabbabharaṇapaṭimaṇḍitaṃ, Dhp-a* III.115). The only commentary that is different is the *Jātakatthavaṇṇanā*. The core of at least some of the *Jātakatthavaṇṇanā* stories, as argued recently by Appleton (2009) and Anālayo (2010b), are likely early, and this can be confirmed by the interest in bodily adornment evidenced in the text. Some of the many examples of this include the queen and other women in the *Mahāsāra Jātaka* (92) who take off their jewels and ornaments to bathe, the description of beautiful Ummadantī (in the jātaka named after her, 527; see Chapter 12) who is said to be adorned with jewel earrings (*āmuttamaṇikuṇḍalā*) and covered with the best

[22] *Ap.* 574. *Idam pi te subhaṃ rūpaṃ passa kantaṃ manoharaṃ 'maṃ bhūsanaṃ alaṅkāraṃ sirisaṅkhatasannibhaṃ. Pūjitaṃ lokasāraṃ va nayanānaṃ rasāyanaṃ puññānaṃ kittijananaṃ okkākakulanandanaṃ.*

sandal perfume (*candanasāralittā*), and the men who wear fine ornaments in the *Bhūridatta Jātaka* (543).

Thus, it would appear, from the evidence of the *Thera-Therīgāthā* most particularly, that the notion of beauty had adornment as its foremost principle in these earlier phases of Indian history. This continued to some extent in the *Apadāna*, but rescinded in the commentaries. In assessing the Buddhist texts alongside the other evidence the following observations can be made. The evidence of art history demonstrates that the notion of adorned beauty was *fully formed* by around the middle for the first century BCE, as it is portrayed comprehensively on even the earliest images, and on sculptures and in narrative scenes found in different regions. The relationship between beauty and adornment also appears fully formed in the *Mahābhārata*, although noting this comes with incumbent dating problems. The adoption of the notion in the *Thera-Therīgāthā*—importantly—in order to reject it also suggests, by the fact of the rejection of it, something fully developed. The *Thera-Therīgāthā* here accords with what we find if we survey other early Pāli texts. In the texts of the four nikāyas, notions of beauty are intertwined with ornamentation and adornment. This is in evidence in the quote in Chapter 12 (pages 213–14), an *Aṅguttara-nikāya* rendering of the important constitutes of masculinity and femininity, which includes, respectively, male and female ornaments. Other examples of this include the previously mentioned discourse on Nandā and his make-up in the *Saṃyutta-nikāya*, the description of the Licchavis dressing for their audience with the Buddha (see Chapter 9), and the list of ten desirable and undesirable things in the *Aṅguttara-nikāya* that tells us that lack of finery and adornment are obstacles to beauty (*amaṇḍanā avibhūsanā vaṇṇassa paripantho AN* V.136).

However, in the *Apadāna* the emphasis on it rescinds considerably, and this appears problematic at first sight, as the *Apadāna* dates to around the time of the other supporting evidence. The most likely conclusion to draw, however, seems to be that the *Thera-Therīgāthā* was composed earlier and is the earliest evidence for this notion, rather ironically as it is tendered to be rejected. And the reason for the relative lack of it in the *Apadāna* may be as follows: as the text is post-Asokan, it was composed at a time when Buddhism was flourishing and expanding. As Buddhism flourished in its own right, it was likely to be less prone to acculturation and religious influence in relation to Brahmanism and other north Indian belief systems. It could, and likely did, establish its own sub-cultural enclaves, within which its own values became normative. The *Mūlasarvāstivāda Vinaya*, dated by Schopen (2007) and others to the period between the empires, to the Kuṣāṇa or pre-Kuṣāṇa period, can provide us with some potential indication of this. In the *Mūlasarvāstivāda Vinaya* we see both some acquiescence to normative cultural ideas of beauty, and also a surprising incident of non-adherence. First, in the story from the *Bhaiṣajyavastu*, the Buddha, in a former life as Prince Sudhana falls in love with a *kinnara*, who is described in these typical ways:

> Prince Sudhana saw the *kinnara* Manoharā, beautiful, lovely and charming ... whose breasts were like golden jars ... with a collection of crest jewels, the palms of her hands reddish, going about with the playful sound made by her anklets, bracelets, necklace and pearls that was a thrill and a delight...[23]

However, there is another story apart from this, from the *Adhikaraṇavastu*, which could be indicative of sub-cultural values and norms. In this story, a woman, the wife of a Sakyan, arrives at Nyagrodha to hear the Buddha teach. She arrived adorned with all her ornaments (*sarvālaṃkāravibhūṣitā*), but was also possessed of a (natural) youthful beauty (*rūpayauvanavatī*). Seeing her, Ānanda spoke to her and said:

> Sister, you are already beautiful, lovely and charming, why now adorn yourself with all these ornaments? You have not made yourself beautiful, when you come concealed by adornments...[24]

[23] Dutt, Gilgit Manuscripts I.136–7. *adrākṣīt sudhano rājakumāro manoharāṃ kinnarīm abhirūpāṃ darśanīyāṃ prāsādikāṃ...kañcanakalaśa... saṃhitamaṇicūḍām āraktamaratalāṃ praharṣanūpuravalayahārārdhahāra-nirghoṣavilasitagatiṃ....* This story is discussed in Finnegan (2009, 237–40).

[24] Gnoli 1978, 62. *Bhagini tvaṃ tāvat prakṛtyaivābhirūpa darśanīyā prāsādikā; kimaṅga punaḥ sarvālaṃkāravibhūṣitā; na śobhanaṃ tvayā kṛtaṃ yad alaṃkāraṃ prāvṛtyāgatā...*

On hearing Ānanda's words, the woman felt shame and removed her ornaments, having her servant take them away, seemingly having been made aware of an axiom. Thus, we see here, in Ānanda's speech, an alternate view—that adornment does not make a body or person beautiful; on the contrary, it rather takes away from natural beauty. Schopen (2007) has previously highlighted the importance, in the *Mūlasarvāstivāda Vinaya*, of beautifying monasteries, as this can attract wealthy donors who might be inspired by the spectacular sights to make generous offerings. Also, the bejewelled Gāndharan bodhisattvas, possibly dated prior to the Common Era, or a little after, demonstrate that while a partial move away from the notion of adorned corporal beauty is evident, this may have been more of a subtle shift which included a continuation of hegemonic notions of beauty and majesty within architecture and for apparel for non-human beings, and so perhaps only included a rejection of ornamentation as an aspect of human beauty, which makes sense doctrinally.

Lack of adornment

The verses in the *Thera-Therīgāthā* on ornamentation both help to establish this as part of the notion of beauty in India prior to the Common Era, and, as well, begin to enable an understanding of certain relationships to the world of sensory pleasure and the human body within early Indian Buddhism. Both within the confines of the tradition (however boundaried they may be) and outside of it, the adorned body is the body that is ripe and ready for sensual and sexual pleasures. This stands against the simple naked body and the ascetic naked body, both of which are considered asexual. In this broad early Indian context, the simple naked body is noted for its absence from the textual and art historical record. With regard to the early sculptures, there has been a longstanding assumption that the figures that adorn monuments are nude, but this is not the case, as identified by Dehejia:

> Sculptors in India depicted their figures seemingly bare, but a close inspection will reveal—at ankles, waist, neck, and arms—hints of the delicate folds of fine drapery.... Sculptors depicted these skirt folds

quite prominently and with considerable attention, but they rarely allowed the folds to obstruct the view of lower limbs, placing them so that they swing away from the body. Frequently, the lower limbs are so clearly visible that viewers assume they are unclothed; but once the eye is trained to notice the skirt folds, they seem to appear everywhere. (2009, 34)

The reason that the simple naked body is not well attested in the art and literature of the period is because it was considered impure, asexual, and a signifier of social exclusion. This may be because it was envisioned through the lens of dharmaśāstric notions of purity and impurity that became applicable more broadly.[25] In the early Buddhist texts, there are examples of how the naked body is considered impure. For example, in the *Mahāvagga*, the lay woman Visākhā wants to give bathing clothes to the nuns because it is impure for women to be naked (I.293). Further, in the *Petavatthu*, the unfortunate souls reborn as ghouls for their past misdeeds are most often naked, such as in the examples quoted in Chapter 12 (pages 217–19). In the stories of naked and ugly-looking petas and *petīs* the connection between nudity and impurity is apparent, as is the connection to social exclusion. These are both also in evidence in the following *Therīgāthā* verses attributed to Vāsiṭṭhī (vv. 133–8), an otherwise little-known nun.

> Afflicted by grief for my son(s), with mind deranged, out of my senses, naked, and with disheveled hair, I wandered here and there.
>
> I dwelt on rubbish heaps, in the street, in a cemetery, and on highways, I wandered for three years, consigned to hunger and thirst.[26]

[25] Dehejia further notes that '[c]ertainly the word "naked" should have no place in the Indian artistic vocabulary...', as drapery is an integral part of adornment (2009, 36).

[26] *Puttasoken' ahaṃ aṭṭā khittacittā visaññinī, naggā pakiṇṇakesī ca tena tena vicari 'haṃ. Vīthisaṅkārakūṭesu susāne rathiyāsu ca, acariṃ tīṇi vassāni khuppipāsāsamappitā* (*Thīg* vv. 133–4 at 136). This verse is discussed more fully in Chapter 10. Chapter 10 is on the well-known nun Paṭācārā, whose biography in the later commentaries includes a period of nudity. Her nakedness is not mentioned in the canonical references to her, but as with Vāsiṭṭhī, here female nakedness is representative of an asexual woman—a woman distraught with grief.

Here, the nakedness of Vāsiṭṭhī is part of the portrayal of her grief-stricken state. Her nudity in no way corresponds to a vibrant or active sexuality but, instead, along with her disheveled hair, represents an asexual state engendered by loss, pain, and suffering. There is also another layer to the taxonomy between the fully adorned body ready for sex and the asexual and impure state of nudity; this is the state of half-undress, or partial adornment. There are, in the epics and some later literature, examples of an unadorned state which either symbolize asexual states of emotional distress or are a trope for feigned emotional distress. In the aftermath of the *Mahābhārata* war, discussed above, when the women become distressed at the battlefield scenes, the wailing women are depicted as 'half-undressed, just wearing a single garment, their untied hair disheveled' (trans. Crosby 2009, 309 *ekavastrārdhasaṃvītāḥ prakīrṇāsita mūrdhajāḥ* 11.24.8), and are also said to have 'all their jewelry scattered about' (*prakīrṇasarvābharaṇāṃ* 11.25.8). Also, Sally Sutherland Goldman has analysed an episode in the *Rāmāyaṇa* in which one of the wives of Daśartha, Rāma's father, attempted to manipulate him. Influenced by an evil servant, Mantharā, Kaikeyī decides to try to persuade her husband to make her own son king, instead of Rāma. Putting on a dirty garment, she enters her private chamber:

> There the lovely lady removed her pearl necklace, worth many hundred thousands, and her other costly and beautiful jewelry. And then, under the spell of the hunchback Mantharā's words, the golden Kaikeyī got down upon the floor and said to her: 'Hunchback, go inform the king that I will surely die right here unless Bharata receives as his portion the land and Rāghava, as his, the forest.' And uttering those ruthless words, the lady put all her jewelry aside and lay down upon the ground bare of any spread ...[27]

[27] *Ram.* 2.9.43–6, trans. Pollock 2008, 57. *Anekaśatasāhasraṃ muktāhāraṃ varāṅganā avamucya varārhāṇī śubhany ābharaṇāni ca. Tato hemopamā tatra kubja vākyaṃ vaśaṃ gatā saṃviśya bhūmau kaikeyī mantharām idam abravit: iha vā māṃ mṛtāṃ kubje nṛpāy' āvedayiṣyasi vanaṃ tu rāghave prāpte bharata prāpsyati kṣitiṃ. Athaitad uktvā vacanaṃ sudāruṇaṃ nidāya sarvābharaṇāni bhāminī asaṃvṛtā āstaraṇena medinīṃ tadādhiśiśye...*

When Daśartha arrives in her private chamber, he reads the visual clues and comprehends that her removal of jewellery, apparel of a dirty garment, and lying on the sparse floor are indications of emotional distress. The private chambers are also usually the place for lovemaking, and Daśaratha also understands that, stripped down as she is, Kaikeyī is 'not sexually available' (Goldman 2000, 135).[28]

Ali also notes this lack of adornment as a signifier of grief—as in the *Abhijñaśākuntalam* when King Duṣyanta removes his ornaments when separated from Śākuntalā, and in later works such as the *Kādambarī* of the seventh-century poet Bāṇa, in which Queen Vilāsavatī refraining from ornamentation as a signifier of her emotional distress at not being able to bear a child.[29] Further, Dehejia notes just one of many Śilahāra inscriptions detailing how the women of defeated armies are made to abandon adornment (Dehejia 2009, 38–9).[30] Although some of these sources are later, all of them together demonstrate that unadorned, barely, slightly, or simply clothed, the body lacks

28 In her article, Sutherland Goldman presents an impressive juxtapositioning of Rāma and Ravana in relation to ornamentation. In quoting long descriptive passages of both, she highlights the excessive adornment and ornamentation of Ravana, as opposed to the more physical description of Rāma as muscular, graceful and majestic. This difference she puts down to the troping of self-control and excess, particularly sexual excess. Rāma is righteous and self-restrained, while Ravana is the epitome of sexual excess (2000, 126–31).

29 Ali (2004, 165–6). He quotes the *Kādambarī* (103) when King Tārāpīḍa asks the queen, 'O thin-waisted one, why have you not decorated yourself? Why haven't you put *alaketa* dye on your feet ... why haven't you favoured with the touch of your lotus-like feet your jeweled anklets, why is your waist silent, your girdle being laid aside, why is the ornament design ... not painted on your expansive breasts ... why haven't you decorated your slender neck with a pearl necklace ...' Ali also notes that '[f]or people of the court, the unadorned naked body had little aesthetic appeal' (103).

30 Verse 18 of the Thāṇā plates of Mummuṇirāja, śaka date 970 (corresponding to 1049 CE), reads, 'He caused the ladies in the harems of his enemies slain by his sharp sword drawn out to have dangling hair, to

its sexual allure, and has become separated from the world of sensual pleasures.

The antithesis of beauty

Buddhism grew up in this ancient Indian world rich in discourse and imagery relating to the pleasures of the senses, and in many ways a society, or communities, particularly preoccupied with the sensory world. How then, can this be challenged? What might be a hard-hitting rebuttal to and rejection of this corporal entanglement? Given that the naked body is already a socio-religious signifier of asexuality, impurity, and social exclusion, what instead might work as a fresh rebuke to cultural norms and mores? Perhaps a sharp focus on the reality of the raw, visceral human body, in all its fleshy, pus-ridden, and foul-smelling gore would do it:

> I, Kulla, going to a cremation ground, saw a woman cast away, discarded in the crematory, her whole body being eaten by worms.
>
> See the body, Kulla, diseased, impure, putrid, oozing, trickling, the delight of fools.[31]

> This two-legged, impure, bad-smelling (body), full of various corpses, oozing here and there is cherished.
>
> Like a lurking deer in a snare, a fish in a fish-hook, a monkey in a sticky trap, they bind ordinary people.[32]

---

discard necklaces from their pitcher-breasts and to have eyes without collyrium' (Mirashi 1977, 93). This same verse is repeated on other Śilahāra inscriptions, such as the Panhāḷe plates of Vikramāditya, śaka date 1061 (corresponding to 1139 CE) on page 136.

[31] *Tha* vv. 393–4. *Kullo sīvathikaṃ gantvā addasaṃ itthim ujjhitaṃ, apaviddhaṃ susānasmiṃ khajjantiṃ kimihī phuṭaṃ. Āturaṃ asuciṃ pūtiṃ passa kulla samussayaṃ, uggharantaṃ paggharantaṃ bālānam abhinanditaṃ.* Apart from the name, this second verse is identical to Khemā's, as are some of the other of Kulla's verses.

[32] *Tha* vv. 453–4. *Dipādako 'yam asuci duggandho parihīrati, nānākuṇapaparipūro vissavanto tato tato. Migaṃ nilīnaṃ kūṭena baliseneva ambujaṃ, vānaraṃ viya lepena bādhayanti puthujjanaṃ.*

O shame on bodies! Bad-smelling, on Māra's side, oozing. There are nine streams in your body that flow all the time.[33]

Full of stains of different sorts, a great producer of excrement, like a stagnant pool, a great tumour, a great wound,

Full of pus and blood, immersed in a privy, trickling with water, the body always oozes foully.

Having a binding of sixty tendons, plastered with fleshy plaster, girt with a jacket of skin, the foul body is worthless.[34]

The decomposing or decaying body, when set alongside the adorned and ornamented body, can be seen as an anathema to it. As the simple naked body was considered asexual and not dangerous (in terms of arousing sexual desire), in order to combat one's arousal/desire/interest in the adorned and ornamented enticing body a more emotive image was needed, something to bring about disgust in the corporal body. I will demonstrate this point with recourse to an idiom found only in the *Thera-Therīgāthā* and the *Vimānavatthu* (to my knowledge). Many of the *Thera-Therīgāthā* verses, such as Khemā's, mention what has been termed and translated as the 'fivefold music' or the 'fivefold ensemble' (*pañcaṇgika turiya*). According to the commentaries, this is music produced by different five instruments; however, it may be that the idiomatic use of the phrase had been lost even by the time of the later canonical texts. The phrase is not one well known within the literature on music in ancient India, and in fact, Roswell (1992), in his comprehensive study of this music in this milieu, does not mention the

33 This set of verses, and those of Sabbakāma preceding them are the only two times that the snare of Māra is mentioned in relation to bodies, but with no mention of ornamentation. *Tha* v. 279. *Dhir atthu pūre duggandhe mārapakkhe avassute, nava sotāni te kāye yāni sandanti sabbadā.*

34 *Tha* vv. 567–9, trans. Norman (Rhys Davids and Norman 1989, 62). *Nānākulamalasampuṇṇo mahāukkārasambhavo, candanikaṃ va paripakkaṃ mahāgaṇḍo mahāvaṇo. Pubbaruhirasampuṇṇo gūthakūpe nigāḷhiko, āpopaggharaṇī kāyo sadā sandati pūtikaṃ. Saṭṭhikaṇḍarasambandho maṃsalepanalepito, camakañcukasannaddho pūtikāyo niratthako.*

term at all.[35] Further, the use of it in the *Theragāthā* verse of Kulla, which follows on from his verses cited, demonstrates that, in some instances at least, it is being used idiomatically, to refer to sense pleasures—the 'music' of five parts being the pleasures of the senses and it is in these that Kulla, as a monk, finds no pleasure.

> There is not such pleasure from the music of five parts as there is for someone with intent mind rightly having insight into the dhamma.[36]

If we understand this to be one of the ways in which engagement with the world of sensory pleasures was envisioned by early Buddhists, we can better comprehend the use of the decaying and decomposing body as rhetoric with a vigorous, stark shock factor, used to drive away the gravitational pull towards pleasure. If we understand the five-fold pleasure to be central to notions of the most sensually enjoyable activities, it becomes clear to see how a decaying, decomposing corpse can be an antithesis to that. Rather than the bejewelled, elegant form of a woman, beautiful to behold, the pus-ridden corpse is a horrific sight. Rather than the fragrance of sandalwood paste and *jujube* flowers, the rotten corpse emits a rancid, disgusting smell. Rather than the delicate soft flesh of a paramour, painted in many hues, delightful to the touch, the corpse is tangibly putrid and vile. Rather than the subtle jangling of earrings and anklets, the only sounds are of the dogs that tear at the flesh or the mass of worms slowing moving through the carcass as they devour it.

Given that, as has been seen, the simple naked body is asexual, to attempt to circumvent desire with recourse to such would be to no avail—an image that quashed the senses was needed. And, sometimes, even to remonstrate with such intensely unsightly figurations was not enough. While the decaying body represents the antithesis of all things beautiful, on occasion, this did not appear to mean that desire was simply eroded upon sight of it. Take, for

35 Although an otherwise impressive survey, Roswell makes little mention of Buddhism and the evidence from Indian Buddhist texts.

36 *Tha* v. 398. *Pañcaṅgikena turiyena na rati hoti tādisī, yathā ekaggacittassa sammā dhammaṃ vipassato 'ti.*

example, the poor monk, Rājadatta, for whom such aberrations continued to engender longing:

> I, a monk, going to a cremation ground, saw a woman cast away, discarded in the crematory, her whole body being eaten by worms.
>
> Seeing someone dead and wretched, some are disgusted, (but) desire for sensual pleasures arose. I was as though blind to the flowing body.[37]

***

Relating the above to Khemā's biography, we can see that the theme was fitting to its day. Khemā's preoccupation with her body and the Buddha's response to her can be seen to be contextually and historically relevant. Khemā's apparent obsession with her beauty does not seem to go against the grain of social mores of the time. Rather, she appears quite typical in her preoccupations that reflect north Indian preoccupations of the time. And the Buddha's lesson to her, highlighting the foulness of the human body underneath the artifice of its youthful skin covering, represents a thoroughgoing rejection of the cultural artifice of beauty. In this instance, perception of the 'true' state of the body is a valuable and powerful lesson to a woman reluctant to follow the path of the Buddha, who, given this apposite teaching, has been given an opportunity to make progress on the path.

The relative popularity and interest in discourse on the decaying and decomposing body in early Buddhism has been perceived, in the past, as anti-women, but in this instance that is not the case. Rather, Khemā's biography is an example of the educational value of perception of the foulness of the body *for a female*. Also, in this chapter, the idea that focus on a beautiful female body problematizes women has also been challenged. What the examples of the *Thera-Therīgāthā* verses also show is, quite clearly, that it is not women *per se* that are conceptualized as the 'snare of

37 *Tha* vv. 315–16. *Bhikkhu sīvathikaṃ gantvā addasaṃ itthim ujjhitaṃ, apaviddhaṃ susānasmiṃ khajjantiṃ kimihī phuṭaṃ. Yaṃhi eke jigucchanti mataṃ disvāna pāpakaṃ, kāmarāgo pāturahū andho va savatī ahuṃ.*

Māra'; it is only certain sorts of bodies—adorned and ornamented—that engender desire. Ergo, it is not women themselves that are the problem. The real problem is desire, which is of course doctrinally endorsed, elicited by the body adorned and prepared for sex. Evident in this context is a social pressure—for both men and women—to paint and ornament their bodies in order to be considered beautiful and attract sexual partners. Men, even monks it would seem, did desire to adorn themselves, and debates about beauty, sexuality, desire, and the body in early Indian Buddhism would benefit from this being foregrounded.

9

Female wanderers

KISĀGOTAMĪ

Themes in the Pāli accounts

Female wanderers and other unattached women

Kisāgotamī is distinguished, in the Pāli accounts, as a wearer of coarse or rough robes.[1] She shares this outstanding characteristic with a male counterpart, listed amongst the monks in the *Aṅguttara-nikāya*, Mogharāja. Although what came to be her biography does not concentrate on Kisāgotamī's life post-ordination, biographies of Mogharāja do give some more detail on his choice of apparel. According to one of the two apadānas on Mogharāja, he takes cloth from the dust-heap (*saṅkharakuṭa*), cemetery (*susāna*), and road (*rathikā*) for his robes (*Ap.* I.488). In the *Theragāthā* commentary, the coarse cloth is described as cloth discarded by

[1] Ohnuma's recent comprehensive study of motherhood in early Indian Buddhism can be read alongside this present study. Kisāgotamī's biography is a moving portrayal of motherhood and has been treated as such by Ohnuma (2012).

caravaners, tailors, and dyers. Robes of early Buddhists are said to be rag-robes or dust-heap robes (*paṃsukūlika*), and in his commentary Dhammapāla does not distinguish between rag-robes and Mogharāja's coarse robes. The Pāli *Vinaya* lists six types of material that can be used for robes (*Vin.* I.281), ranging from a comfortable fabric like silk to coarse hemp, which may be what is being referred to here. Also in the Pāli *Vinaya* are rules forbidding monks and nuns from attempting to secure for themselves robes made of fine materials, thus it would appear that not all disciples chose the coarse hemp robes. The fact of being distinguished as a wearer of coarse robes is an indication of ascetic practice. As Freiberger (2006) has argued, within Pāli literature we find both criticism of asceticism and adherence to it. One of the key sets of ascetic practices described are the *dhutaṅgas* or *dhutaguṇas*. These are forest-dwelling (*āraññaka*), living on alms (*piṇḍapatika*), wearing rag robes (*paṃsukūlika*), living at the root of a tree (*rukkhamūlika*), and avoiding fish and meat (*macchamaṃsa*). Freiberger also notes that elsewhere in the Pāli canon is a list of what are likely non-Buddhist ascetic practices which includes the detailing of various types of cloth an ascetic might wear. This list, in the *Mahāsīhanādasutta*, includes coarse hemp cloth, rags from a dust-heap, cloth made from tree-bark, from antelope skin, and from wood shavings. Thus, for Kisāgotamī to have been distinguished for her wearing of the robes indicates that she was a dedicated ascetic. In a *Saṃyutta-nikāya* discourse, Kisāgotamī goes to the forest to meditate. Here Māra seeks to disturb her, and his choice of taunt is interesting, if she is such a committed ascetic. In this short narrative, after having taken alms, Gotamī goes to the Blind Man's Grove for a day's abiding. Māra approaches her and asks:

> Why now, when your son is dead,
> Do you sit alone with a tearful face?
> Having entered the woods all alone,
> Are you on the lookout for a new man?[2]

2 *SN* 5.3.525, I.130. *Kiṃ nu tvaṃ hataputtā va ekamāsi rudammukhī vanam ajjhogatā ekā purisaṃ gavesasī ti.*

The question addressed to Kisāgotamī, a female mendicant who we understand would have been sitting in the forest with shaven head and ragged robes (or even coarse hemp robes), is an interesting one. This exchange highlights a central question with regard to women in ancient India—the question of assumptions about the social status of nuns, other female wanderers, and other unmarried women. Anālayo (2013b) has recently raised the question again of whom or what Māra represents within the early Buddhist corpus, and reasserts the possible interpretation of Māra as the external community; the 'voice' of those outside of the Buddhist saṅgha who question the motives and intentions of those within. In this verse, the question is one of women being alone, practising alone, going out in the daytime alone, and going to a solitary place alone. The question posed here—to this shaven-headed, rag-robe wearing ascetic—is why might a woman do that, if not to search for a mate. This raises the broader question of the social identity of unmarried women within this milieu, and thus includes (without being reduced to) the social identity of Buddhist nuns in the period.

To understand the question of social identity we will look at the relative status of nuns as compared to other unattached or unmarried women. Prostitutes, while perhaps not obviously on a par with holy women, as unmarried women potentially occupy a social location similar to that of nuns, and this is evident in some cases from the textual records. In fact, in some texts nuns are insulted by being likened to prostitutes. In what follows, I will explore the question of the social identity of Buddhist nuns within the different periods. I will do this in part through comparison. Interestingly, in the texts we can see something of a reversal of fortune between nuns and courtesans. In the early period, before Buddhism was fully established, the social status of nuns was unformed, evidenced by them being likened to low-grade prostitutes, by their practice of bathing with the prostitutes, and by the apparent lack of understanding/acknowledgement of or concern for their commitment to celibacy. By contrast, some courtesans enjoyed a sanctioned social status at this time, being protected by government and sovereigns, and thus were treated with respect. Later, as Buddhism begins to flourish, nuns' social status becomes more solid, and they begin to garner respect—not least, in the commentaries, because of the biographies of the female 'saints'—while within the Buddhist subcultural enclaves at least, courtesans are grouped alongside low-grade prostitutes, and all women of such profession reviled.

Courtesans and prostitutes

As prostitutes are unmarried they might be considered to be unattached women, and thus occupy a social location not too dissimilar to that of Buddhist nuns. However, all classes of ancient Indian courtesans and prostitutes were not considered to be unattached. Some gaṇikās (courtesans) were protected by the state or were under the protection of the king and, as Srinivasan has pointed out, were considered to 'belong to the group'—this being the etymology of the word 'gaṇikā' (from *gaṇa*).[3]

Gaṇikās feature most in the early Buddhist texts. In the *Therīgāthā*, there are verses attributed to three former gaṇikās—Vimalā, Aḍḍhakāsī, and Ambapālī. Vimalā is called a gaṇikā in the *Therīgāthā*, although the other two are not. However, Aḍḍhakāsī and Ambapālī both feature in the Pāli *Vinaya* and are given the title there. Vimalā's and Ambapālī's verses have been discussed in Chapter 8, as they both mention their beauty and accompanying ornamentation. Aḍḍhakāsī's verses are briefer, and in the first verse the focus is the fee charged for her services; an improbable high price must be paid for her company. This fee is also how she comes by her name—Aḍḍhakāsī—as her fee was half the revenue of Kāsi.[4] None of the three sets of verses in the *Therīgāthā* say anything about the nuns being disgusted by their former profession. Each set of verses mentions that they were formerly obsessed with their appearance, and Vimalā talks about how she used this to ensnare men, but while the past enrapture with beauty is reviled,

3 Srinivasan (2005, 347). Srinivasan cites the story of Āmrapālī in the Mūlasarvāstivāda *Vinaya* as a good example of how the 'connotation of *gaṇa* operates in the term '*gaṇikā*'.

4 In the *Therīgāthā* verse, the price of Aḍḍhakāsī's services is said to be as large as the revenue of Kāsi, but this is glossed in the biographies of her to accord with her name.

the fact of a life lived in prostitution is not. In fact, here and elsewhere, that they could gain a high price for their services appears to be an accolade and something that they remain proud of. That this is a socially sanctioned norm is attested to in contemporaneous literature (see the following section). Aḍḍhakāsī's verses have both these elements—seeming pride in price fetched, and disgust towards preoccupation with the physical body:

> My wages were as large as the revenue of the country of Kāsi; the townspeople fixed the price and made me priceless in price.
>
> Then I became disgusted with my beauty, and being disgusted I was disinterested in it. May I not run again through the journeying on from rebirth to rebirth again and again. I have realized the three knowledges, I have done the Buddha's teaching.[5]

Aḍḍhakāsī and Ambapālī are both mentioned elsewhere in the canonical literature, although Vimalā is not. Ambapālī, the best known of the two, features in both the *Vinaya* and the *Dīgha-nikāya*, and her grove, which she donated to the saṅgha, is mentioned at other places (*SN* V.140, 141, and V.301 for example). The story of Ambapālī in the *Dīgha-nikāya* (II.95–8) and *Vinaya* (I.231–3) is essentially the same story, with only one real difference. In the *Vinaya* version of the story, the action takes place at Koṭigāma. Ambapālī, hearing that the Buddha was at Koṭigāma, had some magnificent vehicles harnessed and left Vesālī to travel to see the Buddha. The Buddha gave Ambapālī a talk on dhamma, and Ambapālī invited him with the monks to a meal at her house the following day. The Licchavis of Vesālī also heard that the Buddha was in Koṭigāma, and also set off to see him. Not only did the Licchavis in turn harness their own magnificent vehicles for the journey, but they also dressed for the occasion. Some of them applied dark green make-up and adorned themselves with matching clothes and jewellery, others chose yellow, yet others red, and

5 *Thī* vv. 25–6, essentially Norman translation, but with one change (1969, 4). *Yāva kāsijanapado suṅko me tattako ahu, taṃ katvā nigamo agghaṃ agghe 'nagghaṃ ṭhapesi maṃ. Atha nibbind' ahaṃ rūpe nibbindañ ca virajj' ahaṃ mā puna jātisaṃsāraṃ sandhāveyyaṃ punappunaṃ tisso vijjā sacchikatā kataṃ buddhassa sāsanaṃ.*

so on. The Licchavis met Ambapālī en route, as she was leaving and they were arriving. Ambapālī, seemingly emboldened by the Buddha consenting to take her meal offering, told the Licchavis what had come to pass. The Licchavis offered her money—a hundred thousand gold pieces—to give up her meal offering to the Buddha so that they could make the offering instead. She refused, telling them that even if 'you were to give up Vesālī with its produce, I would not give up this meal'.[6] The Licchavis were annoyed by this, feeling vanquished by Ambapālī. They continued their journey to see the Buddha, and when the Buddha saw them coming in the distance, in a comment that has an air of ridicule about it, he told the monks that any monk who had not seen the realm of the thirty gods (Tāvatiṃsā) should behold these overly made-up and dressed up Licchavis approaching. Once engaged in their audience with the Buddha, the Licchavis invited him for a meal the next day, but he declined telling them he had already accepted Ambapālī's offer. After this, when the Buddha had stayed in Koṭigāma as long as he wanted, he travelled to Ňātikā. Ambapālī prepared her meal in her own park, and invited the Buddha and the monks. Once the meal was finished, Ambapālī offered her grove to the Buddha and his community. The Buddha accepted.

The *Dīgha-nikāya* version differs not in narrative content but in regard to location. The *Dīgha-nikāya* version is said to take place in Vesālī, and in this version the Buddha was staying in Ambapālī's grove, in Vesālī, at the outset. Ambapālī visits him there, and the same narrative unfolds, with the only real difference being that Ambapālī offers the grove while they are resident there already.

In the story, there is no moral comment made in regard to Ambapālī's profession. Her request to host a meal for the saṅgha is accepted, and not rescinded once a second offer is made. The interaction between Ambapālī and the Licchavis has a sense of contest about it—it appears Ambapālī has beaten the Licchavis to it, much to their chagrin. And while the Licchavis express some annoyance at this, they malign neither Ambapālī nor her

6 *Vin.* I.232 trans. Horner, IV.316. *Sace pi me …vesāliṃ sāhāraṃ dajjeyyātha, n' eva dajjāhaṃ taṃ bhattaṃ ti. DN* II.96 *Sace pi me ayyaputtā vesāliṃ sāhāraṃ dassatha evaṃ mahantaṃ bhattaṃ na dassāmīti.*

profession in their anger. If anyone in the narrative is on the receiving end of insult it is the Licchavis, in that the Buddha seems to ridicule them for their apparel. Further, the Buddha accepts the offer of the grove for the saṅgha as there is no shame, it would seem, in taking an offering of grounds purchased through capital accumulated by the act of solicitation.

Like Ambapālī, Aḍḍhakāsī also fares well in the portrayal of her in the *Vinaya*. In this passage, which is repeated in the *Therīgāthā* commentary, Aḍḍhakāsī is ordained through a messenger, so as to circumvent any harm befalling her. The passage reads:

> Now at that time the courtesan Aḍḍhakāsī had gone forth among the nuns. She was anxious to go to Sāvatthī, thinking, 'I will be ordained in the Blessed One's presence.' Rogues heard it said that the courtesan Aḍḍhakāsī was anxious to go to Sāvatthī and they beset the way. But the courtesan Aḍḍhakāsī heard it said that rogues were besetting the way and she sent a messenger to the Blessed One saying, 'Even I am anxious for ordination. Now what line of conduct should be followed by me?' Then the Blessed One on this occasion, having given reasoned talk, addressed the monks, saying, 'I allow you, Monks, to ordain even through a messenger.'[7]

In this instance, the courtesan Aḍḍhakāsī is safeguarded from villainous men who, it would appear, set out to waylay and assault her. Her person and virtue were protected by the Buddha, even though she was an ex-courtesan. Courtesans and former courtesans then, it would appear from both examples, should not be treated differently to others; they are not underserving due to their profession, or former profession.

In the early Pāli literature, low-class prostitutes are often called *vesīs* or *vesīyās* and the few mentions of them suggest this class of

7 *Vin.* II.277, Horner's translation, with two small changes (V 383). *Tena kho pana samayena Aḍḍhakasī gaṇikā bhikkhunīsu pabbajitā hoti, sā sāvatthiṃ gantukāmā hoti bhagavato santike upasampajjisāmīti. Assosuṃ kho dhuttā aḍḍakāsī kira gaṇikā sāvatthiṃ gantukāmā 'ti, te magge pariyuṭṭhiṃsu. Assosi aḍḍhakāsī gaṇikā dhuttā kira magge pariyuṭṭhitā 'ti, bhagavato santike dūtaṃ pāhesi ahaṃ hi upasampajjitukāmā, kathaṃ nu kho mayā paṭipajjiabban ti. Atha kho bhagavā etasmiṃ nidāne dhammiṃ kathaṃ katvā bhikkhū āmantesi anujānāmi bhikkhave dūtena pi upasampādetuṃ ti.* See Collett and Analayo (2014) on the problems with translations of the term *bhikkhave*.

prostitute—so conceived—is not viewed with the same value as that accorded to gaṇikās and ex-gaṇikās.[8] In the *Sutta-nipāta* (v. 108), to be seen with a vesīyā can be the cause of one's downfall. In the nuns' *Vinaya*, nuns are prohibited from bathing alongside vesīs—there are two recorded incidents of this (pācittiyas 2 and 11); the lay woman Visākhā in the *Mahāvagga* wants to offer bathing clothes for nuns after there is a report of them bathing with prostitutes (I.293). Also, in the monks' *Vinaya*, in *saṅghādisesa* 5, a rule prohibiting members of the saṅgha from acting as go-betweens in sexual or romantic encounters, a monk persuades a vesī to go to a park and have sexual liaisons with men there, although there is no suggestion of money changing hands, so it is unclear why she would have agreed to go. Such men would likely be unable to afford a gaṇikā, because of the high price she would demand for her services. According to the early Buddhist texts, these gaṇikās were wealthy women, as is attested already in the example of Ambapālī owning her own grove.

Courtesans such as Ambapālī, it would appear, were so good for the prosperity of the town or city in which they lived that, according to one story in the *Vinaya*, King Bimbisāra was inspired to arrange a courtesan for Rājagaha on the basis of the benefits Ambapālī offered for Vesālī. Once again here there is no moral reprobation for the profession, instead the (economic) benefit of it is in evidence.

The wealth of courtesans would have enabled them to decorate themselves with the finest clothes, make-up, and jewellery, just as Vimalā says she did in her verses. The vesīs, on the other hand, being the poor man's prostitute, were likely to be from poor and perhaps low-caste families and so would not have been able to afford to adorn their bodies in the way courtesans did. Visually, there would have been a striking difference between courtesans and Buddhist nuns, but the difference between nuns and low-class prostitutes would have been less obvious. It is interesting then, that when nuns are insulted they are likened to low-class

[8] There are many different names for and types of prostitute in the early and early medieval Indian milieu, Sternbach, for example, in his study notes 330 synonyms (1953, 199n2).

prostitutes. On three occasions in the Pāli *Vinaya*, townsfolk insult nuns by calling them shaven-headed whores (*bandhukiniyo*). On none of these occasions, as they are recorded in the extant text, does the insult appear to have been generated from the specific context, as in no case do the nuns in question behave in a sexually predatory manner. None of the cases are to do with sex at all. The first incident involves a storeroom that was apparently given to the nuns by a man. When he died, one of his sons wanted the room back, and tried to get the nuns to vacate it. Thullanandā consults ministers, perhaps to get the local establishment on her side, so that the nuns could keep the storeroom. It is this act of manipulation that causes the son to insult the nuns, 'These shaven-headed whores are not recluses.'[9] The second incident involves toilet humour. A nun, having defecated in a bucket, threw the excrement over a wall. An unfortunate brahmin, one in the service of the king, was walking past at the moment and found himself in the wrong place at the wrong time. Standing there covered in excrement, he repeated the same line, 'These shaven-headed whores are not recluses' (*Vin.* IV.265). In the third incident, nuns arrive at a village and ask a brahmin family for overnight accommodation. Only the wife is home, and she asks them to await the return of her husband. They agree to wait, but while waiting make up sleeping places for themselves, and while some sit, others lie down. When the brahmin returns, seeing them he tells his wife, 'Throw out these shaven-headed whores.'[10] The insult seems to be generated from perhaps momentary anger in the first instance, and a combination of anger, malice, and dislike in the other examples.

These differences between gaṇikās and low-grade prostitutes, including the more positive regard for gaṇikās and the acknowledgement of the wealth that can be accrued by courtesans are each borne out, to a lesser or greater extent, by the evidence of the *Arthaśāstra*. The surprising fact in this treatise of urban living is that governance of prostitution is built in to city infrastructure. According to Kauṭilīya's prescriptions for city-life, as with many

9 *Vin.* IV.224 *assamaṇiyo imā muṇḍā bandhakiniyo.*

10 *Vin.* IV.274 *nikkaḍḍatha imā muṇḍā bandhakiniyo.*

aspects of city administration, there should be a person appointed to act as the superintendent of gaṇikās, called a gaṇikādhyakṣa. Kauṭilīya's section on superintendence of courtesans contains many aspects that affect our subsequent discussion:

> The Superintendent of Courtesans should appoint as a courtesan, with one thousand *paṇas*, a (girl), from a courtesan's family or a family not of courtesans, who is richly endowed with beauty, youth and arts, (and) a deputy courtesan for half the family establishment.
>
> ...
>
> He should keep an account of the payment by visitor, gifts, income, expenditure and gains of a courtesan, and should prohibit an act of excessive expenditure.
>
> For handing over her ornaments to the keeping of any one else but her mother, the fine shall be four paṇas and a quarter. If she sells or pledges her belongings, the fine shall be fifty paṇas and a quarter, twenty-four paṇas in case of verbal injury, double that in case of physical injury, fifty paṇas and a quarter and one paṇa and half a paṇa for cutting off the ear.
>
> ...
>
> A courtesan, not approaching a man at the command of the king, shall receive one thousand strokes with the whip, or a fine of five thousand paṇas.
>
> If a (courtesan), after receiving payment, shows dislike, she shall be fined double the amount of payment. In case she cheats in connection with the attendance on visitors staying overnight, she shall pay eight times the amount of payment, except in cases of (her) illness or defects in the man....
>
> If a man robs a courtesan of her ornaments, her goods or the payment due to her, he shall be fined eight times (the amount).
>
> The courtesan shall communicate (to the superintendent) the payment, the gain and the (name of the) man.
>
> ...
>
> (Prostitutes) who live by their beauty (*rūpājīvā*), shall pay per month (a tax) double the (normal) fee (charged by them) (2.27.44) (trans. Kangle [1972] 2003 II.158–61)

Two types of courtesans or prostitutes are mentioned in the *Arthaśāstra*—the gaṇikā and rūpājīvā. A rūpājīvā is 'one who lives/ makes a living by her beauty (*rūpā*)'. This type of prostitute is not protected and governed in the same way that the gaṇikā is. A rūpājīvā must pay her taxes—half her normal fee—but otherwise appears free to operate in any way she wishes.[11] The gaṇikā in the *Arthaśāstra* is a specific type of gaṇikā—one in the service of the king. This type of gaṇikā, as is evident from the quote, has her activities governed, and while her primary occupation is to serve the king, she must entertain others at the king's request. The gaṇikās of the early Pāli texts are different from this. These gaṇikās amass their own wealth and keep ownership of it. However, as noted from the *Vinaya* story above, it does serve a city well to have a gaṇikā, so Bimbisāra allows one to be found for Rājagaha (*Vin.* I.268–9). The short story of the courtesan Sālavatī demonstrates again that these types of gaṇikās were not in the service of the monarchy. In the story, Sālavatī hires herself out for good money, but quite quickly becomes pregnant. Finding out she is with child, she decides to make it known that she is ill and so not able to receive clients for the time being. She keeps this up for nine months, until the child is born, and is able to do this without being disturbed, which suggests she is self-employed with no superintendent to answer to.

This same good status for courtesans seen so far in this chapter—that they can accrue wealth and are admired and perhaps even respected—is attested by inscriptional evidence. There are two known inscriptions in which courtesans feature, one a donative inscription from a Jain site, and the other a declaration of love. The first of these is evidence of the wealth of courtesans, in that the named courtesan who makes the donation is able to offer a great deal to the Jain community. She offers a shrine of the arhat (*ārahato devikula*), an assembly hall for an object of worship (*āyāgasabhā*), a cistern (*prapā*), and a

[11] Although specified in this section of the *Arthaśāstra* as a non-governed type of prostitute, rūpājīvās are also mentioned elsewhere in the *Arthaśāstra* as attendants in the palace (1.20.20). There is one reference to a rūpājīvā who is 'reserved for another' (*anuyoparuddhā*), which, as Kangle notes, seems 'to imply a woman in the exclusive keeping of a person' (3.20.15) (Kangle III.164).

stone-slab (*śilāpaṭa*). This inscription has been dated by Quintanilla to the second century BCE (2006, 187). The second inscription is also from a similar time, the Mauryan period. Salomon calls this inscription unusual, due to its content (1998, 141) as it records the love of Devadina for a temple prostitute (*devadaśikyi*), Śutanukā.

One further piece of datable evidence on gaṇikās calls us back to the positive portrayals in the early canonical literature. The well-known Dīdārgañj figure, dated by Srinivasan (2005, 360) and others to the Mauryan period, is a well-preserved image that Srinivasan, in the same article, argues convincingly is an example of a gaṇikā.[12] This figure, perhaps originally part of a pair, would probably have been either the courtesan or deputy of Kauṭilīya's king. That this figure is quite possibly the earliest stone sculpture we have, along with the size and craftsman's skill it betrays, certainly demonstrates that gaṇikās garnered high regard.[13]

Given the positive epigraphic records of gaṇikās dating from, potentially, the Mauryan period, it is interesting to note that the *Apadāna* takes a very different view of women of the profession.[14] In the *Apadāna* there is a moralizing tone in relation to prostitution. The view of the authors of this text is that those who have

[12] The Dīdārgañj figure may be the earliest Indian sculpture, but there is debate as to her dates. Srinivasan (2005) dates her to the Mauryan period, while Dehejia acknowledges the possible reasons for the Mauryan date but also, following Asher and Spink (1989), notes the possibility of a later date (2009, 27–8).

[13] The Kharoṣṭhi manuscript fragments of the British Library collection, datable to the first half of the first century CE, contain some rather tantalizing references to gaṇikās (Gāndhārī *gangiya*). Although the two manuscript fragments that mention the gaṇikās are too incomplete to offer much information, that the gaṇikās appear to be central figures in the short stories, and that the stories were likely edifying stories about practice of the Buddha's dhamma, strongly suggest that, as Lenz notes, 'the Gandhāran gaṇikās partake of the great tradition of the "benevolent hetera"—in good company with Āmrapālī, Padumavatī, and Aḍḍhakāsī—and somehow acted in support of the Buddha's *dharma* and were portrayed in a favorable light' (2013, 52).

[14] In the *Apadāna* the two words 'gaṇikā' and 'vesī' are undifferentiated, and act as synonyms.

had the misfortune to practice the profession in their present life have found themselves in the predicament because of their own unsavoury actions in the past. There are two biographies of former prostitutes in the *Apadāna*, one of Aḍḍhakāsī (attributed to Aḍḍhakāsikā) and the other of Ambapālī. The two are similar but not identical; however, in both cases, the reason each of these women had to endure the unfortunate circumstances of being a gaṇikā is because they abused a nun in a past life. During the era of Buddha Kassapa, Aḍḍhakāsī's apadāna records that:

> I was evil minded and reviled a nun who was without defilements. 'Prostitute (*gaṇike*)', I called her once. Then, because of that wicked deed I was cooked in hell. Because of the remainder of that deed, having offended, I was repeatedly born into families of prostitutes (*gaṇikākule*), and in my last birth, as a consequence of following the holy life, I was born amongst the people of Kāsi into the family of a wealthy merchant. I was as beautiful as a heavenly nymph among *devas*.
>
> Beholding my beauty, in the magnificent town of Giribbaja, I was established as a prostitute (*gaṇikatte*), that was the consequence of my abuse.[15]

Ambapālī's apadāna is not too dissimilar on this point, although the wording in the extant text does differ:

> [During the era of Buddha Sikhī] I was born in a brahmin family in the delightful town of Aruṇa. Being offended, I cursed a bhikkhunī whose mind was completely released.
>
> I was immoral, like a prostitute (*vesikā*), a defiler of the teachings of the Conqueror. Having abused her in that way, because of that wicked deed, I went to a harsh hell and was subjected to great pain. When I passed from there, I was reborn among men as a female ascetic.

15 *Ap*. II.610. 4–7. *Akkosiṃ duṭṭhacittā 'haṃ gaṇike ti sakiṃ tadā, tena pāpena kammena nirayamhi apaccisaṃ. Ten' eva kammasesena ajāyiṃ gaṇikākule, bahuso 'va 'parādhitā pacchimāya ca jātiyaṃ. Kāsīsu seṭṭhikule jātā brahmacariyaphalen ahaṃ, accharā viya devesu ahosiṃ rūpasampada. Disvāna dassanīyañ maṃ giribbajapuruttame, gaṇikatte nivesesuṃ akkosanaphalena me.* Emended to Lilley's suggestion in the note *disvāna dassanīyañ* from *disvā 'tidassanīyañ*, and *nivesesuṃ* from *nivesiṃsu*.

I performed the profession of a prostitute (*gaṇikattaṃ akārayiṃ*) for ten thousand lives. I was not released from that deed, just like one who has eaten a wicked poison.[16]

This low regard for *gaṇikā*s and all classes of prostitutes continues in the commentaries, and in some cases becomes much worse. I will go into detail of just a few examples, but this negative attitude to prostitutes in the commentaries can be found in many examples such as the following:

1. A gaṇikā in the park, who is awaiting a client but is stood up, wanders around looking to entertain herself and comes across a meditating monk. She decides—for no apparent reason—to try to disturb his meditation practice, and undresses and loosens her hair while standing right in front of him (*Dhp-a* II.201–2).
2. A gaṇikā tries to seduce a monk because his parents have promised her great wealth. She schemes; she moves into a house in the street he goes to beg for alms, and then tells the neighbourhood boys playing outside to be noisy and disruptive so she has an excuse to invite the monk indoors (*Dhp-a* IV.194–9).
3. In the *Mahā-Ummagga Jātaka* (546), a man named Senaka tells his secret to a group, the secret being that he once had sex with a prostitute (vesiyā) and then had killed her to get her ornaments (VI.382).
4. In the *Aṭṭhāna Jātaka* (425, III.474) a prostitute (*nagarasobhiṇī*) refuses to have sex with one of her regulars as on this occasion, unlike the many others in the past, he has failed to bring her money. She is reviled for this, and thought evil and wicked by the whole city.

The three ex-gaṇikās who appear in the *Therīgāthā* all have accounts in the *Therīgāthā* commentary, and the esteem accorded

[16] *Ap*. II.613.4–7, as translated by Pruitt (1999, 268). *Tad' āruṅapure ramme brahmaññakulasambhavā, vimuttacittaṃ kupitā bhikkhuniṃ abhisāpayiṃ. Vesikā 'va anācārā jinasāsanadūsikā, evaṃ akkosayitvāna tena pāpena kammanā. Dāruṇaṃ nirayaṃ gantvā mahādukkhasamappitā, tato cutā manussesu uppannā tapassinī. Dasa jātisahassāni gaṇikattaṃ akārayiṃ, taṃ pāpaṃ na vimuccissaṃ bhuttā duṭṭhavisaṃ yathā.*

to them in the early canon is not continued. The *Therīgāthā* commentary accounts of Aḍḍhakāsī and Ambapālī essentially repeat the *Apadāna* story of them reviling other nuns in the past and by that misdeed being reborn to fall into a life of prostitution. The *Therīgāthā* commentary accounts offer more detail than the *Apadāna*. For example, in Ambapālī's account, rather than the brief reference to her reviling another in the *Apadāna*, Dhammapāla offers a vignette; during the era of Buddha Sikhī she was ordained and since then she followed the discipline for nuns. One day, accompanying a large group of nuns, she went to pay homage at a shrine. An accomplished nun, who was ahead of her, suddenly sneezed. A lump of phlegm fell in the courtyard of the shrine, but the sneezer did not see it. Following behind, Ambapālī noticed it and said, 'What prostitute dropped this lump of phlegm in this place?' (*kā nāma gaṇikā imasmiṃ ṭhāne kheḷapiṇḍaṃ pātesī ti* 198).

In the *Dhammapada* commentary, an unnamed gaṇikā is treated brutally (II.35–6).[17] Four youths decide to spend some time with her in the park to enjoy what she has to offer. Later on, after they have engaged in solicitous acts with her, the four of them decide, as there is no one else around to witness their wrongdoing, that they will take back the thousand pieces they gave her for her service, rob her of her jewellery, and kill her. This is the second instance of murder of a gaṇikā following procurement of her services (see point 3 in the previous page). The four young men proceed to commit the act.

Last is the case of Sirimā, another fairly well-known prostitute whose story appears in the commentaries of the *Aṅguttara-nikāya* (I.446–52), *Dhammapada* (III.302–13), and *Vimānavatthu*.[18] There are two separate parts to her story, and both do not appear in each version. In the *Aṅguttara-nikāya* commentary and the *Dhammapada* commentary, Sirimā's services are purchased by a wife devoted to the Buddha, who wishes to have time off from her domestic and spousal duties to pursue her Buddhist practice. Bringing the

[17] In this instance, the woman is called both a gaṇikā and a nagarasobhiṇī.

[18] For this version, see Horner's translation of commentarial excerpts in her translation of the *Vimānavatthu* ([1942] 2005, 24–32).

beautiful Sirimā into her home allows her to do this. However, after living in the house a few days, Sirimā becomes jealous of the wife, Uttarā, and attempts to throw hot ghee over her. Uttarā is protected by her virtue, and the ghee turns cold the moment it touches her. Sirimā is astonished by this, and then ashamed, she asks for Uttarā's forgiveness. Uttarā tells her to ask forgiveness from her teacher, the Buddha. This she does, and in the *Aṅguttara-nikāya* commentary the Buddha forgives her (*khamāmi te sirime* I.452). However, in the *Dhammapada* commentarial account the Buddha only praises Uttarā for her good actions, and appears to ignore Sirimā's plea for forgiveness.

Although none of these examples demonstrate respect for the profession of prostitution or those who practise it, there are a few examples in the commentaries which suggest women of the profession were not always wholly reviled, and two that stand out in which, respectively, a gaṇikā is proven to be virtuous, and another to be smart. Each of these two cases can be linked to canonized women. In the *Kurudhamma Jātaka* (276) of the *Jātakatthavaṇṇanā* is a story of Uppalavaṇṇā in a past life (see Chapter 6) as a gaṇikā. This gaṇikā is proven to be a virtuous woman by Sakka (in disguise), who, playing the part of client, gives her a thousand pieces of money and says he will return but stays away for three years to prove she will be honourable and await a client's return, which she does. Bhaddā Kuṇḍalakesā's biography is also told in a different version in the *Sulasā Jātaka* (419), with the protagonist this time the gaṇikā Sulasā, and just as we saw in Chapter 5, the gaṇikā is proven to be wise and outsmarts the villain, as does Bhaddā.

These differences that can be discerned from the texts of the various biographical periods suggest certain things. Initially it would appear that gaṇikās were regarded positively; they benefitted a city, and there is no evidence of any desire to undermine or revile them. Some of them were governed, and received either state or royal patronage. And this appears to be the case in the early canon but not in the *Apadāna* or the commentaries. In these cases, to be a prostitute of any description was degrading for one who has been unfortunate enough to have had to endure a life in the profession, and prostitutes were most often considered with such contempt that even to murder them after cruelly taking advantage of them met with no social rebuke. These changes in attitude towards courteseans and prostitutes, when compared to changing attitudes to nuns, as we shall see, appear as something of a reversal of fortune between the two groups, in terms of social status.

Sexual assault

Although in the early texts some types of gaṇikās were protected by state or royal patronage, the same was not invariably the case for nuns. To illustrate this, the question of sexual assault will be discussed, as well as responses to instances of assault, or potential assault, of nuns.

The Pāli *Vinaya* recorded several incidents of, and has a variety of responses to, sexual assault of women. In the nuns' *Vinaya*, saṅghādisesa 3 is a fourfold rule that includes origin stories[19] in which nuns are subjected to sexual attack. First, an unnamed nun who had had a quarrel with other nuns went alone to see her relatives in a neighbouring village. The issue is with her having gone alone. When the other nuns who had been dispatched to find her come across her, they ask if she was violated. She replies that she was not but, nevertheless, a rule is made forbidding nuns to do this due to an apparently strong possibility they might be sexually assaulted if they travel alone. The next section concerns two nuns travelling together and their experience of being coerced by a boatman who tells them he cannot take them both across the river at the same time; they must go one at a time. Once separated, each nun is violated. A rule is made that not only must nuns not travel to villages alone, but must not cross rivers alone either. Third, a man conspires to get a certain nun alone, who is part of a group staying overnight in his village. A rule is made that nuns must not be away from the group overnight. Finally, a nun stays behind from a group to defecate. This

[19] Saṅghādisesa and *pāṭidesaniya* are categories of vinaya rules; each of the rules in each category are numbered. Also, each of the individual rules has at least one origin story to accompany it, that is, a narrative account that is intended to relate why the rule was originally made.

very temporary separation was enough for her to be accosted and violated, so a rule was made that nuns must not stay behind a group. In the monks' *Vinaya* as well, there is a rule which talks about women—but not nuns—who are violated by thieves (*pāṭidesaniya* 4). Also, in the *Cullavagga*, a passage notes other incidents of sexual assault:

> Now at that time nuns were staying in the forest where rogues defiled them. They told this matter to the Buddha. He said 'Monks, nuns should not stay in a forest. Whoever should stay there, there is an offence of wrongdoing.'[20]

The rules made in all cases function to protect nuns against sexual assault, so that they are kept out of harm's way. That this appears to be necessary suggests there may have been a real problem of nuns being assaulted in this way. Another incident of rape is recorded in relation to Uppalavaṇṇā. This is found in the monks' *suttavibhaṅga*, in the section on the first pārājika, on sexual intercourse. Uppalavaṇṇā is not considered to be culpable for her assault thereby not culpable in relation to the first pārājika—as she did not intentionally engage in sexual activity.[21]

Although there are several incidents of sexual assault of nuns recorded in the Pāli *Vinaya*, not all of these are found in other nuns' vinayas. In other vinayas, saṅghādisesa 3 appears differently, and the stories associated with it are less often and less clearly about sexual assault. However, in these instances, the stories that come to be associated with the rules are less cogent, and do not always appear to be directly concerned with the rule which they purport to deal with. In the Mahāsāṅghika-Lokottaravāda versions—both Sanskrit and Chinese—for example, there are three rules rather than one: saṅghādisesas 5, 6, and 9. Saṅghādisesa 5

[20] *Vin.* II.278. *Tena kho pana samayena bhikkhuniyo araññe viharanti dhuttā dūsenti. Bhagavato etam atthaṃ ārocesuṃ. Na bhikkhave bhikkhuniyā araññe vatthabbaṃ. Yā vaseyya āpatti dukkaṭassā 'ti.*

[21] In the origin stories associated with the first pārājika in the Pāli *Vinaya*, there are also apparent incidents of sexual assault of monks by women. However, how to read these is problematic and I have dealt with these in a separate paper (Collett 2013b).

prescribes that nuns should not travel alone, saṅghādisesa 6 that they should not stay behind a group, and saṅghādisesa 9 that they should not swim in rivers. Saṅghādisesa 5, extant in both Sanskrit and Chinese versions, is incongruent; the story does not match the rule. The story in both is of a nun called Rāṣṭrā, whose sister falls ill and dies. Her sister's husband then suggests Rāṣṭrā take her sister's place, and become wife and mother to the family. Although the story is now quite different, the rule is the same—a nun should not travel on a road without another nun. However, Rāṣṭrā is never noted as having explicitly travelled alone in the extant story, although of course this can be implied. Also, although Rāṣṭrā is worried that her sister's husband might be dangerous, and leaves his house quite quickly, these actions of hers and the implied threat of her sister's husband are not directly connected to the rule. Von Hinüber (1996, 13–14), amongst others, has noted previously problematic relationships between vinaya rules and origin stories associated with them, and this instance appears to be one of some sort of disconnect between the rule and the accompanying narrative.

In the *Arthaśāstra* and other later *dharmaśāstras* there are rules that mete out punishments for rape of women, but in some instances there are exclusion clauses for certain sorts of women, as discussed in Chapter 10. Overall, in these codifications of law in ancient India, there are fewer regulations on rape and sexual assault than might be expected. In the section on the superintendence of courtesans, Kauṭilīya prescribes suitable punishments for assaults on courtesans:

> In case of violence against a maiden who is unwilling, the highest fine (shall be imposed), the lowest fine for violence if she is willing. If a man keeps under restraint a courtesan who is unwilling or helps her to run away or spoils her beauty by cutting up a wound, the fine (shall be) one thousand paṇas. Or, there shall be an increase in fine in accordance with the importance of her position, up to double the ransom amount. For killing a mother, a daughter or a female slave living by her beauty, the highest fine for violence (shall be imposed). (2.44.13, trans. Kangle [1972] 2003, 160)

The punishment differs according to the type of attack, but nonetheless it is clear from the above that, according to the *Arthaśāstra* at least, sexual assault of certain courtesans is considered a form of violence on a par with murder. Here the punishment for such assaults is the same punishment accrued for the most severe acts of violence. As we shall see in Chapter 10, there is some suggestion that female ascetics are not covered by proscriptions against sexual assault. Female mendicants are little mentioned in the *Arthaśāstra*, but the most outstanding mention of them is Kauṭilīya's imposing of a fine for anyone who encourages and helps a woman to renounce. This implies that female renunciation—for Kauṭilīya—while itself not a crime, should incur a penance for its perpetrators.

Although in Kauṭilīya's view rape and sexual assault on courtesans in the king's service are forms of violence on a par with murder, the rape and sexual assault of other women was not treated even nearly as seriously in other Brahmanical literature. As noted in Chapter 10, the types of marriage listed in Brahmanical texts include marriage by the act of rape of the woman. Also, in the *Bṛhadāraṇyaka Upaniṣad*, we find condoning of rape. In a section on Prajāpati's creation of woman, who is created as a receptacle for semen, the suggestion is that women are created for the purpose of sexual intercourse. In the passage on a woman who has just changed her clothes at the end of her menstrual period, a most auspicious time, the text suggests that one should invite such a woman to have sex, and then:

> Should she refuse to consent, he should bribe her. If she still refuses, he should beat her with a stick or with his fists and overpower her saying: 'I take away the splendour from you with my virility and splendour.' (6.4.7, trans. Olivelle 1996b, 88–9)

In these two instances—marriage by an act of rape and condoning of rape—the rape of a woman appears to be more an enactment of masculinity than a form of violence that should incur punishment. Taking a woman by force, in these examples, is either a means by which one acquires the woman as a wife or an assertion of male virility. Surveying the evidence of the texts overall, it would appear that the idea of taking a woman by force—that is, forcing her to engage in non-consensual sex—is not in itself considered inappropriate. The only occasion on which it is considered either inappropriate or 'unlawful' is when the woman *clearly belongs to another man or other men*. Thus, in Kauṭilīya, it is unlawful to rape the courtesans who belong to the king, while single women can be subjected to rape and through that act considered to be the new wife of the rapist. Thus, before the social identity of Buddhist nuns is firmly established, as unattached women they are considered sexually available to men, and can be taken by force if the man desires to do so. There is no mention of rape or sexual assault in the nuns' *Apadāna*, and this could well be because by the time of the composition of the text the social identity of nuns was more robustly established—they belonged to the saṅgha, or even perhaps the Buddha; they were holy women and therefore celibate and their choice of a life of sexual abstinence was to be respected.

By the time of the commentaries, the rape of a canonized woman results in earth-shattering damnation for the perpetrator. This incident is recounted in Chapter 6, as Uppalavaṇṇā is the victim. Uppalavaṇṇā is staying alone in the forest and a man, her cousin, comes in to her hut, hides and waits in order to sexually assault her. As a result of his actions the earth quite literally tears asunder and he is cast into hell for the deed. Although the consequences of the act are extreme, nonetheless, the story still demonstrates a lack of awareness of the consequences of sexual assault on the victim, as questions are asked as to whether Uppalavaṇṇā might have taken pleasure from the experience.

Female wandering

If nuns were grouped alongside other unattached women who did not belong to or have a secure identity within the social order, and were then subjected to sexual assault during the early period of the establishment of the Buddhist tradition in north India, perhaps there was a serious concern as to whether they should lead a fully peripatetic, homeless, wandering life. Anālayo (2011c), in a new reading of a well-known passage, suggests that there were real concerns of this nature, and that it was perhaps initially recommended that women do not wander but stay at home. Through comparative study of the Chinese version of the story of the foundation of the nuns' Order, Anālayo argues that the Buddha's refusal to allow nuns into the Order was predicated on his fear of the dangers there were for nuns living the homeless life. Anālayo argues that this is the way to read the Buddha's refusal and that, rather than it being a refusal to allow nuns to practise, the passage instead relates the Buddha telling Mahāpajāpatī Gotamī that 'she should better live a celibate life in the more protected environment at home, having cut off her hair and put on robes' (2011c, 307).

Anālayo's argument can be further substantiated by some evidence from the *Thera-Therīgāthā*. In these two texts, we find different words being used for monks' and nuns' dwellings. A *kuṭi*, a 'single-roomed abode', is often used to describe the monks' dwellings in the *Theragāthā*, but nuns are not recorded to have dwelt in kuṭis. For example, a recurrent verse, and the verse that begins the whole collection, speaks of a well-roofed small hut of Subhūti (see, for example, v. 1, vv. 51–4 and 325, although not all incidents of it are identical), as discussed in Chapter 10. In another example, Gaṅgātirya has a hut made of three palm leaves, situated—unsurprisingly—on the bank of the Ganges (127, Gaṅgātirya means 'on the banks of the Ganges'). This monk is also said to have a robe that is 'a rag from a dust-heap'. There are also two verses attributed to a monk called Kuṭivihārin (v. 56 and v. 57). The name Kuṭivihārin means 'one who lives in a hut/kuṭi'.

The word, however, is not used at all in the *Therīgāthā*. When dwelling places for nuns are mentioned it is almost always the word *vihāra* that is used, except in one instance when it is *vihāraka*. The word 'vihāra' occurs in three instances, and each one is the same verse repeated:

> Four or five times I went out of my cell [vihāra], not having obtained peace of mind, being without self-mastery over the mind.[22]

The word 'vihāraka' occurs in the verses of Mittakālī, recalling how she sat down in her little cell. The word 'vihāra', as has been well documented, changed in meaning over time, with the earlier meaning seeming to encompass smaller dwelling places, until it became the word associated with the larger, permanent resident

[22] *Thī* vv. 37, 42, 169, trans. Norman (1971, 6). *Catukkhattuṃ pañcakkhattuṃ vihārā upanikkhamiṃ, aladdhā cetaso santiṃ citte avasavattini.*

monasteries of the tradition. Often in the *Theragāthā*, when the word is used it appears in a set of verses that also mention a *caṅkamanta*, a cloistered terrace, which suggests that a vihāra in these instances would be a larger dwelling, big enough to have a sheltered walkway within it, such as, perhaps, the site at Thotlakonda, Andhra Pradesh, excavated by Fogelin between 2000 and 2002 (2006).[23] Although the *Thera-Therīgāthā* are composite texts, in the extant version nuns do not appear to stay in single-roomed abodes (kuṭis), rather perhaps the indication here is that they shared rooms or lived in rooms in more complex dwellings. As far as I know, within the biographical accounts and elsewhere in the Pāli literature, nowhere is a nun associated with a kuṭi, with the one exception being the case of Uppalavaṇṇā mentioned earlier, a case that highlights the lack of safety of such dwellings for nuns. Although nuns did, as Kisāgotamī does in the *Saṃyutta-nikāya*, go to the forest alone to meditate during the day, there is no evidence that they stayed alone at night in the forest.[24] In the Pāli *Vinaya*, as in one of the examples mentioned above, we find accounts of nuns who stay together in groups in villages, and mention of nunneries. In the incident recounted earlier (page 144) in which the nuns are insulted, they have arrived in a village in a group and are looking for a place where they can stay together overnight. This is far from the only occurrence of such an incident in the Pāli *Vinaya*. Although the text is composite and shows signs of different types of lifestyle, with mention of both more permanent and more temporary lodgings, both inside and outside urban areas, nuns are never described as dwelling alone. There are also two rules in the nuns' *Vinaya* that advise a nun to carry a weapon if she goes for alms in dangerous places (pācittiyas 37 and 38), and one in the

23 Fogelin notes that this site was likely active from around the second century BCE (2006, 5).

24 In the early accounts as well there are some instances of noble thieves, thieves and rogues who protect the nuns whom they see alone in the forest. There is an account of Uppalavaṇṇā in the Pāli *Vinaya* in which a thief leads his band away from where she is meditating and instead of attacking, leaves an offering for her. There is a similar but not identical story in the Mūlasarvāstivāda *Vinaya*—see Finnegan (2009, 227ff.).

monks' *Vinaya* where monks are given permission to walk along a road with a nun if the road is known to be dangerous (pācittiya 27). The overall impression in the *Therīgāthā* and related literature is that nuns did wander, but perhaps ensured they stayed together at night. Sihā says in her verses that she wandered for seven years (v. 79) and Bhaddā Kuṇḍalakesā recounts:

> I have wandered over Aṅga and Magadha, Vajjī, Kāsi and Kosala. For fifty years without debt I have enjoyed the alms of the kingdom.[25]

However, these are the only two instances that fully suggest a peripatetic lifestyle.

The evidence of archaeology can partially support the notion that regions outside of urban centres were unsafe places, from the fact of fortifications made for towns and cities. Although Deloche (2007) has surveyed and provides detail for the archaeological findings of fortifications in ancient India to date, attempts to map such evidence onto the political, social or economic history of the subcontinent is only just beginning (Shaw 2007). It is not clear from the current state of knowledge, for example, whether fortifications were more necessary during the politically unstable period of the mahājanapadas, for example. The evidence suggests, on the contrary, that even during periods of empire, fortifications continued to be reinforced. For example, Kosambī had an impressive rampart prior to the sixth and fifth centuries BCE, which was raised to a further height of 2.4 metres during the mahājanapada period, and then, during the Mauryan period, guardrooms and towers were added to it. Also, Vesāli initially had only a small ancient fort, and during the Mauryan period a mud rampart was added. Deloche underscores that all fortifications were defensive by nature, and this is further evident from some of the types of sectional doorways built into the structures (2007, 3–27). However, the lack of physical safety for women outside the city walls may not have been a particularly defining factor with regard to whether the nuns were safe in their religious pursuits. What enabled them to wander safely was a shift in attitude; a more complete social

25 *Thī* vv. 110, 134, trans. Norman (1971, 14). *Ciṇṇā aṅgā ca magadhā vajjī kāsī ca kosalā, anaṇā paṇṇāsavassāni raṭṭhapiṇḍaṃ abhuñji 'haṃ.*

awareness of who and what nuns are, and a growing respect for them and Buddhism overall.

***

The social identity of different groups of unmarried women, or women who did not belong to a man or men, can be seen to shift. Courtesans, when considered to be the custody of a man or group (gaṇa), have a fairly defined and clear social role, are part of the social order, and as such are protected by the jurisdiction of those with political authority. However, a changing attitude to them is in evidence in Buddhist texts of different periods, which may have been in part the result of a changing political landscape, and the move to empire.

The social identity of Buddhist nuns took time to become established. The early texts appear to evidence a struggle with this, the *Apadāna* likely helped to more firmly establish this with its biographies of female 'saints' of the past. By the time of the commentaries, the parameters of a social identity for nuns becomes circumscribed around the biographical accounts, which indicate the veneration to be accorded to nuns. However, they also reveal some disparity between female 'saints' and women in general—such that it is far from clear which attitudes underpinned the basis of contemporaneous regard for female practitioners (see chapter 12).

In the early period, if women who lived outside the confines of marriage, or were unattached to a man or men, were viewed as sexually available, then the establishing of a clear and pronounced social identity for nuns was paramount. Celibacy needed to be a binding facet of this, and this could be most easily achieved though showing that the nuns were under the guardianship of men. This may be a reason for the incorporation of the eight garudhammas, or important rules, into the set of rules nuns must be seen to abide by. The eight rules certainly classify the nuns as under the protection and rule of the monks. As such, seen by the broader community to be under the charge of a group of men, nuns would thereby no longer be considered to be sexually available, and attempting to engage in sex acts with them would be henceforth considered inappropriate.

10

Family, marriage, and class

PAṬĀCĀRĀ

Themes in the Pāli accounts

Family and Vaṇṇa

All of the biographical accounts studied in this volume highlight the importance of family for the nuns, especially prior to their ordination. This accords with the more general view of the centrality of family in this historical milieu, as is confirmed by inscriptional evidence.[1] Although family remains important across the Pāli texts of the different periods, the way caste or class status is articulated varies, and highlights a difference between the north Indian and south Indian/Sri Lankan milieus. In the *Apadāna* biographies, in a reflection of earlier canonical works, class—or *vaṇṇa*—is specified or indicated in each case. However, in the commentaries, in a move that seems to reflect the changed

[1] See Shah (2001), who discussed how, in early Indian inscriptions made by women, they situate themselves relationally, that is, as a daughter of a certain father or wife of a certain husband.

socio-political environment of the more southerly geopolitical climates, this is changed to a note on birth into the more ubiquitous 'good families'.

The importance of family is evident in the *Thera-Therīgāthā*, although, as I argue in the following section, it may have been more important still in earlier (perhaps oral) forms of the text. Norman has already, some time ago, identified the way in which verses belonging to members of a family can be grouped together in the *Theragāthā*, along with others that indicate potential family or tribal/clan connections. He says:

> Other verses are linked because of some relationship between the speakers, e.g. 11 is by Cūla-gavaccha and 12 by Mahā-gavaccha; 13 is by Vanavaccha and 14 by his pupil (*sāmaṇera*); 36 is by Kumāputta and 37 by his companion; 56 and 57 are both by theras named Kuṭivihārin; 107 is by Dhammasava and 108 by his father; 112 and 113 are both by members of the Vaccha clan; 129–130 are by Ajina and 131–32 by Meḷajina; 133–34 by Rādha and 135–36 by Surādha; Bharata, the author of 175–76, was the brother of Nandaka, the author of 173–74, and refers to him by name in 175; Bhāradvāja, the author of 177–78, is said by the commentary to have had a son named Kaṇhadinna, although it is not specifically stated that this son was identical with the author of 179–80. (Norman ([1969] 2007, xxviii)

More of these than Norman ventures to claim may have been relatives, as it was not uncommon at the time to name siblings with related names, similar to those he notes, such as Rādha and Surādha, Ajina and Meḷajina. Norman has also previously raised a question as to the internal structure of the *Thera-Therīgāthā*. He notes that the verses on Vaḍḍha (vv. 335–9):

> ...seem at one time to have been a whole with his mother's verses, but the compilers would appear to have divided what was originally a single poem into two parts in an entirely arbitrary way. (trans. Norman, in Rhys Davids and Norman 1989, 72)

Further to this, there are potentially three other verses/sets of verses which attest to an original text (although perhaps not a written one) with a different structure. The first of these relate to the siblings of Sāriputta. The verse attributed to his brother, (Revata) Khadiravaniya (v. 42), includes reference to Cālā, Upacālā, and

Sisupacālā; these three together are usually known as his sisters, and the Pāli endings on the names in the extant text are '–e', the regular singular vocative for the feminine. However, these endings have caused some consternation, since at least the time of the extant aṭṭhakathās. Dhammapāla, alongside modern scholars translating and studying the text, has produced different theories as to why the '–e' ending appears. Dhammapāla (*Tha-a* II.117) suggests the '–e' ending comes about from the text addressing the sons of Cālā, Upacālā, and Sisupacālā. As they are the offspring of these women, the sons are known as Cāli, Upacāli, and Sisupacāli, and the vocative '–e' comes from this. Neumann, the author of the first German translation of the *Therīgāthā*, understands the endings to be feminine (1899, 46), but C.A.F. Rhys Davids understands them as male ([1909] 2000, 46). Norman, aware of these issues, instead suggests the '–e' as the masculine ending in the 'Eastern form' or 'Māgadhism', following Geiger (Norman [1969] 2007, 146; Geiger [1916] 2005, 73). But there are no other instances of the '–e' as the masculine vocative in the entire extant *Thera-Therīgāthā*.[2] However, if an argument from context is combined with the linguistic evidence, what is immediately noteworthy is that there is no other mention in the canon of these three male offspring; there is one mention of two—Cāla and Upacāla—in the *Aṅguttaranikāya* (V.133), but the other instances of the three names together are all references to the sisters of Sāriputta. These sisters are mentioned in quite a few other canonical texts; not only do they have sequential verses attributed to them in the *Therīgāthā*, but each of them also has a sequential vignette in the *bhikkhunisaṃyutta*, and they are also mentioned in the *Vinaya*.[3] Thus, the argument from context—that when the three names appear together they refer to the women—combined with the linguistic evidence of the '–e' endings on the names in Khadiravaniya's verse suggest that it is the sisters who are being addressed here.

[2] Although there are many other Eastern forms in the overall text, see Norman's comprehensive notes to his translation (1969, especially see page 133).

[3] The two sets of verses attributed to the three are disordered, see Bhikkhu Bodhi's note 350 (trans. 2000, 428).

Further, in relation to a separate family group, the verses of Cāpā (vv. 291–311) in the *Therīgāthā* are essentially verses of herself and her husband, whom she calls Kāḷa. The verse details Kāḷa's religious motives, intentions, and desires more so than they do Cāpā's. However, in the penultimate verse, we do find an expression of Cāpā's faith as well, in her asking her husband to make her obeisance to the Buddha for her, when he goes into his presence. The expression of the faith of each, given the way the narrative unfolds, cannot be separated. Finally, and perhaps better known than the other examples, the verses attributed to Bhaddā Kapilānī speak more of the attainments of her husband, Mahākasspa, than her own. All these four examples—Vaḍḍha and his mother, Sāriputta's sisters, Cāpā and Kāḷa, and Bhaddā Kapilānī with Mahākasspa—together suggest that the *Therīgāthā* may originally have been structured differently. Rather than being divided along gender lines, it may originally have been grouped into sets of verses attributed to different families: kinship groups of brothers and sisters, parents and children, and husbands and wives. That this may have been the case accords with some instances in the extant text in which family groupings are still in evidence.

Some supporting evidence for such an argument comes from the extant *Sthaviragāthā* fragments (see Bechert 1961), which suggest a variant structure. Although these fragmentary verses are few in number, it is clear that there are many differences between this recension of the text and the extant Pāli version. Some of these differences, perhaps the majority of them, can be put down to transmission errors. But what they highlight is the fluid nature of texts in the transmission process. Table 10.1 notes the similarities and differences between the Sanskrit and Pāli versions:[4]

In the *Sthaviragāthā* version there appears to be a thematic grouping, around the theme of hut/kuṭi. We can see this in the names for verse 8 and verse 10 and also other verses that mention *kuṭikas*. The section of *Theragāthā* verses that the *Sthaviragāthā* fragments are most similar to is a section of verses which also share

4 In addition to what is given in Table 10.1, the *Sthaviragāthā* fragments also include the opening verses, the beginnings of an *uddāna*, and a few other words/phrases.

Table 10.1 Comparison of *Sthaviragāthā* fragments and the *Theragāthā*

Sthaviragāthā	*Theragāthā*
v. 1 Subhūti	Verse 1 in both is attributed to Subhūti, but the content of the *Sthaviragāthā* verse is not similar to the verse of Subhūti in the *Theragāthā*
v. 2 Subāhu	Looks to be the same as Subāhu v. 52
v. 3 unknown monk	Content similar to Subhūti v. 1
v. 4 unknown monk	
v. 5 unknown monk	
v. 6 Dhanika	As Bechert notes 'Vom Vers nichts erhalten; nur die Unterschrift' (1961, 262). In the *Theragāthā* a Dhaniya has vv. 226-30 attributed to him
v. 7 unknown monk	This verse can be identified as that of Añjanavaniyo v. 55
v. 8 Kuṭikacchāyin	This verse can be identified as that of Ramaṇīyakuṭiko v. 58
v. 9 unknown monk	
v. 10 Kuṭikāvāsin	Again only a name appears on the fragment. In the *Theragāthā* two verses (56 and 57) are attributed to a Kuṭivihāri
v. 11 unknown monk	

a theme of kuṭi, although not all of the verses in the *Theragāthā* that mention kuṭis are in this section. This may suggest, in both cases, attempts to structure around a theme, and what it does show more concretely is that the structure of the extant *Theragāthā* was not mirrored in this Sanskrit version of the text.

As part of the emphasis on family, the biographical accounts highlight the importance of social status with regard to both family of origin and also choice of marriage partner. The way in which social status is conceptualized in the early texts of the

Pāli canon does not, as noted by Uma Chakravarti, conform to the Brahmanical division of class (vaṇṇa) into the fourfold classification of brahmin, *khattiya* (*kṣatriya*), *vessa* (*vaiśya*), and *sudda* (*śūdra*). This fourfold division does appear in the early texts of the Pāli canon in 'situations in which the Buddha converses with a *brāhmaṇa*', and occasionally in conversations with kings (Chakravarti [1987] 2008, 98). What Chakravarti calls the 'Buddhist scheme' is a threefold division into khattiya, brahmin, and householder (*gahapati*), and this scheme, she underlines, is used 'in the context of *kula*' (or family). That is to say, a person is defined by their family status, rather than with reference to the class divisions articulated as part of the Brahmanical vaṇṇa ideology (although the two do overlap to some extent). Besides these primary three, which are considered the high families, there are numerous other workers mentioned in Pāli literature who form parts of the lower kulas—for instance, to name but a few, *kumbhakāra* (potter), *naḷakāra* (basket maker), *cammakāra* (leather worker), and *pesakāra* (weaver). Paṭācārā herself, as we have seen, comes from a good merchant family most often—one of the high kulas—as do most of the nuns whose biographies make up this volume.

Although worker and servant families are considered to be lower than the khattiya–brahmin–gahapati triad, and some types of workers lower than others, they are not denied the opportunity to become members of the saṅgha.[5] Parasher-Sen lists many different types of named former workers who were admitted to the saṅgha—barbers, potters, a vulture trainer, a horse trainer, a fisherman's son, and so on (2006, 441).[6] She also notes that the one mention of a son of a *caṇḍala*, the lowest group by most accounts, is often cited to 'illustrate the early Buddhist concern of not letting birth, occupation ... and social status hinder' entry into the Buddhist Order (2006, 441).

5 And, of course, as noted by Bailey and Mabbett, members of these higher status families would often be employed in professions, even brahmins, so the differentiation is to an extent spurious (2003, 60).

6 Certain of these are identified as particularly low class, see Bailey and Mabbett (2003, 59) and Wagle (1966, 135ff.).

In addition to this one well-known mention of a caṇḍala, on other occasions in the Pāli canon, caṇḍalas are grouped amongst low tribes or workers who are socially excluded.[7] Again, we find here a somewhat dichotomous application of the notion of social exclusion similar to the one Chakravarti finds with regard to Brahmanical vaṇṇa ideology. Just as vaṇṇa ideology is sometimes acknowledged in general terms in a particular way, but differently in specific individual cases, so too is the idea that certain groups should be socially excluded adhered to in general, theoretical terms, whereas individuals from socially excluded groups are admitted to the saṅgha. With regard to social exclusion, it may be the case that this is being indicated in Paṭācārā's biography in the *Apadāna*. Her shadowy lover, the 'man from the country' (*naraṃ janapadaṃ*), with whom she elopes, may well have been a member of a socially excluded group, who were said to live outside of cities and villages.

More generally, with regard to women workers and servants, we find an inclusivist attitude in both the early canon and the *Apadāna*. In the early canon, the *Therīgāthā* contains one clear example of a woman from the working classes becoming a nun. These are the verses of Puṇṇikā, (236–51) which state that she was a water-carrier (*udakahārī*). In the nuns' *Apadāna*, there are more examples of female water carriers and in this proselytizing text, low social standing is used as a rhetorical device to inspire practice. In these examples, the women in question, though low-grade workers or servants, are rewarded with high status and other benefits once they have made an offering, or performed some other comparable good action. For example, in two cases—that of the two nuns Ekuposathikā and Modakadāyikā (*Ap.* II.522 and 524)—the women are said to have been water-carriers in past lives, and then, as a consequence of good deeds done, in the present

7 Bailey and Mabbett (2003, 42) note a repeated passage in the Pāli canon that denotes low families (*nīcakula*)—'a caṇḍala family, a family of hunters, of bamboo workers, of chariot makers, and of refuse removers' (*...caṇḍalaṃ vā nesādakulaṃ vā veṇakulaṃ vā rathakārakulaṃ vā pukkusakulaṃ vā...*) (*MN* III.169, and also see *SN* I.93, *AN* I.107, II.85, *Vin.* IV.6).

Ekuposathikā is born to a wealthy merchant, and Modakadāyikā to a brahmin. In relation to Puṇṇikā, who makes an appearance in the *Apadāna* as well (*Ap*. II.611–12), the reason for her low birth in the present life is imbricated into her biography as induced by kamma. According to the *Apadāna* account, in the past Puṇṇikā was a nun of bedazzling substance; she was virtuous and possessed of zeal, and demonstrated great learning and skill in understanding. Unfortunately for her, her superior skills soon led to a haughty and arrogant nature, and it was this that caused her to be reborn as a servant. In the present, she was a servant in the house of Anāthapiṇḍa and, once she had redeemed herself with a good deed behoving of her past, she was set free and, with Anāthapiṇḍa's permission, went forth. The good deed that brought about this reversal of fortune includes within it an apparent re-emergence of her past accomplishments as a nun. She gave a teaching to a male brahmin, who was promptly converted. This she did while still physically a servant, although the thrust of the text suggests she has cognitively transcended this low state at this juncture, and in the very next verse she is freed. Another nun, Ekāsanadāyikā, of whose parents it is said that they, in the past, 'went to work' (*kammantam agamaṃsu*), in her subsequent births, having done a good deed she declares that, as a consequence, she has 'known two sorts of family—*khattiya* and brahmin' and that she has 'not known life as an outcaste' (*Duve kule pajāyāmi khattiye cāpi brāhmaṇe ... vevaṇṇiyaṃ na jānāmi ...Ap*.526). Even Dhammadinnā and Khemā are said in the *Apadāna* to have been servants in the past, which (according to the lore of the text) just shows what it is possible for a former servant to achieve, if they dedicate themselves accordingly.

In sharp contrast to the nuns' *Apadāna*, the monks' *Apadāna* takes a much more radical step away from any advocacy of Brahmanical vaṇṇa ideology and social identity formulated around kinship/clan/birth/class. The monks' *Apadāna* was composed around the time of the *Buddhavaṃsa* and, as identified by Walters ([1997] 2002, 165), is obviously a later work as it borrows from the *Buddhavaṃsa*. In relation to this issue of social location and self-identity, the monks' *Apadāna* needs to be seen as part of the ambit of the *Buddhavaṃsa*. The *Buddhavaṃsa*, which tenders details of the lineage of twenty-four Buddhas that ends with Gotama, proffers a more defined and fully formulated (mytho-) past than do any earlier books of the Pāli canon. It can and has been argued that the Buddha-lineage is an attempt to rival the Brahmanical notions of genealogy as history. According to this Brahmanical construction of the past, through one's kin/clan/tribe/class one can trace back one's own history and situate oneself within a historical trajectory formulated around the roots of Brahmanical tradition. In Brahmanical terms, through the genealogy of kin/clan/tribe, each individual can trace back their family origins to the Kurus and Pandavas.[8] The radical step of the monks' *Apadāna* (but not the nuns') is to replace this socio-historical ancestral line, that underpins interest in social 'location', with the Buddha lineage. Rather than the individual monks being introduced—or rather introducing themselves, as the text is autobiographical—via an acknowledged family background of either of the three high kulas—khattiya, brahmin, gahapati—or as workers, almost all biographies begin, instead, by delineation of Buddha era. As such, each monk-to-be who has lived during the era of a previous Buddha is defined by that very fact. In these former existences, the monk-to-be will have made an offering to a previous Buddha (or several), or done a good deed, and by so doing will have dramatically affected the trajectory of his life. Thus, existence during the time of the former Buddha cements the future monk's identity as a revered practitioner and faithful disciple, and gives him a more solid socio-historical location rooted in Buddhist tradition, and this replaces family background which, as socially construed, links to Brahmanical constructions of the (mytho-) past.

Further, a more straightforward rebuke to the hegemonic emphasis on social status comes in the apadāna of Jatukaṇṇika (*Ap.* II.558). Jatukaṇṇika, one of the few who tells us he was the son of a merchant, boasts about his inclusivist policy on guests; he enjoys entertaining many people of various classes,

[8] See the excellent papers in conference proceedings from the *Genealogy as History: Social Constructions of the Past in South Asia*, special volume of *Religions of South Asia* 5 (1 and 2), 2011.

occupations, and tribes. In his bountiful list of those who come to visit he includes different types of religious persons *samaṇa*, brahmins, Jains (*nigaṇṭhas*), and Ājīvakas, as well as otherwise little-known or unknown groups such as the *koṇḍa-puggalas*. In welcoming tribes from different regions, he boasts that neighbours from Madhura, Kosala, Kāsi have visited, as well as members of other tribes and clans such as the well-known Pallavas, along with otherwise little-known groups such as the Muṇḍakas. Even those considered to be *mlecchas/milakkha* (foreigners/outsiders, according to Brahmanical vaṇṇa ideology) have been to his house, such as Tamils (*damiḷa*) and Yonakas (Greeks) and the word *babbhara* also appears in this magnanimous list, sometimes translated as 'barbarian', and which certainly refers to those of unknown tongue. Of the different types of workers he has entertained, these include *usukārā*—arrowmakers, *cāpakārā*—bowmakers, *gandhikā*—perfume workers, *rajakārā*—dyers, *tunnavāyā*—tailors, *lohakārā*—metalworkers, and *kaṭṭhahārā*—wood gatherers, to name a few. The list also includes servants (*pessikā*) and watercarriers (*udahārā*) but not, in its extant form, caṇḍalas. However, a few apadānas on is an account of a former caṇḍala, who, through making an offering, gains better conditions for himself (*Ap*. II.377–8).

While the monks' *Apadāna* reveals a seemingly bold reiteration of the new model of history, the apadāna of Jatukaṇṇika does betray a tension that exists within the text overall, as part of its only partially successful manoeuvre. Although labouring under a new purview, the authors of the *Apadāna* are not able to fully rescind pervasive norms—which were likely firmly embedded as hegemonic. The monks' *Apadāna* does mention brahmins and, more often, kings, who are sometimes stated to be khattiya. It also mentions families of high birth (*ucca* kula), and—most problematic for its authors—it is formulated around depiction of kammic trajectory by which those doing good work benefit from this by no longer experiencing negative circumstances in their lives. The text is replete with a phrase formulated along the lines that an individual, having done one good deed or another no longer experiences low birth (*duggati*). While other monks' biographies are ambiguous with regard to exactly what a low birth might be in the ambit of the text, in the apadāna of Jatukaṇṇika the syntax does demonstrate that duggati clearly means low birth into a poor family—the text has Jatukaṇṇika say that, as a consequence of good deeds done, he was not reborn into any low family who dwelt in poverty (... *dalidde duggatimhi nibbattiṃ me na passāmi* ... *Ap.* II.361).[9] Thus, here is clear elision into the high/low *jāti* paradigm.

The commentaries seem to miss the attempted innovation of the monks' *Apadāna*, and instead follow the format of the nuns' *Apadāna*, placing monks and nuns within a twofold social location—that is, at the time of one Buddha or another, and within a suitable family. The commentaries follow the purview of the majority of canonical works, through designating family origin in terms of either the three higher kulas—khattiya, brahmin, gahapati—or as workers or servants. However, the language used to demarcate family of origin changes slightly, such that the more ubiquitous *kulageha* ('home of a good family') predominates. Other than that, *mahābhogakula* ('wealthy family') is sometimes used, but apart from that the narrative prose throws up no surprises here, and we find the monks and nuns hail from—*brāhmaṇakula*[10] (for example, *Tha-a*, II.56, 70, 71, 157; III.7, 26, 45), *khattiyakula* (for example, *Tha-a*, II.11, *Thī -a* 34, 39), *seṭṭhikula* (for example, *Tha-a*, II.57; *Dhp-a* I.239), *gahapatikula/kuṭumbikakula* (for example, *Tha-a*, I.46; II.46, 49, 141 167; III.1; *Thī-a* 51) as well as workers' families—barbers, potters, hunters, gardeners, servants, etc.[11]

9 Emended from Lilley, who has *dalidde duggatimhi vā nibbattiṃ*....The monks' *Apadāna* is not especially concerned with the realms of existence, and while in some contexts duggati can be 'birth into a lower realm', that does not fit the context here.

10 *Brāhmaṇakula* refers to a brahmin family, *khattiyakula* to a family of the warrior caste, *gahapatikula/kuṭumbikakula* refers to the families of respected householders.

11 Sometimes the formulations are slightly different,—that is, another word is added, such as the addition of a third word here in the middle of the compound *khattiya-mahāsāla-kula*, to indicate a wealthy khattiya family, and on other occasions the monk or nun is said to be born as a son or daughter of a householder, brahmin, and so on.

Paṭācārā's unsuitable lover, in the commentaries, is reshaped as a servant in her father's household. And as can be seen from the quote from the *Dhammapada* commentary on page 51, as a result of her reckless deed of eloping, she was forced to perform menial tasks herself, which here is reconfigured as bad kamma. This again demonstrates some level of ambiguity with regard to the question of social equality.

There is one other feature—a striking feature—of the women's biographies that further highlights a perhaps subtle (attempted) acquiescence to Brahmanical vaṇṇa ideology. In the biographies, a woman is rarely recorded to leave a brahmin husband to enter discipleship with the Buddha. Although some of the women are born into brahmin families, they all ordain before marriage, so there are no stories of women choosing to reject their brahmin husbands through their own initiative and abandoning them for a homeless life. There are two stories of adult brahmin women who do become followers of the Buddha, but in one case—that of Bhaddā Kapilānī—she follows her husband into the Order, and in the second case, the woman renounces in imitation of her father, who has just done the same.[12] Generally speaking, the women who are born in brahmin families ordain early, that is, either before or just as they reach marriageable age. There are a fair few examples of girls born to brahmin parents who convert, but none of married brahmin women who do so. There is, for instance, the rather charming story of Rohinī, who is born into a brahmin family, but whose heart is immediately set upon renunciation. As the *Therīgāthā* records, which the *Therīgāthā* commentary glosses as her father speaking to her:

> You fell asleep saying 'recluses', you woke up saying 'recluses', you praise only recluses, you will surely become a recluse yourself.[13]

12 Bhaddā Kapilānī has verses attributed to her in the *Thī* (63–6), and her story is told in the *Ap.* (578–84) and in the *Thī-a* (66–74). The other account appears only in the *Thī-a* (215–22). Sundarī's brother died and her father, overwhelmed with grief, decided to go forth, and thus Sundarī followed him.

13 *Samaṇā ti ... maṃ vipassi samaṇā ti paṭibujjhasi, samaṇānam eva kittesi samaṇī nūna bhavissasi* (*Thī* v. 271)

There is also the example of the 84,000 young brahmin girls in the *Apadāna* who, immediately upon being reborn into a brahmin family, while still 'delicate of hand and foot' (*sukhumālāhattapādā*) went forth and became followers of the Buddha (*Ap*. II.600).

Although there is an absence of categorical examples, some of the verses in the *Therīgāthā* do belie the intimation that adult married brahmin women do not convert. This is seen most clearly in the verses of Nanduttarā:

> I worshipped fire, and the moon and sun, and divinities. Going to pilgrimage-places by rivers, I would go down into the water.
> Undertaking many vows, I shaved my head, made my bed on the ground, did not eat food at night.
>
> Delighting in finery and adornments and bathing and anointing I tended to this body afflicted by desire for sensual pleasure.
>
> Then, having gained faith I went forth into the homeless life, seeing the body as it really is, desire for sensual pleasures is destroyed.
>
> All existences cut off, and wishes and longings too. Unfettered from all ties, I attained peace of mind.[14]

These verses, as with many in the *Therīgāthā*, and as discussed earlier, may be in the wrong order or out of place; that is to say, one might assume that Nanduttarā's affliction with sensual pleasures was something that she experienced prior to her initial renunciate activities. However, this is not necessarily the case, as some female renouncers within Brahmanism did marry following a period of renunciate living.[15] The verses, nevertheless, certainly do convey a sense of an adult female practitioner of Brahmanism, fully fledged

[14] Aggiṃ *candañ ca sūriyañ ca devatā ca namassi 'haṃ, nadītitthāni gantvāna udakaṃ oruhāmi 'haṃ. bahūvatasamādānā aḍḍhaṃ sīsassa olikhiṃ, chamāya seyyaṃ kappemi rattibhattaṃ na bhuñji 'haṃ. Vibhūsamaṇḍanaratā nhāpanucchādanehi ca, upakāsiṃ imaṃ kāyaṃ kāmarāgena additā. Tato saddhaṃ labhitvāna pabbajiṃ anagāriyaṃ, disvā kāyaṃ tathābhūtaṃ kāmarāgo samūhato. Sabbe bhavā samucchinnā icchā ca patthanā pi ca, sabbayogavisaṃyuttā santiṃ pāpuṇiṃ cetaso* (*Thī* vv. 87–91).

[15] See, for example, the *Mahābhārata* story of Bṛhaspati's sister, who was a *brahmacāriṇī*, but eventually abandoned her ascetic ways to marry (*MBh* I.60.26ff. as cited in Dhand 2008, 81).

in various religious pursuits prior to her conversion to Buddhism. The *Therīgāthā* commentary, however, glosses these verses as if they were those of a brahmin girl. According to the *Therīgāthā* commentary, Nanduttarā was born into a brahmin family in the town of Kammāsadhamma and said to have 'learned some of the branches of study and the arts' (*ekaccānī vijjāṭṭhānāni sippāyatanāni ca*). There is no mention of her being married and the implication is, instead, that she practised Brahmanism at home, with her family of origin.

The Pāli canon rarely records a married brahmin woman abandoning her husband and family to live a homeless life, and this is the case not only in the canonical material but is also taken up and sponsored by the commentaries. This even appears to be the case with female renouncers within the Brahmanic tradition, although evidence of these female ascetics is sparse. Of the relatively few female renouncers recorded in contemporaneous Brahmanic literature, Dhand notes that they 'practiced *brahmacarya* as a vocation right from childhood' (2008, 81). The vaṇṇa of these women is not always stated, some were daughters of ascetics, and one, Sulabhā, whose story is told in the *Mahābhārata*, was from a khattiya family but as no suitable husband could be found for her she became an ascetic (*MBh* 12.308.184 as cited in Black 2007a, 72).

There are a few references within the Brahmanic corpus which highlight that marriage to a brahmin male is of greater significance than other marriages, but this is not a consistent or prominent theme in Brahmanical literature. The *Atharvaveda*, however, does deem marriage to a brahmin the most real. In discussing polyandry, the text reads:

> And, when a woman has ten former husbands, not brahmins, and a brahmin seized her hand, he alone is her husband.[16]

And:

> A brahmin only is her husband, not a *rājanya*, not a *vaiśya*, this the sun goes proclaiming to the five races of men.[17]

[16] *Uta yat patayo daśa striyāḥ pūrve abrāhmaṇaḥ, brahmā ceddhastam agrahīt sa eva patirekadhā* (AV V.17.8).

[17] *Brāhmaṇa eva patirna rājanyo na vaiśyaḥ, tat sūryaḥ prabravanneti pañcabhyo mānavebhyaḥ* (AV V.17.9).

Such ideology may have had something to do with the lack of instances of women leaving brahmin husbands to renounce and follow the path of the Buddha but, as this is not a prominent theme in Brahmanical literature, it may well have been the case that excluding any such depictions from the Pāli texts was an attempt at compliance to some assumed Brahmanical norms, but a somewhat misguided one.

Women choosing their own marriage partners

According to all of her Pāli biographies, Paṭācārā runs off with an unsuitable man, whom she then marries. But each account does not give the same details about her lover. In the *Apadāna* he is said to be, as mentioned, a man from the country, but the commentaries say instead that he was a servant in Paṭācārā's family home.[18] Each account at least suggests, even if it does not specifically say, that Paṭācārā's indiscretions were much to the displeasure of her family. This is suggested in the *Apadāna* account, and explicitly stated in the other accounts. For example, in the *Dhammapada* commentary, her parents guard her very

[18] Both the manuscripts used for the Pāli edition of the *Apadāna* and the *Therīgāthā* commentary have either *janapada* or what appear to be either variations or corruptions of janapada (*jānapada, jāna para*), but Pruitt emends to *jārapati* in the text and Lilley suggests it as a possible emendation (Lilley [1925] 2006, 558; Pruitt 1999, 111). If this is the correct emendation, as far as I know this would be the only occurrence of the term 'jārapati' in Pāli. The other uses of *jāra* are concerned with women who commit adultery. The term more often used for adultery is *paradāra* or *paradārika* ('someone else's wife'), as this seems to be the parameter for adultery in the ancient Indian context; the fear of one man 'sowing his seed in another's field', as the often-used textual metaphors would have it. Adultery in ancient India is not usually concerned with an unfaithful husband (jārapati) per se, focusing more on the status of the husband's love-interest than on his fidelity to his own wife. As noted by Doniger, male infidelity is 'easily overlooked in the polygamous world of The Laws of Manu ... and in the two great epics, the *Mahābhārata* and the *Rāmāyana*' (Doniger 1995, 161).

keenly, and in order to escape their home to be with her lover, she has to disguise herself:

> Very early in the morning, having put on soiled clothes, disheveled her hair and smeared her body with red powder, she took a water-pot to give the appearance of one who is part of a group of slaves.[19]

Apparently possessed of an independent disposition, Paṭācārā disregards her parents in favour of her own personal choice of marriage partner. Of the nuns discussed in this volume, Paṭācārā is not the only one who chooses her own marriage partner; Bhaddā Kuṇḍalakesā does the same (see Chapter 5). In Bhaddā's case, she becomes infatuated with a thief as she sees him being led off to execution. At great expense to the family (according to some accounts), her father secures release of the thief for Bhaddā so that the two of them may wed. Thus, amongst the six biographies, we have two instances of women who choose their own marriage partners, one with not only the consent but also the assistance of her parents and the other without parental consent. In neither case is the match a good one in terms of kula (family), that is, although the women are generally from good families, this is not the case with their desired suitors. In Bhaddā's case, one of her biographical accounts situates her husband-to-be as someone from a brahmin family of a high status, but the rest only give his status as that of a renegade thief. What is also of interest here is that this–a woman's agency in choice of spouse—is one thing that remains static across the *Apadāna* and commentarial accounts. If Walters (2013) is correct about women authoring the *Apadāna*, this may be the reason for these portrayals in the first place, although we do find similar depiction in other texts as well. However, such agency was not presumed for women in the marital arena in this milieu.

According to the Brahmanic legal texts, eight types of marriage are enumerated, although the exact differences between certain types are not entirely clear (Jamison 1996, 215).[20] Amongst these

19 *Sāpi pāto va kiliṭṭhavatthaṃ nivāsetvā kese vikiritvā kuṇḍakena sarīraṃ makkhetvā kuṭaṃ ādāya dāsīhi saddhiṃ gacchantī viya* (*Dhp-a* II.261).

20 The list of marriage types is mentioned many times in the literature, such as at *MDS* III.2034; *Āp. DS* II.17–20, 12.1–3; *GDS* IV. 6–15; *BDS* 1.20.

eight types, there are marital arrangements by which the father makes the choice of suitor for the bride-to-be, and at least one type by which the union appears to have been established through love and the mutual consent of the lovers—this is called the gāndharva-type—and yet others which to varying degrees circumvent female agency and choice, involving abduction or rape of women and girls.[21] In addition to these types described in the *dharmasūtras* and dharmaśāstras, they are also discussed in the *Mahābhārata* by Bhīṣma (1.96.8–11 and 13.44–2–9), Kṛṣṇa (1.213.3–5) and Duḥṣanta (1.67.8–9), though here the lists show some minor alterations.[22] Although there is some discussion as to the exact constituents of each type, the types can be broadly categorized for our present purposes as:

1. *Brāhma*—in which the father gives his daughter to a suitable man
2. *Daiva*—the father gives his daughter to a priest
3. *Ārṣa*—the daughter is given on receipt of a gift from the bridegroom
4. *Prājāpatya*—the specific features of this type are unclear, but it may have originally been a marriage by mutual consent (Jamison 1996, 217–8)
5. *Āsura*—the groom's family pays a bride-price to secure the bride
6. *Gāndharva*—the union comes about through love
7. *Rākṣasa*—the woman or girl is taken through abduction
8. *Paiśāca*—the woman or girl is raped

For present purposes, these types will be discussed under the three broad rubrics of parental control of the union, female choice, and male choice (the latter of which are often cases in which some amount of force is used). These types of marriage are not, to my knowledge, discussed or referred to in the Pāli canon and

[21] See Jamison for a discussion of abduction and re-abduction, and female agency as evidenced in the extent to which women go willingly or resist (1996, 281ff.).

[22] These discussions in the *MBh* have been noted by Allen (2007, 180) and Brodbeck (2009, 46).

commentaries; however, the broad rubrics of them are reflected in the textual discourses concerning martial unions. Although the Pāli texts do not contain their own comparable list of types of marital arrangements, there is, in the *Vinaya*, a list of types of wives, which includes within it some indication of how a wife can be procured. Some descriptions on this list can add to the discussion of the question of female choice, however, this list should in no way be considered to be some sort of a Buddhist equivalent to the Brahmanic list just mentioned. The ten types of wives are:

1. One who is bought for money
2. One who stays out of love
3. One who stays because of wealth
4. One who receives clothes
5. One who can provide water
6. One who carries vessels on her head
7. One who is a slave (*dāsī*) and a wife
8. One who is a servant (*kammakārī*) and a wife
9. One who is won through battle ('flag-brought' *dhajāhaṭā*)
10. A temporary wife[23]

The extent of female agency and female choice is difficult to discern in this list of ten, as some of the Pāli compounds can be read in various ways. For example, with regard to the third one in the list, *bhogavāsinī* can be read as 'one who stays because of wealth', and indeed this seems to be how both the commentary in the extant Pāli *Vinaya* and Buddhaghosa, in his *Vinaya* commentary, understand it. However, although Horner has it in her translation of the *Vinaya* as 'a kept woman', elsewhere she

[23] *Dasa bhariyāyo dhanakkītā chandavāsinī bhogavāsinī paṭavāsinī odapattakinī obhatacumbaṭā dāsī ca bhariyā ca kammkārī ca bhariyā ca, dhajāhaṭa muhuttikā.* (*Vin.* III.139). The meaning of some of these only becomes clear with the aid of the commentaries. For example, the wife who is 'one who dwells in receipt of a cloth' (*paṭavāsinī*) is said by Buddhaghosa to be referring to a woman who is raised from vagabond status by being given a cloth or garment (*Sp* III. 555). There is another list of five types of wives in *AN* IV.92–3.

records this category of wife as 'one to be enjoyed or made use of occasionally' (Horner [1930] 1990, 43), thus reading it more along the lines of a translation as 'one who dwells for [the] enjoyment [of the man]'. In this same way, there could be an issue with the second kind on the list, *chandavāsinī*, which could be read along the lines of male choice as 'kept for passion', however, again, both the attached commentary and Buddhaghosa make it clear that they read this as a union of mutual consent, and that the wife stays of her own free will, because she is in love and enamoured with her husband.[24]

In the *Vinaya* list, some of the wives can be seen to have been acquired through male choice, such as through purchase of the bride (*dhanakkītā*), as in the first one, although it is possible that this may be a Buddhistic understanding of the mechanisms of exchanging gifts which underlie Brahmanical marital arrangements and thus include considerable involvement of the parents. Also, listing a type of woman who is both a slave and a wife suggests the acquiring of women through some type of male initiative, but there is not sufficient detail on this type for any further speculation. Third, the wife acquired through victory in battle is also indicative of male choice, but these are the only three on the list that are obviously indicative of male choice. Returning to the three rubrics of parental choice, female choice, and male choice, both the lists include male choice of partner through means sometimes governed by use of force and, notably, both include and have in common one mention of marriage brought about by mutual consent. In these instances, female choice looks to be at least half the equation. The Pāli list does not include any mention of parental choice, and this is the most noticeable difference between the two, but is easily accounted for, in that the two lists are intended for different purposes.

In assessing and surveying the ways in which marital unions are convened from the Buddhist texts detailing women's lives, it appears that parental choice was by far the overarching factor. As this is the case, marriage in these instances appears to accord

24 *Chandavāsinī nāma piyo piyaṃ vāseti* (*Vin.* III.140); *chandena attano ruciyā vasatīti chandavāsinī* (*Sp* III.555).

more with the Brahmanical models outlined earlier than with what can be gleaned from how men 'attract' wives from the *Vinaya* list. In the Buddhist texts which recount the lives of the women, once the woman's or girl's own kula has been established, the texts then often recount that the woman or girl is given to another family, which is sometimes specifically said to be a family of similar rank. Of the nuns whose biographies make up this volume, we know from Chapter 1 that Dhammadinnā was born into a merchant's family, and her hand was given in marriage to Visākha, a rich merchant from Rājagaha. Chapter 2 documents that Khemā was born into a khattiya family, as a king's daughter, and married into the royal line in the majority of her accounts. Kisāgotamī was born into a poor merchant's family, as noted in Chapter 3, and married into a wealthy family who despised her because of her impoverished heritage, until she provided them with a male heir. Chapter 5 illustrates that Bhaddā Kuṇḍalakesā was born into a wealthy merchant's family and Chapter 6 that, amongst the various accounts of her, there are some that record Uppalavaṇṇā to have been born into a merchant's family and sought after by many merchants' sons. While these kula-specific marital unions take place, there are times when the texts simply say that the woman or girl, when she came of age, 'went to another family' (*parakulaṃ gantvā*, for example, *Ap*. 569) or to her 'husband's family' (*patikulaṃ*, for example, *Ap*. 577). In these more sweeping statements and from the detail of the texts, parental control of the marital union is visible. Girls and women were also taken to another family as if it had been pre-arranged and was something that had been organized for them. For example, Isidāsī in the *Therīgāthā* is born into a merchant family and does not make her own choice of partner:

> Then, from Sāketa men came from the best families offering marriage. My father gave me to a merchant with many jewels, as daughter-in-law.[25]

Further, there is also evidence that girls were betrothed at a young age, and this becomes part of the narratives when, as young

[25] *Atha me Sāketato varako āgacchi uttamakulīno, seṭṭhi bahutaratano tassa maṃ suṇhaṃ adāsi tāto* (*Thī* v. 406).

women, they resist, such as in the case of Sumedhā in the *Therīgāthā*, who, as the daughter of King Koñca's chief queen, had been betrothed to a king from a neighbouring district (*Thī* vv. 448–522). Thus we can see reflected in the evidence of the Buddhist texts, the broad application of this first rubric of legal marriage types from Brahmanism—that parents, or sometimes solely fathers, take responsibility for arranging the marriage of their female children.

It would be easy to expect, and accept, that for both Buddhist and Brahmanical traditions, if one or both parents, or indeed the wider family, orchestrated the marital arrangements of their children, then in these cases women had no control over this aspect of their lives and had to consign themselves, willingly or not, to the cards that they had been dealt. However, in many of the Buddhist stories of nuns, the opposite is the case, as these women, by virtue of their subsequent discipleship, wholly reject household life. Thus here, a substantial degree of either resilient female agency or familial and communal acceptance of women's choice reveals itself. Indeed, the protagonist under discussion, Paṭācārā, according to some later commentarial accounts, had to battle against parental pressure to marry a suitable man in order to run off with her paramour. Similarly, Sumedhā, mentioned earlier, categorically refuses to marry King Anīkaratta, saying instead, 'I am disgusted with sensual pleasures. They are like vomit, to be uprooted like the palm and its base' (*Thī* v. 478).[26] And she tells Anīkaratta that sensual pleasures are 'great poisons' (*mahāvisā*), 'like a heated ball of iron' (*ayoguḷo va santatto*), 'the root of evil' (*aghamūlā*), 'like lumps of flesh' (*maṃsapesūpamā*), 'a disease' (*rogo*), 'a tumour' (*gaṇḍo*), and 'evil destruction' (*aghaṃ nighaṃ*) (*Thī* vv. 489–91). The nuns and laywomen of the Buddhist literature frequently assert themselves in similar situations, demonstrating a great deal of female agency and empowered choice.

This might, superficially, be counterpoised with the pervading circumstances for women in Brahmanism, who can be viewed as the property of men, or at worst, as observed by Brodbeck of

[26] *Nibbiṇṇā me kāmā vantasamā tālāvatthukatā.*

khattiya women, the unwanted appendage unfortunately attached to the womb necessary for the heir (Brodbeck 2009, 44). However, even within Brahmanism, and in relation to the marital rubric of parental giving of a girl for marriage, some female agency is visible from the texts. There is, for example, the otherwise rather disconcerting story of Mādhavī in the *Mahābhārata* (*MBh* 5.113ff.). Jamison discussed this story under her section on wives as commodities (1996, 208ff.), as it is essentially the story of a woman being sold and re-sold for a bride-price (*śulka*). In this tale, the brahmin student Gālava at the end of his studentship insists that his teacher allow him to offer a gift. Annoyed at Gālava's constant questioning on this, the teacher makes an outrageous demand for eight hundred moon-white horses, each with a black ear. Gālava goes to kings known to be rich to beg for these horses, or the means to acquire them. The first king he approaches provides him with neither the animals nor the money to buy them, but rather a bargaining tool, that is, his daughter Mādhavī, whom Gālava is to exchange for horses. Gālava does this; he successfully exchanges Mādhavī three times to different kings whom she marries and provides with an heir, for a score of two hundred horses per exchange. Thus far, not a tale of female choice or agency; however, the finale of the tale provides us with some recompense. Following her fourth marriage, to Gālava's teacher to whom she also provides a son, Mādhavī is returned to her father and offered a *svayaṃvara* (discussed in the following section), a ceremony by which a woman could choose her own marriage partner. Mādhavī, instead of choosing for herself a fifth husband, decides upon a different option:

> It is perhaps not surprising that Mādhavī bypasses all the assembled suitors and chooses instead the forest as her bridegroom ... where she proceeds to live alone, practicing austerities among the gentle beasts (Jamison 1996, 210).

Thus Mādhavī, in the end, does have a choice, and not just the sort of choice usually the norm at a svayaṃvara, that of which man to take as her husband, but also the choice of not having to marry again.

Additionally, even within the dharmaśāstras, the Brahmanical texts which prescribe strict control of women by men, evidence for female agency in terms of sexuality, as well as economics, can be discerned. Olivelle notes that, although within the ideology of the dharmaśāstras overall, 'the ownership of women passes from the father to the husband' (2004, 496), as evidenced above in some of the types of marriage and reflected in Buddhistic mores, there is acknowledgement of (though not acceptance of) certain types of independent women. Following pronouncements on punishments for rape and adultery, the *Mānavadharmaśāstra* says:

> The above rule does not apply to wives of traveling performers or to wives who earn a living on their own, for such men get their women to attach themselves to men and, concealing themselves, get them to have sexual liaisons. When someone engages in secret conversations with such women, as also with female slaves serving a single master and with female wandering ascetics, he shall be compelled to pay a small fine.[27]

In an observation that resonates with the actions of the Buddhist women described above, and with the actions of Paṭācārā and Bhaddā Kuṇḍalakesā, Olivelle notes that 'the reality behind these prescriptions probably is that within certain classes of society there were strong and independent women, both economically and sexually' (2004, 499).

Further acceptance, of both Paṭācārā and Bhaddā Kuṇḍalakesā and of other independent women who have free agency in the arena of marriage as well as elsewhere, appears to have been found in one of the marriage types not yet discussed: the gāndharva marriage, and its sometimes related ceremony, the svayaṃvara. However, although these two things superficially suggest themselves to be avenues for female agency and free choice, the evidence is more convoluted. The svayaṃvara ceremony is not mentioned in the legislative texts of Brahmanism, although there is some evidence for at least the idea or possibility that a woman chooses a marriage

[27] Translated by Olivelle (2004, 499). In the *Dharmasūtra of Baudhāyana*—that is, an earlier dharmasūtra rather than a later dharmśāstra—the second sentence on female wandering ascetics is missing and only actresses and wives of minstrels are mentioned as women who 'lure' men away (2.4.1–3).

partner for herself (*svayāṃ sā vṛṇīte*) in the *Ṛg Veda*, which may have been indicative of 'an already ritualized social institution' (Jamison 2001, 304). Most evidence of the occasion for svayaṃvara is to be found in the narrative plots and subplots of the epics, although, as Brockington notes, there are fewer instances than is often imagined (2006, 35). Within this amalgam of stories, there are those which portray women making their own choices, but the majority only nominally depict the bride-to-be with some agency. The celebrated marriage of Rāma and Sītā in the *Rāmāyaṇa* is itself an instance of a svayaṃvara, and is itself evidence of only nominal female agency. Janaka, Sītā's father, is the instigator of Sītā's svayaṃvara, and in the text leading up to the marriage, the focus is more on Janaka and his arrangements to offer his daughter in marriage to the best of suitors. In a conversation with Viśvamitra, Janaka decides that if Rāma can perform a heroic feat proving his worth, he will give Sītā to him.

> If Rāma can string this bow, Sage, I will offer Sītā, my non-uterine daughter, to Dāśaratha's son.[28]

Similarly, with other examples of svayaṃvaras in the epics, it is generally the case that the father decides upon the date and makes all the arrangements for his daughter's ceremony. There are one or two instances in which this is not the case, but parental instigation is the typical pattern found. In the *Nalopākhyāna* of the *Mahābhārata* (III.51–79), Damayantī is involved in two svayaṃvaras. In the first her father makes the arrangements, realizing it is time for his daughter to marry. However, the second is her own idea, as she decides she needs to find a second husband not knowing if her first, Nala, is dead or alive.

Interestingly, although the svayaṃvara is not well attested in the Pāli literature,[29] there are some other Indian Buddhist examples of it, which do intimate more female choice than the instances just mentioned. Several of the stories in the *Avadānaśataka* narrate potential occurrences of it (see Muldoon-Hules 2013, 192–220).

[28] *Yady asya dhanuṣo rāmaḥ kuryād āropaṇaṃ mune sutām ayonijāṃ sītāṃ dadyāṃ dāśarather aham* (*Rām.* I.65.25).

[29] As noted by Horner, a svayamvara is mentioned in the *JA* 536 for the king's daughter, princess Kaṇhā (Horner [1930] 1990, 30).

The sections in each story are quasi-formulaic, in that they narrate a recurring incident. In each case, the protagonist's father ponders on his predicament. For example, in the story of Suprabhā (71), in her vital youth she become popular with many suitors—sons of kings, ministers, and merchants. Her father puts his hand on his cheek (*kare kapolaṃ dattvā*) and thinks, 'If I gave her to one, the others will become my enemies.'[30] He eventually resigns himself to a svayaṃvara, to which all potential suitors would be invited and in which his daughter would have complete free choice amongst those offering themselves. In each one of the cases in the *Avadānaśataka*, either through some magical intervention of their own making, or by simple verbal assertion, the girls reject all suitors, opting instead for a life of renunciation as devotees of the Buddha.

Although the gāndharva type of marriage is mentioned in the Brahmanical list of types, it is otherwise not often discussed. Though specified as a marriage of mutual consent, the dharmasūtra and dharmaśāstra acknowledgements of it are sometimes voiced from a male perspective, such as in the *Dharmasūtra of Gautama*, 'When a man on his own has intercourse with a willing woman ...'[31] (4.10, trans. Olivelle 1999, 85), sometimes as wholly mutual, as in the *Dharmasūtra of Āpastamba*, 'When a couple in love engages in sexual intercourse ...' (2.11.20, trans. Olivelle 1999, 55), and at other times from a female perspective, as in the *Mānavadharmaśāstra*, 'When a girl and her lover join together in sexual union ...' (III.32).[32] Usually, in these texts the marriages are said to be listed in ascending order, the best one first, and either the initial members of the list or just the first one are most suitable for brahmins, however, the *Mānavadharmaśāstra*, usually distinguished for its negativity in relation to women, makes an interesting addition:

> For Brahmins, the gift of a girl with a libation of water is the best [marriage]; but for the other classes [the best is] when they desire one another.[33]

[30] *Yadyekasmai dāsyāmi, anye me amitrā bhavisyantīti* (*AŚ* 71).
[31] *Icchantyāḥ svayaṃ saṃyogo...*
[32] *Saṃyogaḥ kanyāyāśca varasya ca ... maithunyaḥ.*
[33] *Mānavadharmaśāstra III.35* (Doniger and Smith 1991, 46).

There is evidence here both of license for female agency and choice; an addenda in the *Mānavadharmaśāstra* also suggests that a union brought about with the consent of the female is the most desirable. Other narrative textual examples of gāndharva or gāndharva-type marriages seem to support this liberal view. In the *Mahābhārata*, Sāvitrī, a woman so beautiful that no man would attempt to woo her, is instructed by her father to go out and find her own suitor, which she does, and once determined insists upon her choice, even though her father is not happy with the match. Also, in some of the earlier depictions of Śakuntala, such as the portrayal of her in the *Mahābhārata*, she makes her own decision with regard to the king's advances.

***

Both the Brahmanical and Buddhist literatures indicate that women were sometimes allowed and/or enabled to make their own choices when it came to choosing a life-mate. The most notable difference between the two corpuses of literature is that the evidence from Brahmanism is more occluded from view, and needs to be sought out and brought to the surface, whereas in the Buddhist texts female choice is more obvious, more commonplace, and appears less discomfited. In setting these Buddhist stories alongside the evidence from Brahmanism, it is clear that the core of the Buddhist narrative provides a level of disambiguation not found in the Brahmanical sources. Two levels of female agency are evident: those sanctioned by parents/family and those unsanctioned. In the case of Bhaddā Kuṇḍalakesā, the subject of the next chapter, her choice—after some brooding—was accepted by her parents. However, with Paṭācārā, her choice did not meet with parental approval, and this seems to be because she had married beneath her—he was an unsuitable man from a lower family, or with lower social status. The *Apadāna* example is the only instance I have come across in the Pāli texts that perhaps allows for the idea that one who becomes a respected nun might have been intimately involved with a social outcaste.

In relation to social status more broadly, the Pāli canon appears generally to keep with inclusivity, such that members of both families of high status and families belonging to the working classes could join the saṅgha. The nuns' *Apadāna*, in what appears to be part of its proselytizing remit, underscores the opportunities for any member of any family. However low status a woman may be, she has the potential to make good progress on the path and by so doing improve her lot in life. One outstanding difference, however, is that in contrast to the plethora of Buddhist monks who hail from brahmin families, far fewer nuns do the same, as the notion that a woman might abandon a brahmin husband to enter discipleship under Gotama seems to be problematized in the canon and commentaries. But this seeming acquiescence to assumed Brahmanical ideology overall makes little impact on the historical memory of these good women, from respectable families, who become virtuous and noble disciples.

11

Female conversion

BHADDĀ KUṆḌALAKESĀ

Themes in the Pāli accounts

Female conversion

One of the most prominent features of Bhaddā Kuṇḍalakesā's biography is her conversion. As mentioned earlier, the account of her conversion varies significantly between the canonical and commentarial versions. However, one thing that does remain static between the different versions is Bhaddā Kuṇḍalakesā's accomplished ability—in both cases she is a skilled, wise debater who, in the first case has a realization and in the second is finally defeated in debate by one of the few more accomplished than herself—the eminent Sāriputta. In this chapter, I will discuss the broad question of female conversion from one samaṇa tradition to another in early Buddhism, and in particular look at this variation in the accounts of Bhaddā's conversion. Whatever the reason for the two different versions, it appears that the commentarial version can be linked thematically to south India. The sad fact is that we know very little about Buddhism in Tamiḻakam during the period in which the Pāli commentaries were transcribed/translated/collated/redacted, and, as Anne Monius notes of the commentators connected to south India, they looked 'towards Sri Lanka ...' (2001, 5) perhaps at least as much as they attempted to establish Buddhism in Tamiḻakam. However, one of the strongest links between the commentators writing in their south India monasteries in Pāli and the practice or adoption of Buddhism by the Tamil-speaking population around them is Bhaddā's story. Unlike any other of the biographies of Buddhist nuns in the Pāli canon, Bhaddā's biography seems to have been the inspiration for a Tamil text bearing her name—the *Kuṇṭalakēci*.[1] This now lost text links Bhaddā's biography, perhaps more than any other parts of the commentaries collated and composed in south India, with Buddhists in the Tamil-speaking world.[2]

Female conversion in the early texts

Although it is clear that women were part of the samaṇa tradition, there are no recorded examples of female (*samaṇī*) debaters, in the act of debating, in the early texts of the Pāli canon that reflect the account of Bhaddā in the commentaries. As discussed in Chapter 9, there is a question as to whether women who were part of the tradition did wander alone, but nonetheless there is sufficient evidence for female renouncers to assume they were a historical reality. There are various names for female renouncers, both within the Pāli texts and in contemporaneous literature, as noted by Jyväsjärvi (2007) such as *śramaṇī*/samaṇī, *parivrājikā/paribbājikā*, *tāpasinī/tāpasī*, *tapasvinī*, *yoginī*, *bhikṣukī*.[3] Jyväsjärvi has done a study of two of these—*parivrājikā/paribbājikā* and *pravrajitā*—and concludes that

[1] As noted in Chapter 11, and discussed by Richman (1988, 79–100), there is also a 'branch-story' that is a version of Kisāgotamī's biography in the Tamil *Maṇimēkalai*.

[2] Anne Monius does not think the phrase 'Tamil Buddhists' to be an appropriate one. She prefers that 'we speak of Buddhist thought and practices among native Tamiḻ speakers' (Monius as cited in Schalk and Nahl 2012, 25).

[3] I have chosen to call them renouncers, although other English words used for women following these lifestyles might be 'recluses',

the former of these is a term often used for those outside one's own tradition (2007, 89). The words 'samaṇī and paribbājikā are the ones used most often in the Pāli canon, although the *PED* (*Pali-English Dictionary*, Rhys_Davids and Stede 1921–5, hereafter *PED*) records only a few instances of each. Samaṇī is used once to refer to female renouncers of other traditions in a *Vinaya* passage. In this episode, the nun Caṇḍakālī quarrels with other nuns and sanctimoniously declares she is off to live with other female renouncers (samaṇī) who are 'conscientious, scrupulous and desirous of training' (*lajjiniyo kukkuccikā sikkhākāmā Vin.* IV.235). In another occurrence, samaṇī is used as more of an umbrella term, to apply to female renouncers of all persuasions, Buddhist included. In this verse, which appears in the *Therīgāthā* and *Saṃyutta-nikāya* in almost identical form, the nun to whom it is addressed—Cālā in the *Therīgāthā* and Sisupacālā in the *Saṃyutta-nikāya*—is asked:

> Following whose teaching do you shave your head? You look like a *samaṇī*, but do not approve of sectarians ...[4]

Śramaṇī is also used in this way in the Mahāsaṃghika-Lokottaravāda *Bhikṣuṇī Vinaya*, as an umbrella term for female renouncers, and in this case it is often used interchangeably with *bhikṣuṇī* (see, for example, Roth *niḥsargika-pācattika* 19, p. 178 and *pācattika* 81, p. 219). Instances of the use of paribbājikā include further examples from the Pāli *Vinaya* that mention other female renouncers, and there are rules made that such female renouncers should not be given food or robes meant for the Buddhist monks or nuns. Examples of this can be found in the stories relating to *pācattikas* 28 and 36 in the nuns' *Vinaya*, and *pācattika* 31 in the monks'. Pāli feminine forms of the other words for female renouncers such as tāpasī, and the feminine equivalents for *bhikkhaka* and *yogin* do not appear in the Pāli canon, and only appear infrequently in the commentaries.[5] However, this can be similarly

---

'wanderers', 'ascetics', and so on. I chose renouncers as this seems to be an action they all categorically do—that is, within whatever samaṇa tradition, they all 'go forth' from the home to homelessness.

4 *SN* I.133, *Thī* v. 183. *Kim nu uddisa muṇḍā si samaṇī viya dissasi, na ca rocasi pāsaṇḍe...*

5 Tāpasī however does occur in the *Mil.* (125).

noted of the male forms. According to the *PED* and Cone, *tāpasa* also does not appear in the canon, and *yogin* appears only once, in the *Theragāthā* (v. 947). Also, *bhikkhaka* appears only once in the canon, in the *SN* (I.182), but as a proper name of a brahmin, rather than to indicate a mendicant.

This trend, of there being few occurrences of names of female renouncers but not much more for males, is reflected in the ratio of female to male samaṇī/samaṇa debaters as recorded in the canon. While there are no examples of such women in the canon, there are also less of male counterparts being converted through debate than might be imagined. There are only a few examples of non-Jain samaṇa males being converted in this way.[6] The most frequently mentioned non-Jain samaṇa male convert may be the naked (*acela*) ascetic Kassapa, if indeed all three accounts of his conversion are about the same Kassapa.[7] In each of the three accounts, Kassapa is converted, but by different individuals in each case, and not always via debate. In the *Dīgha-nikāya* (8) version, he is converted in debate by the Buddha and in the *Majjhima-nikāya* (124) account he is inspired to convert by his former friend Bakkula, now a monk himself. In the *Saṃyutta-nikāya* version (IV.300–2), he is convinced by the householder Citta that he will make better progress on the path Citta is following than on the one he has trodden for thirty years, which has borne him no fruits.

While there are a fair few examples of Jain lay-followers being converted in debate, there are less of more committed Jain practitioners. A typical example of a Jain lay-follower being converted through debate can be found in the *Majjhima-nikāya*, in a discourse in which Prince Abhaya (*MN* 58), son of Bimbasāra, is coerced by Nātaputta.[8] The Jain leader tells Abhaya that if he can defeat the

6 I will use the term 'samaṇī'. I use the term 'debate' more broadly than Manné (see discussion later)—for Manné, a debate must entail a defeat and an acknowledgement of that. What is interesting in relation to Jains is that there can be acceptance of a good debate and a trajectory identical to those that lead to defeat and acknowledgement of it, but then no defeat occurring.

7 Malalasekera ([1937] 2003, 26) believes that two accounts are of the same person, but the third is a different Kassapa.

8 Nātaputta is the name for Mahāvīra in the canon.

Buddha in debate, news of this will spread and he will gain renown. Prince Abhaya is not at all sure how he might do this, so Nātaputta instructs him to put a 'two-horned question'(*ubhatokoṭikaṃ pañhaṃ MN* I.393) to the Buddha; that is, one which can be easily challenged irrespective of whether the opponent answers with a yes or no. The question, in this case, is whether Buddha utters a speech that is disagreeable and unwelcome.[9] Seduced by the desire for renown, Abhaya approaches Gotama and puts the question to him. The Buddha replies that there is no categorical, straightforward way to answer this question, and hearing the answer, Abhaya sees that Nātaputta's attempts to outsmart the Buddha are flawed. Following the full exposition on right speech then given by the Buddha, Abhaya requests to become a lay-follower.

Two examples of committed Jain adepts being converted through debate are Vappa (*AN* II.196) and Sīha (*AN* V.179 and *Vin.* I.233), who are both converted by the Buddha in the *Aṅguttara-nikāya*. Vappa may be a committed adept, although this is not entirely clear from the account of him, but Sīha is undoubtedly a firm disciple of Nātaputta, as he requests permission from his teacher to go and visit the other teacher, Gotama. Apart from these two examples, there are other examples of debates—both with Jains and other wanderers—during which conversion does not happen. An example is the case of Saccaka the Jain 'regarded by many as a saint' (*MN* 36). In the sutta in question, Saccaka debates with the Buddha, and in the end acknowledges the Buddha's deft ability, but remains unswayed, simply concluding the exchange by politely making his excuses—he is busy and has much to do—and leaving.

Although there are no examples in the canon of female debaters who match the person of Bhaddā in the commentarial accounts, there are a plethora of examples of women who have the potential to engage in samaṇa-style debate. As has been seen in Chapter 7, once a nun Dhammadinnā was renowned as a skilled debater, as someone who could speak about the dhamma well, and Khemā

9 This is two-horned because if the answer is yes, then the Buddha has positioned himself as no better than any ordinary mortal, but if the answer is no he can be challenged as to why he says certain things that could be argued to be disagreeable and unwelcome.

also shows her ability in this regard. Further, there are the well-known female debaters of the *Upaniṣads*, discussed in scholarship a great deal (most recently Lindquist 2008 and Black 2007b) and there are also examples of female Brahmin wanderers (see Dhand 2008) and of Jain women renouncers (from inscriptions as well as Buddhist texts). Also, as already discussed in Chapter 7, we have records on inscriptions of able and adept women, competent in memorization and recall. Then, there is also Kajañjalā, a classifier of the teachings, and other women with roles that suggest they were skilled in these samaṇa-type encounters from the *Ekottarika-āgama* list (see Anālayo 2013a). Further as well are the inscriptions discussed in Chapter 7 which denote that women were direct disciples of men, a situation which lends itself more to a suggestion of samaṇa-type relationships and lifestyles than do many of the other texts. Further there is Nanduttara, whose *Therīgāthā* verses are discussed in Chapter 8 and who, like Bhaddā, is described in the *Therīgāthā* commentary (the only one that recounts her biography) to have been converted by Mahā-Mogallāna in the same way as Bhaddā was by Sāriputta. As well, in another set of *Therīgāthā* verses Rohiṇī (271–90) seems set on taking up the samaṇa way, although does not herself appear to hold sectarian affiliation, instead praising samaṇas more broadly. It is her parents who advise that, if she wants to practice in this way, she is best off with Gotama.

Dundas (2003) and Brekke (2003) have noted that conversion from one samaṇa tradition to another would obviously not result in a significant change of lifestyle. Therefore conversion, they each argue, would not be the 'Pauline' type experience it is more usually understood to be. Instead, conversion between samaṇa traditions would simply be a case of changing one's views and following a different path laid out by a different teacher. Thus, while we have some examples of male samaṇas converting through debate, and evidence of different sorts of samaṇī women who have the potential to debate, it may also be the case that conversion in this sense—change to a different teacher and different teachings—may be implicit in sets of verses or suttas even when no other tradition is mentioned. In Bhaddā's verses there is no explicit mention of Jainism; this comes only in the colophon that tells us her name. Similarly, in the case of Jambuka in the *Theragāthā*, no other specific tradition is mentioned, and conversion is a simple and seemingly painless shift:

> For 55 years I wore dust and dirt; eating a meal once a month, I tore out my beard and hair.
>
> I stood on one leg, I avoided a seat; I ate dry dung; and I did not accept special food.
>
> Having done many such actions leading to a bad transition, being swept along by a great flood, I went to the Buddha as a refuge.
>
> Seeing the going to the refuge; see the essential rightness of the doctrine. The three knowledges have been obtained, the Buddha's teaching has been done.[10]

Although there is only the clear example of Bhaddā as a female samaṇī from another tradition being converted to become a disciple of the Buddha in the canon, it is possible to read other examples from the *Therīgāthā* as examples of conversion, although in these cases no other sect or tradition is mentioned. Other verses attributed to nuns in the *Therīgāthā* can and perhaps should be read in this way—as female renouncers and their conversion to the dispension of Gotama Buddha. While conversion is obvious when another tradition is mentioned or specifically referred to, this does not mean that we should fail to read conversion into a set of verses if it does

[10] *Tha* vv. 283–6, trans. Norman ([1969] 1997, 36). *Pañcapaññāsa vassāni rajojallam adhārayiṃ, bhuñjanto māsikaṃ bhattaṃ kesamassuṃ alocayiṃ. Ekapādena aṭṭhāsiṃ āsanaṃ parivajjayiṃ, sukkhagūthāni ca khādiṃ, uddesañ ca na sādiyaṃ. Etādisaṃ karitvāna bahuṃ duggatigāminaṃ vuyhamāno mahoghena buddhaṃ saraṇam āgamaṃ. Saraṇagamanaṃ passa passa dhammasudhammataṃ tisso vijjā anuppattā kataṃ buddhassa sāsanan ti.* In the *Tha-a* (II.118), after taking rebirth in hell for reviling another monk, Jambuka is then reborn into the human realm for five hundred lives as a Jain (*nigaṇṭha*) for having eaten dung. In the *Dhammapada* commentary (II.52–63) Jambuka is a naked ascetic who eats only dung because of bad deeds done in the past. In the present, he joins the Ajīvakas, who throw him out when they realize he eats dung, as they do not want to be associated with someone who does such a thing, thinking it will tarnish their reputation.

not contain any specific references to another tradition. However, the difficulty that arises when attempting to do this is that expressions of frustration with lack of progress in following the teachings can appear similar to possible accounts of conversion. Each case is concerned with lack of progress in practicing the path and the occluded, undifferentiated variable would be between practice of the right path and practice of the wrong one. For instance, compare the following two sets of verses on long-time wandering:

Another Sāmā

Twenty-five years have passed since I went forth. I am not aware of having obtained peace of mind at any time.

Without peace of mind, without self-mastery over the mind, then I reached a state of religious excitement, remembering the teaching of the conqueror.

Delighting in vigilance because of many painful objects, I have obtained the annihilation of craving. I have done the Buddha's teaching. Today is the seventh day since my craving was dried up.[11]

An unknown nun

It is twenty-five years since I went forth. Not even for the duration of a snap of the fingers have I obtained stilling of the mind.

Not obtaining peace of mind, drenched with desire for sensual pleasures, holding out my arms, crying out, I entered the vihāra.

I went up to a nun who was fit to be trusted by me. She taught me the doctrine, the elements of existence, the sense bases, the elements. I heard the doctrine for her and sat on one side. I know that I have lived before; I have purified the divine eye; and there is knowledge of the state of mind of others; I have purified the ear-element; I have realised supernormal power too; I have attained the annihilation of the

[11] *Thī* vv. 39–41, trans. Norman (Rhys Davids and Norman 1989, 173). *Paṇṇavīsati vassāni yato pabbajitāya me, nābhijānāmi cittassa samaṃ laddhaṃ kudācanaṃ. Aladdhā cetaso santiṃ citte avasavattini, tato saṃvegaṃ āpādiṃ saritvā jinasāsanaṃ. Bahūhi dukkhadhammehi appamādaratāya me, taṇhakkhayo anuppatto kataṃ buddhassa sāsanaṃ, ajja me sattamī ratti yato taṇha visositā.*

āsavas; I have realised these six supernormal knowledges; I have done the Buddha's teaching.[12]

We need to acknowledge that the text is a composite text, and be aware that the ordering of verses can change significantly during transmission processes. But with this in mind, with the text as it stands, the question begged by the second of these is—how could it be that a nun had been practicing the path laid out by the Buddha for twenty-five years and in all that time had not been taught the doctrine? This seems unlikely. Therefore, a more obvious reading of these verses by an unknown nun is to read them as an account of conversion; formerly, for twenty-five years, the woman was a wanderer of another tradition, and then finally she was introduced to the teachings of the Buddha and thereby was able to make great progress.[13] However, such a reading is confounded by the prior verse above, concerning frustration with practice. Even when following the right path, frustration can reach extremes and both a monk and nun in the *Theragāthā* and *Therīgāthā* respectively contemplate suicide, and come close to committing it, as a result (*Tha* vv. 405–10, *Thī* vv. 77–81). Also, the 'wrong path' can be an articulation of simply not practicing well, rather than following the teachings of another (see for example Mittakālī's ambiguous *Therīgāthā* verses).[14] Nonetheless, the possibility for reading the verses of the unknown nun (and other similar ones) as conversion remains.

12 *Thī* vv. 69–71, trans. Norman (Rhys Davids and Norman 1989, 178) with one change—replacing *bhikkhunī* with 'nun'). *Sā bhikkunim upāgacchiṃ yā me saddhāyikā ahu, sā me dhammaṃ adesesi khandhāyatanadhātuyo. Tassā dhammaṃ suṇitvāna ekamante upāvisiṃ, pubbenivāsaṃ jānāmi dibbacakkhuṃ visodhitaṃ. Ceto paricca ñāṇañ ca sotadhātu visodhitā, iddhi pi em sacchikatā patto me āsavakkhayo, cha me 'bhiññā sacchikatā kataṃ buddhassa sāsanaṃ.*

13 This is not how the verses are glossed in the *Thī-a*.

14 'I went forth in faith from the house to the houseless state, and wandered here and there, greedy for gain and honour. I missed the highest goal, and pursued the lowest goal. Gone under the mastery of defilements, I did not know the goal of the ascetic's state (*sāmaññattha*). I experienced religious excitement, as I sat in my little cell; thinking "I have entered upon the wrong road; I have come under the mastery of craving ..."' (Mittakālī's verses, *Thī* vv. 92–4, trans. Norman, [Rhys Davids and Norman 1989, 180]).

This account of possible conversion of the unknown nun strikes a similar cord to a conversation between Citta the householder and the naked ascetic Kassapa (mentioned above) in the *Saṃyutta-nikāya*. In this discourse, Citta and Kassapa are reunited after thirty years. During that time, the naked ascetic has not achieved any notable religious accomplishment, whereas Citta the householder has, by his diligent practice of the path outlined by the Buddha. In lamenting this, Kassapa recalls:

> In these thirty years since I went forth, householder, I have not attained any superhuman distinction in knowledge and vision worthy of the noble ones, no dwelling in comfort, but only nakedness, and a shaven head, and the brush for cleaning my seat.[15]

Citta, on the contrary, though a layman, has made great progress by following the path laid out by the Buddha. After hearing of Citta's ability in meditative absorption, Kassapa desired to 'go forth in the *dhamma* and discipline'.

Conversion in the Apadāna and other late canonical works

The *Apadāna*, although consisting of (auto)biographies, does not focus on, or appear to be particularly concerned with, conversion. By the time of the *Apadāna*, the notion of kamma had become more prevalent than it appears in the sutta collection, and as such the biographies are less about conversion to discipleship under the Buddha than they are about tracing the trajectory of past actions to present consequences. The biographies often begin at the time of Padumuttara Buddha, and in some it is almost that a prior or preconverted state is assumed. That is to say, the person in question makes an offering to Padumuttara as if it were a simple, everyday occurrence, and there is no mention of conversion. This is far from always being the case, but can be seen in for example, the apadāna

[15] *SN* IV.300, trans. Bodhi 2000, 1328. *Imehi kho me gahapati tiṃsamattehi vasehi pabbajitassa natthi koci uttari manussadhammā alamariyañāṇadassanaviseso adhigato bhavissati phāsuvihāro aññatra naggeyyā ca muṇḍeyyā ca pāvāḷanipphoṭanāya cāti* with Bhikkhu Bodhi's two emendations according to the Burmese and Sinhala script editions of *SN* (2000, 1447n325).

of Sattuppalamālikāya, who offers garlands to a Buddha (*Ap*. 517–8), and with the monk Cuḷa Panthaka, who offered flowers to Buddha Padumuttara when he was living in the Himalayas (*Ap*. 58). Apart from the suggestion of something akin to a pre-converted state, other assumptions are also made by the author(s) of the text. These are that, first, if one lives during the era of a Buddha, it would be natural to go and listen to a discourse, despite the fact that one may not be a devotee. Second, that once one heard a teaching by a Buddha one would naturally be converted. That conversion would naturally and instantaneously occur in this way is so completely assumed that mention of it, or even a passing comment that faith arose upon first hearing the Buddha teach, is often left out of the narrative altogether, although obviously implied. This transformative effect of listening to a Buddha's discourse is made clear in the apadāna of Bhaddā Kāpilāni, which notes that such discourses 'cause the destruction of all suffering' (*Ap*. 578 *sabbadukkhakkhayāvahaṃ*). Similarly, when Kisāgotamī hears the teaching of Padumuttara, she comments that such teachings 'produce happiness and peace in the heart' (*Ap*. 564 *cittasantisukhāvahaṃ*). Such assumptions are interesting because they reveal a great deal about the popularity of Buddhism during the composition period of the later canonical works. There is a sense here of something akin to innate discipleship, coupled with an intimation of innate credence to teachings of Buddhas. With this as the backdrop to the biographical accounts, conversion in the present life becomes incidental. Conversion in the present life does happen as part of the narrative tract in some cases, which perhaps is an example here of already circulating narrative accounts of prominent monks and nuns being incorporated into the text's autobiographical accounts. Bhaddā's own case is a good example of this. Bhaddā, as is the case with many, heard a teaching by Padumuttara Buddha and was converted upon hearing. Nonetheless, although already converted in a previous life, her present life account includes a subsequent conversion.

Conversion in the commentaries

Similarly, in the commentaries, there is no particular focus on conversion, which again seems to be secondary to kammically delineated fate. For example, a typical way in which what we might call religious conversion is envisaged in the *Therīgāthā* commentary is as in this passage about the nun Muttā:

> She too having acquired the necessary moral qualifications under former Buddhas and having accumulated good deeds in various lives, was born during this Buddha era in the district of Kosala.... When she came of age, her parents gave her to a certain hunchbacked brahmin. Not approving of household life with him, she obtained permission from him to go forth and devoted herself to the gaining of insight.[16]

One thing that does appear to be discernible in relation to conversion stories of women in the commentaries, but discernible with a caveat, is that women do seem to defer to men more, and have less agency themselves. If we compare the stories of the six nuns discussed in this volume, we can see that the three cases that involved conversion by the Buddha remain the same, while the other three, in their commentarial versions, now more fully involve a man. In Bhaddā Kuṇḍalakesā's case, as I am arguing in this chapter overall, this does not appear to be an attempt to make her subservient to a male, but in the other two cases, male agency in women's lives is at least foregrounded. As argued in Chapter 7 in the case of Dhammadinnā, there is some loss of agency. In the commentarial accounts, Dhammadinnā goes forth because she is abjectly rejected by her husband. In Uppalavaṇṇā's case (Chapter 12), in the *Apadāna*, her many suitors do not tempt her towards the world of pleasures and she decides herself to renounce whereas, in the commentarial accounts it is her father that prompts her to leave the world. Her father, worried that if he gives her in marriage to one of the

[16] *Ayam pi purimabuddhesu katādhikārā tattha tattha bhave kusalaṃ upacinitvā imasmiṃ buddhuppāde kosalajanapade...taṃ vayappattakāle mātāpitaro ekassa khujjabrāhmaṇassa adaṃsu. Sā tena gharāvāsaṃ arocantī taṃ anujānāpetvā pabbajitvā vipassanāya kammaṃ karoti* (*Thī-a* 13 [trans. Pruitt 1999, 23]). Although here Muttā has to ask permission from her husband to abandon the household life and her role as his wife, she is not conceptualized as so subservient to him that either *a*) she is too submissive to even take her leave of him in the first place or *b*) she lacks awareness of her own ambitions.

suitors the others will be displeased with him, asks her instead to become a nun, and she agrees.[17]

This addition of male involvement in the conversion process is evident in other narrative accounts in the commentaries as well. Dhammā, whose biography is recounted in the *Therīgāthā* commentary wants to go forth but her husband does not allow it. Abhayamātā who, although in her apadāna simply makes an offering of alms and through that is predicted to become a nun by Tissa Buddha, in the *Therīgāthā* commentary is converted by her son, who teaches her the dhamma, and this is her route to gaining faith. Vimalā, the courtesan, in the *Therīgāthā* commentary goes forth out of shame and fear, having been castigated for her wayward life by Mahā-Moggallāna, whom she is said to have tried to seduce. The three sisters of Sāriputta, Cālā, Upacālā, and Sisupacālā, mentioned in Chapter 10, follow their brother into the Order thinking 'surely that *dhamma* and discipline is not inferior, going forth is not inferior in which our noble [brother] has gone forth'.[18] And, as above, Nanduttarā, for whom there is no Pāli apadāna, is converted in debate by Mahā-Moggallāna, in the very same way that Bhaddā Kuṇḍalakesā is by Sāriputta.

Although there is evidence of increased male involvement in female conversion in the commentaries, the overall purview of the commentaries on conversion seems to be that it is just not really that important; that is, how it happens is incidental, such that whether one is converted by a male or female (or both or neither) is really by-the-by. The increase in male involvement appears to be likewise incidental and rather than there being an agenda concerning women that is adhered to and enacted in the commentaries, as was evident in Chapter 7, and has been indicated at other times in this volume, this does not appear to be the case with regard to conversion on the whole.

[17] This same narrative trope is used in the stories of women in the *Avadānaśataka*—see Muldoon-Hules (2013, 192–220). In these stories, there is male involvement in conversion, but also female agency, as the women often choose to go forth in order that their father does not suffer at the hands of spurned suitors.

[18] *Thī-a* (159) ... *na hi nūna so orako dhammavinayo na sā orikā pabbajjā yattha amhākaṃ ayyo pabbajito...*

This is evident in accounts of the nuns Sakulā and Soṇā. In both cases their conversion is detailed differently over the range of texts. In her *Therīgāthā* verses, Sakulā is the only nun said to be converted by a monk. In her apadāna, the involvement of the unnamed monk is absent, and in this account, she sees the Buddha and from that has an inclination to go forth. In the *Therīgāthā* commentary, once again, the monk appears and teaches her and through this is she is converted. In the case of Soṇā, her accounts always involve her family, but the husband's involvement changes in each case. In her *Therīgāthā* verses, she is said to have had ten sons and then, when old, to have approached a nun. In the *Apadāna*, her husband, who is not mentioned in the *Therīgāthā* verses, goes forth and she follows him into the Order. In the *Therīgāthā* commentary, her husband is mentioned to have gone forth again, but this time he is not the cause of her volition to renounce. In this case it is her sons. After her husband's going forth, she remains a householder to bring up her children. However, once grown, although they respect her for a short time, the children begin very soon to treat Soṇā with contempt, and it is this—her sons' contempt for their mother—that motivates her to go forth. The *Aṅguttara-nikāya* commentary's account of Soṇā is similar to this, but lacks any mention of her husband at all, and this time she goes forth again out of despondency, it would appear, at the lack of respect her children show her.

Bhaddā Kuṇḍalakesā's conversion

Overall, in the *Apadāna* and the biographies as they appear in the extant commentaries, conversion is envisioned differently to how it is configured in the early canon. It is interesting to note then, that the account of Bhaddā's conversion in the commentaries reflects more the accounts in the early canon. Although it is possible to speculate about the reason for the two different recensions of Bhaddā's conversion, the extant evidence raises more questions than it answers. As noted in the introduction to this volume, there are three known recensions to the *Apadāna*, although the full text is only available in the one recension that makes up the European edition. It is possible, therefore, that the account now only in the commentaries was originally in another recension of the *Apadāna*. Further, although the biographies in the commentaries are most often reproduced accounts, in cases such as this we do not know when or by whom a change might have been made—that is, it may have been Buddhaghosa himself, or the earlier Sinhala commentators. The extant textual record does not furnish us with any more clues than this. Similarly, although it seems that there is a link between Bhaddā's biography and south India, such an assertion also remains speculative. As mentioned, Bhaddā is linked to south India through the lost Tamil work, and the admixture of themes (in the commentarial accounts) of a female heroine who outsmarts her husband, and a Jain converted via debate, may have been a combination that was appealing in the south Indian context.

Peter Schalk has examined the evidence for Buddhism in south India, and from the few remaining artefacts, he concludes that there is no evidence of Buddhism in south India prior to the fourth century. In contrast, Vēluppiḷḷai finds evidence for a Jain presence prior to this time (Schalk and Vēluppiḷḷai 2002, on the Jains, see 167–93). As Monius notes, between the composition of classical Tamil literature (second to fourth centuries) and the development of Hindu *bhakti* literature from the seventh century 'the majority of poetic works produced in Tamil were written by either Buddhists or Jains' (2001, 3). However, overall it appears that the Buddhists of south India did not fare well within this changed socio-political milieu, which was far removed from the post-Asokan era of privilege and prestige for Buddhists. The Pallavas, who ruled from the fourth to the ninth century did not favour Buddhism, and a Pallava court text, the *Mattavilāsaprahasana,* dated to the seventh century, depicted Buddhism as a religion in decline (Schalk and van Nahl 2012, 30). In this new setting, there may have been a shift back to an emphasis on debate as a means of conversion, which is suggested by the later texts—the *Maṇimēkalai* and *Nīlakēci* (see below), but cannot be verified with regards to earlier periods (see Vēluppiḷḷai 1997, 223–40).

In this context, the role of the south India monasteries in which many commentaries were composed is far from clear. As Monius writes:

> Evidence of a different sort for an early monastic Buddhist presence in the Tamil region—evidence that is similarly incomplete and difficult to interpret—can be found in the oldest commentarial literature of the Theravāda tradition composed in Pāli. ...clearly, there must have existed flourishing Buddhist monasteries looking towards Sri Lanka and the Mahāvihāra for authoritative guidance, yet were these monks and monasteries all Tamil-speaking? Were Tamil commentaries produced there alongside the Pāli? ...Did such monasteries enjoy royal patronage? Does the existence of such monasteries in the era of the three great Pāli commentators imply a Buddhist monastic presence in the Tamil region earlier than the fourth century? The historical record is maddeningly incomplete. (2001, 5–6)

Nonetheless, if there was a shift back to conversion via debate in this changed religio-political environment, this may have made Bhaddā's commentarial account an attractive story to tell.

Female debaters in Tamil texts

Subsequent to the commentarial accounts, the story of Bhaddā appears to have become a popular story for Tamil-speaking Buddhists. A now lost Tamil text, the *Kuṇṭalakēci*, appears to be another version of Bhaddā's story, in which Bhaddā seems to have been cast more fully as an erudite expositor of Buddhist doctrine.[19] Although the text is now lost, eighty-two verses of it are extant in the *Nīlakēci*, the Jain rejoinder to it, and there are about a hundred verses of it is various Tamil commentaries (Monius, email 2011). Schüler called the *Nīlakēci* a 'refutation of Kuṇḍalakasī's philosophy' (2009, 35), and notes the emphasis in the Jain text on contest and debate, centred on the female protagonist, Nīlakēci.[20] If indeed one were to extrapolate from the content of the *Nīlakēci* (the response) as to the nature of the lost work, one might well imagine

[19] While some scholars assume a connection between the protagonist of the Tamil text and Bhaddā, Monius remains sceptical. The first firm textual evidence for the connection between the two is in the work of Tivakara Mamunivar, a commentator from perhaps the fourteenth century (email communication 2011).

[20] In the *Nīlakēci*, the heroine is 'defeated and becomes a disciple of a Jain ascetic, Muṉicantiraṉ' (Schüler 2009, 36).

Kuṇṭalakēci to have been depicted as a highly competent expositor of sharp and well-reasoned arguments in support of Buddhist doctrine. The *Maṇimēkalai*, the second Buddhist work written in Tamil that was later to come to be known as one of the two main Buddhist Tamil works, alongside the *Kuṇṭalakēci* (Monius 2001), also has a female protagonist, and as Anne Monius has noted, this became commonplace in Tamil literature:

> Virtually all Tamil narrative literature until the substantial influence of Sanskrit literary forms begins in earnest in the twelfth century features heroines over heroes; the classical poetic anthologies—even those dedicated to battle and war—more often than not speak from a perspective gendered female. In other words, what is so striking about the *therī/bhikkunī* in Pāli literature is simply commonplace expectation in ninth-century Tamil literary culture. (Email 2011)

The *Maṇimēkalai* has been tentatively dated to the sixth century, although previous attempts at dating it have ranged from the second to the tenth centuries. It is recognized that the text has earlier and later parts to it (Vēluppiḷḷai 1997, 223). The *Kuṇṭalakēci* is, of course, much more difficult to date, but Vēluppiḷḷai notes that the *Nīlakēci* 'disputes the same philosophical systems as found in the *Maṇimēkalai*' (1997, 24).

Further to this, Leslie Orr has noted that in some inscriptions from Tamil Nadu, especially a set dated to the eighth century, there are records of Jain female teachers (*kuratti*, a term which may be related to the Sanskrit *guru;* 1998, 195 and n19). In her study of these inscriptions, Orr also mentions an eighth century statue of an apparent noted female teacher, similar to counterpart male images (1998, 190). She notes that this emphasis on female teachers in the inscriptions does not accord with Jain texts:

> Jain texts prescribe that nuns were to be dependent on male teachers for her ordination, in establishing penances, and for protection, education and supervision. Certain texts were not to be studied by nuns, nor were nuns expected to engage in debate. (Orr 1998, 190)

The statue and set of inscriptions from one area do show that, at least in some parts of Tamil Nadu in the medieval period, there was a fairly strong presence of female Jain teachers. It may well have been the case that the change to Bhaddā's conversion account was part of something that developed into a more fully blown, (relatively) positive situation for women. The new image of the illustrious female debater, Bhaddā, may have captured the imagination of the Buddhist and Jains in Tamil-speaking south India, as it prefigures some literary and epigraphic evidence for strong female role models in the Buddhism and Jainism of medieval south India.

***

Although there are no explicit examples of female samaṇīs being converted by debate in the Pāli canon, there is ample evidence for the existence of women samaṇīs. Bhaddā is named as a female convert from Jainism, and takes her place amongst a select group of male Jain adepts who are converted, and converted through debate. Later canonical works and the commentaries, inscribed with the indelible ink of the kamma doctrine, occlude the importance of conversion in favour of kammic trajectory. However, unlike the *Apadāna* account, the version of Bhaddā's account in the commentaries is reminiscent of the canonical conversion accounts.

Evidence speculatively suggests that in the south Indian milieu there was a move back to conversion via debate, which may have made Bhaddā's commentarial account an attractive and popular tale to tell, especially as this combines in her biography with a portrayal of woman who outsmarts her morally incorrigible husband. Bhaddā's story appears to have been an inspiration for a later Tamil work that was likely part of a genre that depicts women as sharp, skilled and articulate debaters. It also prefigures other evidence from a strong presence of female teachers within medieval south Indian Jain communities.

12

Female characteristics

UPPALAVAṆṆĀ

Themes in the Pāli accounts

Female characteristics

With such a range of depictions of Uppalavaṇṇā in Pāli accounts of her, there are many themes that could be picked up and explored: the issue of her verses as co-wife in the *Therīgāthā*, her potential blood relationship to the Buddha, how she captivates the bodhisatta in many jātakas with her beauty, and how she teaches him in others. However, what I will focus on in this chapter is an examination of female characteristics in both the canon and the commentaries. I will argue that Uppalavaṇṇā, who herself remains good and virtuous throughout her many and manifold depictions (with only one exception), exemplifies the female characteristics more often met with in the canon, while the jealous wives who feature in her biography epitomize the worst a woman can be—a type of scheming and plotting woman often found in folkloric literature (not only within Buddhism, but also outside of it). While women in the canon are more likely to be teachers, or esteemed in some way or another, just as Uppalavaṇṇā is in her classification as a chief disciple and exemplar for others, as we saw in Chapter 7 on Dhammadinnā, there are rarely new depictions of nuns (or other women) as teachers in the commentaries. Alternately, just as there are many stories of scheming and manipulative women in the commentaries, like the jealous wives who plot against Uppalavaṇṇā, portrayals of women who doggedly set out to manipulate a situation to their advantage are much less common in the canon, really only appearing in one late canonical text, the *Petavatthu*.

Positive characteristics of women in the canon

In the canonical literature, Uppalavaṇṇā is esteemed in two ways explicitly; first, she is included, as the others in this volume are, on the list of distinguished nuns in the canon. As noted by Anālayo in his study and translation of the Chinese *Ekottarika-āgama* version of the list, the list demonstrates that, as these women are said to be foremost (within the community), there would have been other nuns with these same qualities (Anālayo 2013a, 112). Second, Uppalavaṇṇā is also said in the canon to be one of the two chief nuns, along with Khemā. This is stated in the *Aṅguttara* and *Saṃyutta-nikāyas*, as well as in the *Buddhavaṃsa*, and this appears to be the basis for her becoming one of the 'intimate community' (as Walters calls them, 2003, 18ff.), who, in the *Jātakatthavaṇṇanā*, are reborn alongside the Buddha in many previous lives. This group of intimates include his nuclear family—Rāhulamātā (Yasodharā), and Rāhula—as well as his attendant and cousin Ānanda, his two chief monks, Sāriputta and Moggallāna, and the other chief nun, Khemā. The group also sometimes includes his mother, father, and stepmother.

As a chief nun, Uppalavaṇṇā is declared an exemplar of the teachings, and someone who the other nuns could look to emulate. This exemplary status is recorded in two identical passages in the *Aṅguttara-nikāya* and the *Saṃyutta-nikāya*. In the latter, the Buddha proffers that a mother, who is a lay follower, should instruct a daughter thus:

> 'But if, dear, you go forth from the household life into homelessness, you should become like bhikkhunīs Khemā and Uppalavaṇṇā'—[and the Buddha then adds] for this is the standard and criterion for my female disciples who are bhikkhunīs, that is, Khemā and Uppalavaṇṇā.[1]

Apart from being an example to others and a distinguished nun herself, there are only a few specific personal qualities associated with Uppalavaṇṇā. As discussed in Chapter 7, and mentioned elsewhere, many of the biographies of the nuns seem to be somewhat divorced from their exemplary qualities and characteristics. This is not always the case; at times a certain quality shines through from the pages, such as in the case of Bhaddā Kuṇḍalakesā and her quick witted nature. In some instances, the outstanding quality defines the nun, such as with Dhammadinnā, as in most accounts she is a distinguished teacher, although this is not depicted as fully as it might be in her *Apadāna* biography. At other times, as can be seen in this volume with the biographies of Paṭācārā and Kisāgotamī, the distinguished characteristic declared to be that of the nun in question is no longer part of their biography. In Uppalavaṇṇā's case, the relationship between her outstanding quality—her supernormal powers—and her biographies is tenuous. Uppalavaṇṇā's male counterpart on the *Aṅguttara-nikāya* list, Moggallāna, on the other hand, is clearly distinguished for his supernormal powers in various parts of the canon, such as in the humorous *Udāna* tale of Sāriputta's headache. In this instance, Sāriputta is sitting meditating in the open air (and in so doing exemplifying one of his own distinguished characteristics) and Moggallāna, through his supernormal powers, sees a demon

[1] *SN* II.236 (trans. Bhikkhu Bodhi 2000, 689). *Sace kho tvam ayye agārasmā anagāriyam pabbajasi tādisā āyye bhavāhi yādisā khemā ca bhikkhunī uppalavaṇṇā cāti. Sā bhikkhave tulā etam pamāṇaṃ mama sāvikānaṃ bhikkhunīnaṃ yadidaṃ khemā ca bhikkhunī uppalavaṇṇā ca.* And the *AN* passage is: *Saddhā bhikkhave bhikkhunī evaṃ sammā āyācamānā āyāceyya tādisā homi yādisā khemā ca bhikkhunī uppalavaṇṇā cāti. Esā bhikkhave tulā etam pamāṇaṃ mama sāvikānaṃ bhikkhunīnaṃ yadidaṃ khemā ca bhikkhunī uppalavaṇṇā cāti* (*AN* I.88, II.164).

(*yakkha*) come along and give Sāriputta an almighty thwack on the head. When Sāriputta arises from his contemplative state Moggallāna asks him is he is alright, and Sāriputta replies that he had a slight headache (*Ud.* 4.4, 39). Uppalavaṇṇā, on the other hand, is not often demonstrated to be in possession of her own supernormal powers, however, she is linked to supernormal realms within her biographical accounts, through her many different rebirths, such as her arising as a nāga princess, birth in a lotus flower, lotus begetting footsteps, and her many manifestations as various goddesses in the *Jātakatthavaṇṇanā*. Two of her *Therīgāthā* verses mention her powers, and these relate to the incident in which she is said to have offered to perform a miracle for the Buddha.[2]

Positive characteristics of women in the commentaries

Just as Uppalavaṇṇā typifies the esteemed women of the canon, both in being distinguished in certain qualities and characteristics, and in her declared status as an exemplary nun, so too, on the whole, with only one exception, she typifies the esteemed women who inhabit the commentarial literature. In the *Therīgāthā* and *Aṅguttara-nikāya* commentarial biography of her, she remains a good and virtuous woman, despite her ill-treatment at the hands of other women. In the face of such hostility from the jealous wives, she neither retaliates nor seeks revenge, but unassumingly tries to resolve the situation as best she can and, in so doing, is rewarded for her efforts and eventually reunited with her lover, the king. This humble virtue she exhibits is characteristic of good women of the commentaries.

[2] In the *Thī-a*, she offers to perform a miracle if the Buddha will permit her. The text does not comment on the Buddha's reply, but seems to assume consent as then declares she 'roared the lion's roar' (*sīhanādaṃ nadi*), and the Buddha took this as an occasion for placing the nuns in order, and affirmed her as foremost of those with supernormal powers (*Thī-a* 195). In the *Dhp-a* she offers to perform a miracle, but the Buddha declines her offer, as he does with offers from other disciples (*Dhp-a* III.211–12).

Although not always and categorically the case, many of the nuns of the canon have become sacred, revered women of the past, in some way akin to 'saints', and this role as positive and 'good' women is extended into the commentarial literature initially and most significantly through the reproduction of the *Apadāna* biographies, and then—and this especially in Uppalavaṇṇā's case—through other stories. However, what constitutes a 'good' woman changes, such that the general largesse of the liberal characteristics of the nuns illustrated in the canon is replaced by a more constricted and conservative view of the 'good' woman in the commentaries.

What constitutes the social construct of the good woman in the commentaries—whether she be an exemplary nun, ideal wife or noble queen—can be illuminated by a review of the past lives of Uppalavaṇṇā in the *Jātakatthavaṇṇanā* and the characters she portrays within them. In all cases but one—with the exception of those instances in which she is mentioned at the end but has no role in the jātaka—Uppalavaṇṇā in her past life is benevolent, virtuous, intelligent, altruistic, servile, and at times the epitome of feminine beauty. The following is a list of her main roles:[3]

1. A caring mother: In the *Kharādiya Jātaka* (15, I.159) she was a deer, the sister of the bodhisatta, and a mother with an unruly son. In the *Tipallatthamiga Jātaka* (16, I.160) she was the mother of Rāhula, then born as a stag, and she is depicted as a caring mother, eager for her son to do well. In the *Kaṇha Jātaka* (29, I.193) she is an old woman with the bodhisatta as a bull that she reared like her own child, and is the most loving and caring of mothers, even though her 'child' in this case is not her own species. As the goddess of the sea called Maṇimekhalā in the *Mahājanaka Jātaka* (539, VI.30), she saved the bodhisatta

3 In the few examples not included here she is a character of a similar ilk to this fourfold typology—such as the tree-spirit (*nibbattadevatā*) in the *Jāgarajā Jātaka* (414, III.403) from whom the bodhisatta gains merit. There is also some overlap between these types—in some instances, for example, she is both an upholder of dhamma and a virtuous goddess.

and is said to have taken him to Mithilā on her breast, as if he were her dear child (*ure nippajjāpetvā piyaputtakaṃ ādaya*). As the goddess Bahusodarī in the *Sāma Jātaka* (540, VI.68), she is said to have been a mother to the bodhisatta formerly, and this is what inspires her to help him.

2. An altruistic female: In the *Mudulakkhanā Jātaka* (66, I.302), the bodhisatta, as a sage (*isi*), is bewitched upon sight of Uppalavaṇṇā and is overcome with desire. She helps him to forget his infatuation by being purposefully demanding and thus vanquishing his lust. As the doe sister of the bodhisatta in the *Rohantamiga Jātaka* (501, IV.413) she puts his welfare before her own. The bodhisatta is caught in hunter's trap, but she will not leave him, even at fear of her own life.
3. An upholder of the teachings: As the courtesan in the *Kurudhamma Jātaka* (276, II.365), she keeps the five precepts, and when questioned as to whether she does, is proven to be one of virtue. As the brahmin's daughter in the *Uraga Jātaka* (354, III.162), she was one of the family who did not weep at the death of the son, who understand that from the perspective of the teachings, it is pointless to do so. In the *Tesakuna Jātaka* (521, V.109), she was one of three birds, along with Sāriputta and the bodhisatta, who teach the king about righteous kingship. As the goddess of the parasol in the *Mūgapakkha Jātaka* (538, VI.1), although she features only briefly, in a pivotal scene she instructs the bodhisatta on how to rid himself of the burden of kingship and live an ascetic life.
4. A virtuous and knowing goddess: As the goddess Siridevī in the *Sirikālakaṇṇi Jātaka* (382, III.257), she is the good and righteous one, in comparison with the other goddesses. Again, as the goddess in the *Bhisapuppha Jātaka* (392, III.307), although challenging to the bodhisatta, she is benevolent. In the *Sankha Jātaka* (442, IV.15), she is a compassionate goddess of the sea, as she is again in the in the *Kiñchanda Jātaka* (511, V.7), and again as Maṇimekhalā in the *Mahājanaka Jātaka* (539, VI.30). As goddess Bahusodarī in the *Sāma Jātaka* (540, VI.68), she is able to repair and restore a somewhat desperate situation with the use of her powers.

Negative characteristics of women in the canon

In the Pāli canon, the only real examples of something akin to the scheming and plotting, jealous wives in Uppalavaṇṇā's biography and other similar women of the commentaries are found in the *Petavatthu*.[4] Apart from that, there are examples of, not named women, but types of women who apparently seek to ensnare men. There are also examples of conniving nuns in the *Vinaya*, who try to flout the rules, but these are matched by stories of equally scheming monks. There are some references to general negative female characteristics, some of which again are matched by similar references for men, but lacking in the canon overall are the characterizations of women as debase (*pacchimikā*) and lowly (*lāmikā*) that are not uncommon in the *Jātakatthavaṇṇanā*, and are also found in the *Dhammapada* commentary. Before looking at the depictions of formerly jealous women in the *Petavatthu*, now made ghoulish by their envy and scheming, I will look at some of these other apparent examples of negative characteristics of women.

First, in relation to female sexuality, a rhetoric has become established within modern scholarship on early Indian Buddhism, and most especially on the Pāli canon, that women are often—if not invariably—portrayed as Salome-type temptresses, whose sole intention is to wrench men away from the path of practice. I have challenged the pervasiveness of this ideation within the Pāli canon elsewhere, citing examples which counter the more commonly presented quotations (Collett 2013b). However, while I do deny the pervasiveness of this characterization of women in the Pāli canon, I do not deny that the characterization exists. The following quote from the *Aṅguttara Nikāya* is a good example. This passage

4 A few other tenuous examples exist—such as the example of the servant Kālī, from the *Majjhima-nikāya*, who decides to test her mistress. The mistress Vedehikā is well-known to be kind and gentle and her servant, Kālī, deciding to push her to see how deep her calm demeanour goes, constantly gets up late and shirks her duties. Vedehikā eventually becomes so displeased that she hits Kālī over the head, causing her to bleed. Kālī does this, it would appear, just because she cannot quite believe a person would be kind and gracious through and through (*MN* 21, I.125–6).

appears twice in the *Aṅguttara Nikāya*, but not in identical form (*AN* I.1–2 and III.68). In the first instance, there is a parallel passage for women and how they become besotted with men, but in the second instance, there is only one passage, with women perceived as the problem:

> I do not see, Monks, even one other form so enticing, so desirable, so intoxicating, so binding, so infatuating, such a hindrance to winning the supreme peace from bondage than, Monks, the form of a woman. Monks, those who cling to a woman's form—impassioned, greedy, enslaved, infatuated, attached—they grieve for a long time, besotted by the female form... (*AN* III.68)[5]

Although passages like this can be found within the canon, much less often cited and referenced are passages which balance the sexuality of men and women, such as the *Saññogasutta*, again in the *Aṅguttara Nikāya*. This sutta talks about how a woman, aware of her femaleness, is attracted to and interested in a man and his maleness, and vice versa, employing exactly the same language in the converse. As a teaching on how men and women are bound (*saññoga*) to the world, the sutta says:

> Monks, a woman attends inwardly to her feminine faculties; her feminine charms, manners, ways, desires, her female voice and feminine adornments. She is excited by that, takes pleasure in that. Being excited and pleased she attends outwardly to masculine faculties; masculine charms, manners, ways, desires, the male voice and male adornments. She is excited by that, takes pleasure in that. Being excited and pleased, she longs to be bonded with what is outside her, longs for

5 *Nāhaṃ bhikkhave aññaṃ ekarūpaṃ pi samanupassāmi evaṃ rajanīyaṃ evaṃ kamanīyaṃ evaṃ madanīyaṃ evaṃ bandhanīyaṃ evaṃ mucchanīyaṃ evaṃ antarāyakaraṃ anuttarassa yogakkhemassa adhigamāya yathayidaṃ bhikkhave itthirūpaṃ. Itthirūpe bhikkhave sattā rattā giddhā gadhitā mucchitā ajjhopannā te dīgharattaṃ socanti itthirūpavasānugā...* This passage is not found in parallel texts to the *Aṅguttara-nikāya*, so is only extant in the Pāli version. Bhikkhu Bodhi, in the introduction to his translation of the text, notes that many of the suttas in the *AN* that are unfavourable towards women 'do not have counterparts in the Chinese Āgamas' (Bodhi 2012, 61).

whatever happiness and joy arises based on the bond. Monks, a woman taking pleasure in her femininity goes into bondage in relation to men. In this way, Monks, a woman does not overcome her femininity.

Monks, a man attends inwardly to his masculine faculties; his male charms, manners, ways, desires, his masculine voice and male adornments. He is excited by that, takes pleasure in that. Being excited and pleased he attends outwardly to feminine faculties; female charms, manners, ways, desires, the female voice and feminine adornments. He is excited by that, takes pleasure in that. Being excited and pleased, he longs to be bonded with what is outside himself, longs for whatever happiness and joy arises based on the bond. Monks, a man taking pleasure in his masculinity goes into bondage in relation to women. In this way, Monks, a man does not overcome his masculinity. (*AN* IV.57–8).[6]

Although women can be and are characterized as sexually manipulative in the canon, this is not the only model of female sexuality that can be located in the corpus. In addition to the above passage which indicates an equity between male and

6 *Itthi bhikkhave ajjhattaṃ itthindriyaṃ manasikaroti itthikuttaṃ itthākappaṃ itthividhaṃ itthicchandaṃ itthissaraṃ itthālaṃkāraṃ. Sā tattha rajjati tatrābhiramati sā tattha rattā tatrābhiratā bahiddhā purisindriyaṃ manasikaroti purisakuttaṃ purisākappaṃ purisavidhaṃ purisacchandaṃ purisassaraṃ purisālaṃkāraṃ. Sā tattha rajjati tatrābhiramati sā tattha rattā tatrābhiratā bahiddhā saṃyogaṃ ākaṅkhati yañ c'assā saṃyogapaccayā uppajjati sukhaṃ somanassaṃ tañ ca ākaṅkhati. Itthatte bhikkhave abhiratā sattā purisesu saṃyogaṃ gatā. Evaṃ kho bhikkhave itthi itthattaṃ nātivattati. Puriso bhikkhave ajjhattaṃ purisindriyaṃ manasikaroti purisakuttaṃ purisākappaṃ purisvidhaṃ purisacchandaṃ purisassaraṃ purisālaṃkāraṃ. So tattha rajjati tatrābhiramati so tattha ratto tatrābhirato bahiddhā itthindriyaṃ manasikaroti itthikuttaṃ itthākappaṃ itthividhaṃ itthicchandaṃ itthissaraṃ itthālaṃkāraṃ. So tattha rajjati tatrābhiramati so tattha ratto tatrābhirato bahiddhā saṃyogaṃ ākaṅkhati yañ c'assa saṃyogapaccayā uppajjati sukhaṃ somanassaṃ tañ ca ākaṅkhati. Purisatte bhikkhave abhirato satto itthīsu saṃyogaṃ gato. Evaṃ kho bhikkhave puriso purisattaṃ nātivattati.* (The phrases 'attends inwardly to her feminine faculties' and 'attends outwardly to masculine faculties', and vice versa for males, are Thanissaro's [Thanissaro Bhikkhu, 'Access to Insight', 4 July 2010, http://www.accesstoinsight.org/tipitaka/an/an07/an07/an07.048, retrieved on 13 November 2012]).

female sexuality, there are also vinaya stories that describe monks speaking inappropriately to women about sex, or attempting to persuade or cajole women into having sex with them, such as in saṅghādisesa 4 of the monks *Suttavibhaṅga*, in which Udāyin tries to persuade a laywoman into having sex with him by telling her it is the highest form of gift she can offer to a monk. This, of course, is suggesting the converse to be the case: rather than women being the temptresses, it is men who are the sexual predators (see Collett 2013b).

In the *Vinaya*, we also find examples of conniving nuns and monks, who try various schemes to either get around rules, or to manipulate others into giving them what they want. In the nuns' *vibhaṅga*, we meet with aggressive women, and others who bargain for their own ends, those who hoard with some apparent capitalist intention, and others who revile and slander. Pācittiya 6 tells of a nun who is the former wife of a monk who talks down to him when she is attending him at a meal time. He is not pleased with her behaviour and so they quarrel and she hits him.[7] In an act of misappropriation for her own ends, in pācittiya 127, Thullanandā offers ordination to a novice if she gives her a robe. *Nissaggiya* 1 tells of nuns who have hoarded a stock of bowls. The belief of those who rebuke this action is that these nuns are (perhaps) intent on selling them for their own ends. Finally, in pācittiya 126, the nun Caṇḍakālī wants to be promoted to ordain other women, but she is not granted this privilege, so, although appearing to acquiesce graciously, goes off and criticizes the other nuns in return. This is far from the only case of slander in the nuns' vibhaṅga. However, similarly, and in a true reflection of the nuns' less-than-edifying behaviours, the monks match the nuns for their inapposite acts and actions. As well as Udāyin trying to persuade a laywoman to have sex with him, in the previous saṅghādisesa 3, monks speak in lewd words to women and make sexual innuendos to them about 'sowing'

7 A fuller version of this vinaya story appears in the Mahāsaṅghikā-Lokottaravāda nuns' *Vinaya*—in which the nun is said to be fed up with her former husband 'prattling on', see Langenberg's translation (2013, 87–8). See also Clarke (2014, 97f.).

and 'rough coarse hair' (see Collett 2013b). In a story connected with the first pārājika, of what turns out to be a gross attempt to get around the rules governing sexual conduct, a monk is said to have sexual relations with a female monkey and when challenged on this by other monks and told this is not appropriate, argues that it is only sex with human women that is not allowed. In terms of vivid examples of scheming and plotting behaviours, a group of six monks turn a good trick or two. Pācittiya 16 sees them scheming to get the best sleeping places, while the story attached to pācittiya 17 has them lying to get a good dwelling for the rainy season. Other monks also commit similarly devious acts as, for example, in pācittiya 35, in which monks are rebuked for eating at one house, and then going to another for a second meal.

It could be argued that the most comprehensive ascription of negative characteristics to womenkind can be found in the *Mātugāmasaṃyutta* of the *Saṃyutta-nikāya*.[8] Negative characteristics of women are documented here, including those for which they would take rebirth into hell. However, the section recommends that, through practice of the precepts and through attaining the five powers of women (essentially good qualities and deeds) a laywoman, if she observes the teachings well, can become fully aware of the essence of herself and this bodily existence. The negative characteristics noted of women are as follows:

1. Three qualities—heart obsessed with taint of selfishness; heart obsessed with taint of envy; heart obsessed with sensual pleasure.
2. Five characteristics leading to rebirth in hell—being without faith, without shame, unafraid of wrongdoing, angry, and unwise (and listed alongside are malice, envy, stinginess, loose conduct, immorality, lack of learning, laziness, and muddle-mindedness).[9]

8 This *saṃyutta* has no counterpart on the Chinese *Saṃyukta-āgamas*.

9 The fourth item on the list changes as the five are reiterated nine times. In place of anger, sequentially, are malice, envy, stinginess, loose conduct, immorality, lack of learning, lazy, and muddle-mindedness.

The other parts of the section are sympathetic to what we must assume is understood to be the lived reality of everyday life for women. As well as listing negative characteristics of women, there is a section on the five kinds of sufferings particular to women. These five kinds of suffering include, for example, having to go and live with her husband's family once married, and missing her own family, giving birth, and having to serve a man. However, interestingly, following the first section of the *Mātugāmasaṃyutta* on women and their agreeable and disagreeable characteristics is an identical corresponding passage on men. The text tells us that the five characteristics that make women disagreeable to men are the same five characteristics that make men disagreeable to women. With this as the preface to the whole section, it is difficult to know how to read the remainder, and whether other parts of it should be imagined to have a corresponding passage on men. The next section is section 3, that details the forms of suffering particular to women, and the section on powers delineates gender differences, detailing powers that women have and separate ones for men. But the other sections, including those outlined earlier—on envy, selfishness, lust and faithlessness, shamelessness, lack of fear of reprisal for actions done, anger, and ignorance—could just as equally apply to men. These are just the types of human traits that, it could be argued, the entire Pāli canon and whole edifice of the Buddha's teaching of dhamma therein is intent to rescind.

If we turn to the *Petavatthu*, it is here that we find some examples of jealous women, who mirror the jealous wives in Uppalavaṇṇā's tale. The *Petavatthu*, a verse text, tells of the ghoulish appearance of male and female petas/petīs, born into their suffering existence due to past misdeeds. In the text as a whole, we find, again, a parity between men and women. Although many hideous and ugly female petīs are met with, equally there are tales of ghoulish, frightful males. There are a few more tales of male petas than female, and if there is any disparity it may be true to say that the descriptions of the female petīs are just slightly more foul than the male ones. One of the female petīs, reborn into this state as a result of being jealous of a co-wife, is described as follows:

> You are naked and ugly in form; you emit a foul-smelling and putrid odour; you are covered with flies...[10]

A male reborn as a *peta* for stinginess is described in equally ghastly terms:

> You are naked and ugly in form, thin, and with your veins showing. Your ribs stand out, you are emaciated...[11]

A few of the women have taken rebirth into this realm as a result of jealousy. In fact, this is the most common reason a woman is born into this depraved state, as there are three examples of it as opposed to only one or two for other reasons given. In the first instance of a wife who feels jealous of another and acts upon it (I.6, 4), in a mirror of Uppalavaṇṇā's story, the woman in question caused the other, pregnant wife to miscarry, then lies about it and, reborn as a petī, is forced to 'eat the flesh of children, stained with the blood of the past'.[12] The second story, sequential to the first, is very similar. A jealous wife causes a miscarriage of another, and this time is forced to eat the flesh of seven children—rather than the five in the first example—for her misdeeds. The other account of a jealous wife (II.15, 19) is longer, and contains a list of several misdemeanours the jealous wife commits against the other. Her bad behaviour includes using abusive language, throwing dust, putting a substance in the other's bed to cause itching, stealing her garments, throwing her perfumes into a cesspool, and lacking in generosity.

Men are reborn as petas for various reasons, the most common being meanness with money, but they never find themselves in the peta realm for jealousy themselves. Thus, while there is a relative parity here in the ratio of male–female petas/petīs, and their ghoulish appearance, there is a discernible difference with regards male and female character traits. Women, at their worst, are jealous, abusive, tight-fisted, and unfaithful, while the most reviled traits of

10 *Pv* 5. *Naggā dubbaṇṇarūpāsi duggandhā pūti vāyasi makkhitāparikiṇṇā va...*

11 *Pv* 26. *Naggo dubbaṇṇarūpo 'si kiso dhamanisanthato upphāsuliko kisiko...*

12 *Pv* 6, 5. *...puttamaṃsāni khādāmi pubbalohitamakkhitā...*

men are meanness, greed, dishonesty, aggression, maliciousness, and an abusive nature. The jealousy of women as compared to the apparent lack of it in men is the most prominent difference, but in the polygamous world of these texts this is hardly surprising. Even with regards to aggression, although the detail of the acts may be different, there is not much in it between the two sexes.

Negative characteristics of women in the commentaries

The jealous wives in the story of Uppalavaṇṇā in the *Dhammapada* commentary and *Jātakatthavaṇṇanā* are typical of a type of scheming and plotting, manipulative woman found in folkloric literature. Both these commentarial texts do contain stories that are folkloric in origin, and have been adapted (sometimes not very successfully) for their Buddhist context.[13] In what follows I will explore several things: first, I will comment upon the folkloric elements of some of the content of the *Dhammapada* commentary and *Jātakatthavaṇṇanā*, then, I will assess characterizations of both women and men in such folkloric literature, and end by assessing the extent to which caricatures of women as seen in such texts can, or should, be classified as Buddhist views on women.

The tale of the jealous wives can be easily seen as a folkloric tale, as very similar stories exist in folklore traditions in other countries. For example, the following is one of Galland's so-called 'orphan stories' from his French translation of *A Thousand and One Nights*:[14]

> One day, King Khusraw Shâh of Persia dressed up in disguise as a merchant. Together with his vizier, he set out to inspect the circumstances of his subjects. Soon they overheard three sisters in a

[13] See the discussions in Appleton (2009) and Anālayo (2010b) of the jātaka genre for more on the *Jātakatthavaṇṇanā* relationship to folklore.

[14] Galland included stories in his French translation not found in the fifteenth century manuscript he worked from. His journals reveal that he was told these apocryphal stories orally, by a Persian woman called Hanna (see Larzul 2004). These stories were termed the 'orphan stories' by Gerhardt (1963, 12–14). In quoting the story, I have omitted Burton's internal references.

house telling each other about their dearest wish. The first one wanted to marry the king's chief baker; the second dreams of marrying the king's chief kitchener; while the third, who is the most beautiful and clever, wishes to marry the king himself.

The next day the three are introduced to the king and their wishes fulfilled. The eldest and second sisters, however, envy the youngest one, who married the king. When the youngest sister gets pregnant, the other two dispose of the baby in a basket they put into the canal while exchanging the baby for a puppy. The next time she is pregnant, they exchange the baby for a kitten, and the third time they replace it with a muskrat. The children, two sons and a daughter, are found by the keeper of the royal gardens, who raises them as his own. (Marzolph, Van Leeuwen, and Wassouf 2004, 425)[15]

Eventually, after the children are grown, the truth is revealed to the king by the intervention of a speaking bird and the envious sisters are executed. There is also a similar north European folkloric tale of Oriant, son of King Pyrion and Queen Matabruna of Lillefort.[16] Out hunting one day, Oriant encounters a beautiful young woman, Beatrix, whom he immediately falls in love with and decides to marry. His mother disapproves and when Beatrix bears seven children, the mother replaces them with puppies, so that she can falsely claim Beatrix had sex with a dog. In surveying such tales from around the world, Duggan argues that while other forms of folkloric persecution of wives have male instigators, 'stories in which a wife is persecuted for having given birth to animals are initiated by female characters who compete for status' (2005, 412). In the case of Uppalavaṇṇā, the animistic connection is not present but, nonetheless, the story arc, theme, and caricatures are all distinguishable enough for this to look like a comparable tale.

In folklore, both male and female characters are caricatured, such that amplified versions of manipulative women and idiotic men, for example, populate the pages of such literature. While it is the case that women can be—and are, especially in the

15 There also may be a version of the story in which a log of wood is substituted for a newborn, but I have not been able to find out much about this (see 'Narrative Men' by Todorov in Marzolph 2006, 228).

16 For a telling of this story see Gallagher (2009, 243ff.).

Dhammapada commentary and *Jātakatthavaṇṇanā*—vilified for their unsavoury characteristics, if we turn for a moment to some of the characterizations of men, we find that men don't come off that much better. For example, if we take the stories of slapstick humour in the *Jātakatthavaṇṇanā*, there are two similar stories in which first a man and then a woman are the butt of the joke. The story is essentially the story of a slapstick blow on the head of a parent, first a father and then a mother, that proves to be fatal although well intended.[17] Other examples of less-than-edifying male characters in the *Jātakatthavaṇṇanā* and *Dhammapada* commentary include fat Tissa, who is obstinate and disrespectful (*Dhp-a* I.37), mean brahmins and merchants, who will not pay for a doctor even when their beloved son falls ill (*Dhp-a* I.25), or are never satisfied with what they have (*Dhp-a* II.25). Then there are jealous, vindictive, and insolent monks, who scheme to humiliate former friends (*Dhp-a* I.133), shirk duties, and take credit for others' work, or might even, due to the grudge they bear for small rebukes, set fire to another's hut (*Dhp-a* II.19). There are also men who cannot see the complexities of a situation, and kings who cannot solve their own problems, needing to seek the counsel of their wives (*Dhp-a* II.1). In one such instance, the queen, hearing the advice her husband has taken from a brahmin tells him:

> You are a simpleton, your majesty. You have an abundant supply of food, you may feast upon viands flavoured with all manner of sauces and curries cooked by the bucketful, you may rule over two kingdoms, but all the same you have very little sense.[18]

In these commentaries, we find stories of both sexes, each of whom exemplify good and evil—both illustrious and foolhardy

[17] See the *Makasa Jātaka* (44), in which a carpenter's son, intent to kill the mosquito that has landed on his father's head, picks up an axe for the job, and the *Rohiṇī Jātaka* (45), in which Rohinī kills her mother with a pestle, while attempting to keep the flies off.

[18] *Andhabālo 'si mahārāja kiñcāpi mahābhakkho 'si anekasūpavikatikaṃ doṇapākaṃ bhuñjasi dvīsu raṭṭhesu rajjaṃ kāresi paññā pana te mandā* (II.8, trans. Burlingame Vol. II, 105).

kings, noble and manipulative queens, both virtuous and scheming laymen and women, and either vengeful or honourable monastics. The category of persons least often cast in an ignoble role is nuns, in part because the compilers of the commentaries appear to be least concerned about generic nuns, and given the way the female saints of the past are regarded in historical memory, they are unlikely to be cast in these roles, as they are almost always exemplars of the path.

The reproduced biographies of nuns, or other accounts and stories of them in other manifestations of their former lives, are, overall, exceptionally positive.[19] But in the cases in which either folkloric stories are being reproduced with their accompanying women characters, or in which the commentators (whoever they may be, Sinhala or Indian) are left more to their own devices, a different sort of woman can emerge from the pages. While men and women are caricatured in folklore and folkloric tropes exaggerate character traits—and this happens both within and outside of Buddhist contexts—something more than this exists in some commentaries. In contrast to how men as a group are portrayed, women are maligned and vilified with blanket one-liners that revile the generic woman, or womankind overall. These one-liners appear most often in the *Jātakatthavaṇṇanā*, and some of the most salient of these are as follows:

> ...women are naturally wicked and ... plot evil against you....[20]
>
> ...women are disagreeable, mean, and inferior...[21]

[19] One exception is the *Jātakatthavaṇṇanā* story of Uppalavaṇṇā as Ummadantī. In this instance, Ummadantī seeks revenge on a king who chooses not to marry her, and conspires to ensure he will catch a glimpse of her, knowing this will engender a mesmerising infatuation. However, although Uppalavaṇṇā's behaviour in this story is not especially virtuous, other jātaka stories have the Buddha as bodhisatta portrayed in a less virtuous way still. Another exception is the way Dhammadinnā is reconfigured by the commentators (see Chapter 7).

[20] The line is: *...mātugāmo nāma pāpo tumhākaṃ pāpakam pi cinteyya...* (6, I.128)

[21] *...itthiyo nāma āsā asatiyo lāmikā pacchimikā...* (61, I.285).

...all women become wicked.[22]

...women are ungrateful and deceitful...[23]

...women are feckless and immoral...[24]

...women are common to all, this immorality defines them...[25]

...women have insatiable sexual appetites...[26]

What is interesting about these examples is that they occur much less often in the *Dhammapada* commentary than in the *Jātakatthavaṇṇanā*, which suggests that these comments could be particular to the compiler(s) of the extant text, who may have been especially gynophobic. The *Dhammapada* commentary is not without some share of such malignant discourse, but vilification of women, as a group, occurs less often. One of the most noteworthy examples from the *Dhammapada* commentary is a story of wicked and promiscuous men. Suggesting all women would prostitute themselves for the right fiscal sum, the leader of this group says:

> '...no woman is without passion if we tell her we will give her money. Let us offer money to other's wives and commit adultery'. 'Good, good!' all of them said. From then on they sent money to beautiful women, and for twenty thousand years committed adultery with them...[27]

[22] The entire verse, which reflects on innate nature, is *sabbā nadī vankagatā, sabbe kaṭṭhamayā vanā, sabbitthiyo kare pāpaṃ labhamānā nivātake ti*, 'all rivers wind, all forests are made of wood and, given the opportunity, all women become wicked' (62, I.289).

[23] *...ittiyo nāma akataññu mittadūbhā...*(63, I.295).

[24] *...itthiyo nām[a]...anācārā dussīlā...*(64, I.300).

[25] *...itthiyo nāma sabbasādhāraṇā tāsu dussīlā etā ti...*(65, I.301–2). 'Common to all' here refers to sexual infidelity.

[26] *...itthiyo nāma methunadhammena atittā...* (120, I.440). The context for this line is a tale in which a queen, sent home without her king, seduces sixty-four messengers in turn that he sends to her. The use of *methunadhamma* here could be implying women are never satisfied with monogamy, that is, one sexual pairing.

[27] *...dhanaṃ dassāmā ti vutte anicchamānā nāma natthi dhanaṃ payojetvā payojetvā pāradārikakammaṃ karissāmā ti. Sadhu, sadhu ti sabbe*

The men were reborn in hell for their misdeeds; not for their disrespecting of women, but rather because they committed adultery with wives of other men.[28]

Similar contempt for women can be found in other Indic non-Buddhist folkloric tales, such as in the *Pañcatantra*, as well as in other texts of Brahmanism. In the later *Kathāsaritsāgara*, a male parrot and female myna bird—coupled together here as in the *Tesakuṇa Jātaka*, in which Uppalavaṇṇā is the female myna bird—argue as to whether men or women are better. The parrot asks the myna bird to marry him, but she declines, and in her reply retorts:

> 'I don't want to get involved with you because all men are wicked and ungrateful.' 'Males are ungrateful', said the parrot, 'It is females who are hard-hearted.' (trans. Sattar, 1994, 202)

The two cannot resolve their argument, so ask the king to adjudicate. They each present their case to him with recourse to a narrative tale, and the king, after consideration, decides:

> Females are wicked. Males sometimes behave badly but females are wicked always and everywhere. (trans. Sattar, 1994, 207)

Olivelle offers an overview of depictions of women from the *Pañcatantra*, which he describes as—like the world of Indian politics it imitates—'predominantly, if not exclusively, a male domain'. In relation to the few female protagonists and characters found within the text he says:

> A pattern emerges from these animal stories: wife-mother is the only positive role for a female, while other females, even wives, who do not play maternal roles always pose a threat to the males either as sexual objects or by their nefarious activities.
>
> This pattern is even more pronounced when we look at the stories with human characters. (1997: xxvi)

---

tassa kathāya aṭṭhaṃsu. Te tato paṭṭhāya abhirūpānaṃ itthīnaṃ dhanaṃ pesetvā pesetvā vīsativassasahassāni pāradārikakammaṃ katvā... (II.10). The act of adultery is expressed as an act which involves taking a woman belonging to another, *pāradārikakammaṃ katvā*.

[28] See note 18 in Chapter 10 on adultery and how it is conceptualized only as the taking of one's wife by another man.

This pattern Olivelle discerns is not mirrored in the Buddhist commentaries, although it reflects some aspects of the commentarial typologies of women. In the Buddhist case, there is a more broadly conceived group of women that are, or can be, perceived positively. One aspect that does not reflect Olivelle's observations is that mothers are not always portrayed positively. As noted above, Uppalavaṇṇā is often portrayed in a nurturing, maternal role, but women with children can be manipulative as well. An example of a devious mother can be found in the story of Kumbhaghosaka in the *Dhammapada* commentary, in which a scheming female servant uses her daughter—in a version of the folkloric 'bedtrick'—for her own ends. In attempting to discover if Kumbhaghosaka has some hidden wealth, she damages his mattress such that it is no longer possible for him to sleep on it, then suggests that he share her daughter's bed, conniving for a marriage between the pair. What underscored the possibility for a female to be 'good' in both these Buddhist and Brahmanical cases appears to be a loosely conceived application of dhamma, which thus differs respectively. The noble female Buddhst 'saints' of the past are almost invariably good, and other women most often conceptualized in a positive light are women who follow the teachings of the Buddha. Queen Mallikā is one example of such a woman, as is the lower-ranking wife of a jeweller who tries to dissuade him from torturing a monk. In this *Dhammapada* commentary story, the jeweller's heron has swallowed a gem, and the jeweller accuses the monk. But his wife says:

> Husband, say not so. During all the years the Elder has visited this house, I have never observed a flaw in him; it was not he that took the jewel.[29]

Also, although, as the above quotations from the *Jātakatthavaṇṇanā* intimate, there is an implication that women are innately unscrupulous and immoral, this is not borne out by the detail of some of the stories. In one case, for example, a story is told of a laywoman who stood up to social pressure to do what she considered right, to honour the Buddha and his monks, even at the fear of being

[29] *Dhp-a* III.35 (trans. Burlingame [1921] 1995, 285). ...*sāmi mā evaṃ avaca ettakaṃ kālaṃ mayā therassa na kiñci vajjaṃ diṭṭhapubbaṃ na so maṇiṃ gaṇhātī ti.*

beaten. The *Vimānavatthu* commentary relates this narrative, in which a woman offers the Buddha and monks water, despite the village brahmins' interdiction that the Buddha and his community should be ignored.[30] This confirms again that while women who do not follow the path can be lowly and debase, those who do—in imitation of the canonized 'saints' of the past—can be as robust in their discipleship as any man.

Overall, although the king's summation in the *Kathāsaritsāgara* might prove to be the most astute in relation to depictions of men and women in Indian folklore, the Buddhist commentaries of the *Therīgāthā* and *Aṅguttara-nikāya* do not share the rhetoric, recounting only the lives of the nuns and rarely venturing into folkloric narration. The commentaries that do contain more folklore share some of these assumptions, and go even further astray in the vilification of women than other Indic texts. However, underlining this is the philosophy of Buddhist doctrine and the belief—not always appearing to be adhered to in the rhetoric, but there in the detail—in the transformative power of human nature, both male and female.

***

What I have attempted to show in this chapter is that Uppalavaṇṇā exemplifies both the positive characteristics associated with women in the canon and in the commentaries. Further, the jealous co-wives that we meet with in some of the biographies of her represent some of the worst characteristics associated with women across canon and commentary.

Both good and bad character traits of women are documented in the canon and commentaries, with some commentaries, especially the *Jātakatthavaṇṇanā*, exhibiting a particularly virulent gynophobia. However, overall, with the exception of the *Jātakatthavaṇṇanā* and *Dhammapada* commentary, and especially in the canon, more of a parity is evident between men and women—both corpuses provide opportunities for us to glimpse the social construct of both male and female, and masculine and feminine, and see both the best and the worst that both men and women can be.

30 *Vv-a* 14. As a result of this deed, the woman was beaten to death by her brahmin master, and reborn in a heavenly place.

Conclusion

This book is a re-examination of different aspects of women's lives as presented in the Pāli canon and commentaries. The first remit of the work is to question past scholarly methods in using the evidence of the commentaries to augment understanding of the canon. I attempt, instead, to understand the two genres of texts to have been produced in different socio-historic milieus.

In revalourizing and re-examining the evidence, something of a new picture emerges. In relation to women as teachers and pupils, we find examples of female teachers in texts and epigraphic evidence. The inscriptions also reveal nuns as firm actors in relational saṅgha networks and teacher–pupil lineages. Given that the epigraphy that details this is found across a broad range of sites in north and central India, and can be dated to a broad time-frame, this challenges the textually prescribed, formalized role of monks as advisors to nuns, and raises questions as to the extent to which the formalized scheme was enacted.

The book also challenges interpretations of the female body in the Pāli literature. In Chapter 8, I argue that it is not women's bodies per se that are being conceived of as the problem, but rather the adorned and ornamented body (which could be either male or female). In this chapter, male adornment is discussed and references to women's bodies—most often ornamented ones—nuanced. Thus conceived, the problem being highlighted is reimagined as the doctrinally endorsed problem of desire. The adorned and ornamented body is the ideal of beauty, the conventional standard, and disciples' (normative) pre-occupation with this is challenged with a focus on the visceral, corporal nature of flesh.

Notwithstanding the notion that the ideal form of the body is the most desirable, it would appear that even a shaven-headed, rag-robe wearing nun continued to arouse desire in some men. The concept of sexual availability seems to, in this context, revolve around the question of whether a woman belonged to a man or a group of men. If she was deemed not to, she was considered sexually available, and the question of her consent or otherwise was not particularly a factor. In the early period of Buddhism, before the social identity of nuns was fully established, the threat of sexual assault appears to have been a very real one. This may have been because Buddhist nuns were considered available, as they did not belong to men. Thus, the garudhammas, or eight chief rules, may have been instituted as a way to communicate to the wider community that Buddhist nuns were under the protection and rule of monks—that is, of a group of men—and were thereby not to be considered sexually available.

Although a woman's choice does not seem to figure centrally in relation to questions of non-consensual sex acts, there are some surprising incidents of an unusually weighty focus on women's agency when it comes to choice of spouse, and this even though the importance of family still chimes strong in the Buddhist literature. Both Bhaddā Kuṇḍalakesā and Paṭācārā chose their own husbands, rather than the choice being made for them. In Bhaddā Kuṇḍalakesā's case, she did gain eventual parental consent, following a somewhat dramatic, emotive display. Paṭācārā, however, acted without parental consent—running away from home to be with her lover. Other compelling aspects of female agency come in the discussion of women as debaters and those who chose to convert to follow the path of the Buddha. Although Bhaddā Kuṇḍalakesā stands as the only named example of such, the literature demonstrates a great deal of potential for other debaters amongst the female population of early communities.

Finally, and in the last chapter, the differences between the canon and commentary crystallize in a focus on how men and women are represented in terms of their characteristics. Challenging past scholarship that tends to equate the best of men with the worst of women—that men are exemplars but women can tend to be weak and emotional—I argue instead we need to ensure we compare like with like. The canon and commentaries present to us both the best and worst that both men and women can be. At best, monks and nuns are each exemplary teachers and devoted disciples and at worst women are jealous and manipulative and men foolhardy, aggressive, and greedy for wealth. Drawing out this parity, by examining negative portrayals of men, introduces a new angle to the debate.

In the biographies in this volume, as discussed throughout, given their historical distance, it is not possible to know the extent to which they reproduce the lives of actual historical women who were direct disciples Gotama Buddha. As highlighted in the Introduction to Part I, it is also not possible to know if the names attached to each account were the actual names of women who lived in India over 2,000 years ago. Despite the limitations of the evidence available to us, certain features in these portrayals of women's lives materialize repeatedly—that women struggled to be taken seriously as persons of good character, as exemplary disciples and devoted practitioners, and as adept teachers. The textual record is multivalent on this, with such things either variably accepted or rejected, considered possible or not, viewed as axiomatic or denied, allowed or disallowed. This focus appears to reflect fundamental aspects of the lives of nuns in early Indian Buddhism.

As a conclusion to this volume, Martin Seeger kindly agreed to write an afterword on work he has been doing on modern Thai Buddhist nuns. He focuses, in the afterword, on the life of one nun, Khunying Yai. In Seeger's work, unlike the historical texts and other evidence that make up this volume, the biographies are known to be based upon actual historical women. What is striking about the lives of these modern Thai nuns that Seeger studies, when compared to the nuns whose life stories make up this volume, is the resemblance between the two. Khunying Yai has remained somewhat occluded from history, both in terms of her biographical account and works authored by her. A major text composed by her is an impressive work, and as such, the anonymized text was attributed to a well-known male teacher. Khunying Yai is lauded as a nun with an extraordinary memory and ability to teach, which means we can align her with our nuns of early Buddhist history such as Dhammadinnā and Khemā, the exemplary teachers, as well as Paṭācārā, the vinayadhārā.[1] She was also, like the women who feature in the inscriptions in Chapter 7, a nun with a male monastic teacher. Of further note is that Khunying Yai takes inspiration from the lives of some of the stories of women found in the Pāli literature, and is herself part of a network of female practitioners, just like those presented in the historical record.

These accounts of modern Thai Buddhist nuns such as Khunying Yai can be seen to be part of an ongoing biographical lineage tracing the lives of Buddhist nuns through history. Khunying Yai is not well known, even in Thailand, although some of her contemporaries, such as Ki Nanayon are. All of these stories, past and present, as they increasingly continue to be made known, will no doubt continue to inspire generations of Buddhists to come—both male and female alike—around the world.

[1] Given her extraordinary competence in understanding the dhamma, Khunying Yai even taught monks. This is something the historical texts are silent on in relation to early Buddhist women, even those who are accomplished teachers.

Afterword

THE INSPIRING LIFE STORY OF A TWENTIETH-CENTURY THAI BUDDHIST WOMAN: KHUNYING YAI DAMRONGTHAMMASAN (1882–1944)*

Over the course of the last eight years, I have researched the (auto-) biographies, homilies, and the veneration of a number of

* This article is an abridged and slightly modified version of my article 'Orality, Memory, and Spiritual Practice: Outstanding Female Thai Buddhists in the Early 20th Century', which was published in *Journal of the Oxford Centre for Buddhist Studies* (Seeger 2014). The original paper is the result of a development of ideas presented during a talk I gave at the University of Oslo as part of The Oslo Buddhist Studies Forum on 1 April 2014. I would like to thank Khun Naris Charaschanyawong, who has sent me a number of sources relevant for this article. In addition, he has given valuable comments on previous drafts of this paper and was my co-researcher on the research I have done on Khunying Yai Damrongthammasan (Seeger and Naris, 2556a/b). I am very grateful to Than Mae Chi Vimuttiyā for her many most interesting and valuable comments on Khunying Yai's literary work. I also would very much like to thank Bhikkhu Anālayo, Richard Gombrich, Justin McDaniel, Caroline Starkey, Victor King and Adcharawan Seeger for their comments on and help with this paper. I am also very grateful to Khun Prasop Wisetsiri, the adopted son of Khunying Yai, for his most generous support in the

female Thai Buddhist practitioners.[1] I have studied in some depth the inspiring life story and Buddhist practice of Khunying Yai Damrongthammasan, who until now has hardly been known in Thailand and in academic literature. This came about as a result of a series of astonishing discoveries with regard to the (wrong) attribution of authorship of a 'valuable' Thai Buddhist treatise (see later). Given Khunying Yai Damrongthammasan's extraordinary life story, her advanced understanding of Buddhist doctrine as reflected in her texts, and the fact that her biography allows valuable insights into various aspects of modern Thai Buddhism, an appraisal of her life is overdue. Another important reason why a study of Khunying Yai's life is needed is that she appears to have produced one of the first significant Buddhist treatises ever authored by a Thai woman.

Dhammānudhammapaṭipatti is the title of a collection of five dialogical texts, which were first published anonymously and separately between 1932 and 1934.[2] These five texts, which are still being reprinted and widely disseminated either together or as single texts, have widely been praised as outstanding and valuable pieces

course of this research project. The translations from Thai are my own unless stated otherwise. I wish to thank The British Academy for a grant that allowed me to do research on the life of Khunying Yai Damrongthammasan and the authorship of the text *Dhammānudhammapaṭipatti*. I also wish to thank the School of Languages, Cultures and Societies (LCS), University of Leeds, for providing me with a grant that enabled me to conduct additional interviews in Thailand. I have used my own standardized phoneticization of Thai script except in cases where the author's or person's name mentioned in this paper have an established transliteration. Throughout this article, Thai words are differentiated from Pāli words by underlining (Pāli words are italicized; Thai words are italicized and underlined).

[1] See Seeger 2009, 2010, 2013, and 2014. At the moment I am working on a book project that is based on the biographies and venerational practices of numerous Thai Buddhist women of 20th century Thailand; many of these women have been revered as saints.

[2] [No author mentioned], 2475a [1932a]; [no author mentioned], 2475b [1932b]; [no author mentioned], 2476a [1933a]; [no author mentioned], 2476b [1933b]; [no author mentioned], 2477 [1934]. These texts have also been published as a collection with the title 'Achieving Awakening within Seven Days' (*jet wan banlu tham*), Praphot Setthakanon (ed.), [no date].

of Thai Buddhist literature. This is thanks to the profundity and obvious extraordinary scholarly competence with which numerous difficult Pāli canonical teachings have been explained in these texts. The original editions of these five texts have been published without naming an author. Moreover, they exhibit an unusually advanced understanding of the dhamma of its author. These two factors combined must have lent to the authorship of these texts being attributed to the 'Father of the Thai Forest Tradition', Luang Pu Man Bhūridatto (1870–1949). This happened probably some 20 years ago, if not earlier, but it is not clear as to how exactly this attribution took place. Luang Pu Man certainly is one of Thailand's most respected and famous monks and often referred to as a 'national saint', many people believing that he has achieved full awakening. This attribution of authorship happened despite the fact that Luang Pu Man never claimed to have written these texts. In fact, the content and style of the *Dhammānudhammapaṭipatti* texts together with the major biographies of Luang Pu Man clearly show that it is extremely unlikely that he was involved in the production of these texts.

In recent research, together with my Thai co-researcher Naris Charaschanyawong, I have been able to find evidence that conclusively shows that the real author of these texts is Khunying Yai Damrongthammasan.[3] Thus, Khunying Yai can be regarded as one of, if not the first, female author of a significant Buddhist treatise in Thai Buddhist history.

Unfortunately, despite her extraordinary life, her high social status, and closeness to a number of high-ranking monks, there is a scarcity of biographical sources on her. One reason for this may be her humility; people who knew her personally consistently described Khunying Yai as a very humble person (*thom tua*).[4] Her

[3] See Seeger and Naris, 2556a [2013a] and 2556b [2013b]; Seeger, [forthcoming]; see also Dissanayake, 2013.

[4] Here it should also be noted that authorship questions in Thai Buddhism are often complex. Many Buddhist texts have emerged with the (partly significant) help or input of monks, *mae chis* or laypeople; but despite this, often the text is then ascribed to a single teacher (who may not have had a significant, if any, impact on the final text version) or, as in the case of Khunying Yai's texts, is published anonymously (see, for example, McDaniel, 2008, 180; Seeger, [forthcoming]).

humility is also likely to be a reason why she published her major texts anonymously. The biographical data we have on her life make consistently clear that Khunying Yai was not interested in promoting herself, despite the high respect many people had for her deep understanding of Buddhist doctrine and what was perceived to be highly developed Buddhist practice. At the moment, we are in the process of reconstructing her fascinating and inspiring life story, and there are still numerous significant gaps in what we know about her biography. In the following, I will largely focus on aspects of her biography that are relevant for the understanding of her Buddhist practice and how she received and perceived Buddhist knowledge.[5]

Khunying Yai was born into the nobility and received private education at home. She belonged to one of the richest families in Thailand. She had been interested in the study of Buddhist teachings since a very early age. She was married to a famous judge, Phra Ya Damrongthammasan (Sang Wisetsiri), who was a noble and a devout Buddhist too. From a young age she suffered from a severe form of diabetes. As a consequence of this she must have been in a lot of physical pain, and increasingly so towards the end of her life. In 1922, together with her husband, she started to build the monastery Wat Thammikaram in the southern province of Prajuabkhirikhan. The construction of this monastery was supported by the King of Siam, Rama VI (r. 1910–25), who even visited the construction site. In 1931 Khunying Yai won the first prize of an essay writing competition for which participants were asked to submit answers to 'Eight Questions on the *Dhamma*' (*Aṭṭhadhammapañha*).[6] The Buddhist author Prince Krom Muen Wiwitwanpricha, a son of Rama IV, made the decision that Khunying Yai submitted the best answers, on the level of *Ek-U*. The expression *Ek-U* probably derives from

5 At the moment, together with Khun Naris I am working on a book with the title *pucchā-vissajjanā wa duai kan patibat tham* (*pucchā-vissajjanā on the Practice of Dhamma*) that will contain all her texts and a detailed and comprehensive biography of her.

6 *Aṭṭhadhammapañha* is the title of the book in which the best essays of this writing competition were published.

the Pāli words *eka* (one) and *uttama* (highest, best), and may be translated as the 'Most Excellent One'. As an award Khunying Yai also received a silver cup from Chao Phra Ya Mukhamontri (Uap Paurohit), a high-ranking member of the nobility.

During the last ten years of her life she was living in the white robes of a *mae chi* (*mae chis* are women who shave their hair, keep either the eight or ten Buddhist precepts and wear white-coloured robes). After the death of her husband in 1940, she spent most of her time practising Buddhist meditation at Wat Thammikaram, which has become one of the most important temples in the whole province. Her cremated remains, together with those of her husband, are buried in this monastery underneath the major Buddha figure in the ordination hall (*uposathāgāra*).[7]

Much of what we know about her knowledge acquisition and Buddhist practice comes from the recollections of the abbot of Wat Sattanartpariwat in Ratburi, Phra Thepsumethi (Yuak Cattamalo, 1914–2002), who as a young monk listened to Khunying Yai's explanations of Buddhist teachings. He reported: 'She had an excellent memory and was able to recollect the content of long-ago discussions with a high degree of precision.'[8] According to Phra Thepsumethi, from a young age she was able to recite all the 423 verses of the canonical book *Dhammapada*. In addition, she was also able to memorize a large number of dhamma principles/teachings (*lak tham*). Based on her unusually advanced knowledge, Khunying Yai was teaching monks. Even highly educated monks were in awe of Khunying Yai's vast knowledge and precise understanding of Buddhist teaching. At a very early age she herself was a student of the still highly revered monk Somdet Phra Wanarat (Thap Buddhasiri, 1806–91)[9] of the prestigious Bangkok temple Wat Somanaswihara. Later she then became

7 Khunying Yai's husband, Phra Ya Dhamrongthammasan (Sang Wisetsiri), was a student of Pāli language; he was ordained as a monk for a short period of time and later pursued a career as a judge. He generously supported the famous Bangkok monastery Wat Mahadhatu as well.

8 In Somphong Suthinsak, 2537 [1994], 95.

9 As Khunying Yai was born in 1882, she must have been rather young when she became a student of Somdet Phra Wanarat Thap.

a student of another highly revered and high ranking monk: Somdet Phra Buddhaghosajarn, abbot of the Bangkok monastery Wat Thepsirin. While still living in Bangkok, in the tallest building in Siam at the time (owned by her family), she is reported to have been able to develop a highly concentrated state of mind of one-pointedness (*ekaggatā*) and then able to recollect former lifetimes. But according to Phra Thepsumethi's account, she was not only capable of remembering her own former lives, but could also recollect (huan raluek) the lives of some relatives. Phra Thepsumethi writes that these types of knowledge are comparable to *pubbenivāsānussatiñāṇa* (recollection of one's former life times) and *dibbacakkhu* (divine eye). He also seems to believe that Khunying Yai may have achieved transcendental states of mind.[10] This is of course highly reminiscent of the Buddha's own biography: during the night he found awakening the Buddha went through these stages of insight into the workings of kamma before he finally gained complete liberation (*vimutti*). Thus, Khunying Yai's life has been understood to integrate successfully the theoretical study of Buddhist doctrine (*pariyatti*), Buddhist practice (*paṭipatti*) and, possibly, 'penetration' (*paṭivedha*).

When compared to her own biography, the *Dhammānudhammapaṭipatti* texts seem to contain several clues to key events in her own life and concerns. Thus, even though not certain, it is at least possible, that the themes of *viveka* (seclusion) and renunciation that recur throughout these texts seem to correspond to key events in her own life, such as when her adopted son, Khun Prasop Wisetsiri,[11] was starting school, which allowed her to become a mae chi.

Her texts contain numerous highly interesting features that deserve much more detailed study. One of the most interesting features is the many lists that can be found throughout Khunying Yai's texts, such as the 10 *saṃyojanas* (the fetters that bind human beings to rebirth), the 4 *vesārajjas* (types of self-confidence), the 10 *balas* (types of power), or the 15 *caraṇas* (practices/conducts).

10 Somphong Suthinsak, 2537 [1994], 95.

11 Khun Prasop Wisetsiri was the son of Phra Ya Damrongthammasan with another wife, but Khunying Yai brought him up since birth.

There are also numerous quotations in Pāli with their translations given in Thai. The way that these lists and quotations are embedded in these dialogues makes clear that they had been learned by heart by the people involved in these dialogues[12] and their function was to trigger discussions and explanations. The content of the texts makes it clear that the author must have had a close familiarity with Abhidhammic teachings; in fact the popular tenth or eleventh century abhidhamma compendium *Abhidhammatthasaṃgaha* is referred to and seems to have been an important source text for Khunying Yai's own work.[13] Also, another prominent feature of Khunying Yai's texts is the comparison between different dhammas. Often dhamma teachings are explained by showing the differences (*tang kan*) from seemingly similar teachings. The structure of Khunying Yai's texts is also quite obviously similar to the textual structure of the Pāli canonical suttas, incorporating numerous repetitions and embedding dhamma lists in a narrative. In addition, there are numerous references to orality. Thus, rather than being read, a book is 'listened to' (*fang nangsue*), and the study of dhamma teachings is often described with the word *fang* (to listen) rather than with 'to read' or 'look at'. The word 'listen' (*fang*) is mentioned more than 80 times in the *Dhammānudhammapaṭipatti* texts,[14] often in phrases such as 'to listen to' 'an explanation', 'a speech', 'teaching', or 'sermon' (*thet*), specific suttas or 'verses from the Buddha' (*tam khatha phra phutthaphasit*), the dhamma or '*dhamma* expositions' (*thammapariyai*). In addition to this, *sadap*, which also has the meaning 'to listen to', occurs eight

12 As I argue elsewhere, it is not clear how far, if at all, these conversations may have actually taken place or are imaginary (Seeger, [forthcoming]).

13 Interview with Mae Chi Vimuttiyā on 13 November 2013. At that time this influential Pāli text *Abhidhammatthasaṃgaha* had already been available in a Thai translation.

14 I should mention that this includes the occurrences of the word *fang* when it is used in connection with the Buddhist teaching on the six senses (*āyatana*), which is referred to quite frequently throughout the texts. Here it is of course not surprising that *fang* is used.

times in the texts. The words 'to write' (khian) and 'to read' (an), however, are not mentioned once. In the 'Eight Questions on the *Dhamma*' (*Aṭṭhadhammapañha*), a text she authored before the publication of the *Dhammānudhammapaṭipatti* texts (and which crucially helped to prove conclusively her authorship of her subsequent, anonymously published texts), when not familiar with a specific phrase in one of the questions she literally replies, 'I have never heard and never listened to this within the tradition.'[15] Another typical statement can be found in *paṭipattivibhāga*, one of the five *Dhammānudhammapaṭipatti* texts, where she states that 'We are very fortunate in that we were born [into a time period during which] the Buddhist teaching is available; this enables us to *listen* [*fang*] to the *Dhamma*...'[16] Moreover, in her texts Khunying Yai rather often refers to memorization, using words like 'to recollect/recall' (*raluek*) and 'memorize' (*jamsongwai*). Her texts make it abundantly clear that for Khunying Yai there is a close connection between (right) memory, (real) knowledge, and (right) Buddhist practice. This is also evidenced in the following dialogical passages:

Question

I am a [Buddhist] practitioner, which means I observe the precepts and lead a virtuous life [*mi tham*]. I also possess an understanding of numerous *dhamma* teachings. Why then am I still affected by worldly conditions [*lokadhamma*]?

Answer

Your knowledge is only on the level of *saññā* [perception, recognition]; you have not gained insight [*ru hen*] on the level of *paññā* [wisdom]; but you understand that you know because when thinking about a specific *Dhamma* teaching you have memorized [*jam song wai*] you gain clarity about it on the level of *saññā*; but this is not really knowing, which would be knowing on the level of *paññā*, like the knowing of a noble disciple [*ariyasāvaka*] ... Remembering numerous *dhamma* teachings is called *pariyatti*...[17]

15 Khunying Yai Damrongthammasan, 2474 [1931], 9.
16 [No author mentioned], 2475a [1932a], 35, my emphasis.
17 [No author mentioned], 2475a [1932a], 6–8.

Elsewhere Khunying Yai gives the following explanation:

Question

Paying homage [to the triple gem], using flowers, incense and candles, and saluting the Triple Gem, reciting holy texts [suatmon], such as the daily morning and evening chanting and the chanting of other texts that are the words of the Buddha [*buddhabhāsita*], does this all not [simply] constitute worship by offering material things [*āmisapūjā*], as it is [not the practice of] *sīla*, *samādhi* and *paññā*?

Answer

Do not misunderstand this point! For example, when showing respect to and prostrating in front of the triple gem, this constitutes right action [*sammākammanto*], to recite the virtues of the Buddha, *dhamma* and *saṅgha* constitutes *sammāvācā* [right speech]; both of them are parts of the *sīla* group. As for the mind that recollects the virtues of the Buddha, *dhamma* and *saṅgha*, this should be seen as a part of the *samādhi* group. As for the morning chanting that describes the five *khandhas* as impermanent [*anicca*] or not-self [*anattā*] and the reciting of other *suttas* that contain the teaching of the three characteristics [*tilakkhaṇa*], when recited with a focussed and attentive mind [*jai kamnot tam*], clarity about impermanence, un-satisfactoriness and not-self will arise. Thus, when reciting [in this way] this should be seen as a part of the *paññā* group. This means that the threefold training is complete and thus constitutes *paṭipattipūjā*, the worship through practice.[18]

These passages show that for her reciting Buddhist texts with a correctly focussed and attentive mind constitutes mind-development (*citta-bhāvanā*) in accordance with the spiritual path. This is in line with early Buddhist ideas about recitation, as observed by a number of Buddhist Studies scholars. Thus Bhikkhu Anālayo, for example, argues that 'early Buddhist oral tradition also served as a way of meditating or reflecting on the *Dhamma* ... recitation undertaken for its own sake does seem to function as a means of mental development (*bhāvanā*) in a wider sense, and as such could become a tool for progress on the path to liberation'.[19] Similarly,

18 [No author mentioned], 2475b [1932b], 15–16.
19 Anālayo, 2007, 16.

Collins states that 'the oral/aural dimension of Buddhist texts is not only a matter of learning and public performance: it plays a role in meditation also'.[20] Or as expressed in the words of Gethin: 'mindful recitation of a text ... operates as a kind of recollection of Dhamma (*dhammānusati*), a traditional subject of meditation'.[21]

What is also remarkable is that one of her major source texts for the *Dhammānudhammapaṭipatti* texts is *Soḷasapañha*,[22] which forms the last part of the canonical book *Suttanipāta*. The fact that Khunying Yai refers to or quotes from this text quite often is noteworthy for several reasons. First of all, like the structure of the *Dhammānudhammapaṭipatti* texts, *Soḷasapañha* is also based on questions and answers: sixteen Brahmin students approach the Buddha with questions, to which the Buddha provides answers. But what is at least equally interesting is the fact that in the *Nandamātāsutta* of the *Aṅguttara-nikāya*, the female lay-follower Veḷukaṇṭakī Nandamātā is reported to have risen in the morning and recited this very text. The deva king Vessavaṇa, who happened to overhear her chanting, praised her for this with the words *sādhu, sādhu* ('well done, well done!' *AN* IV.63). Also, in the *Aṅguttara-nikāya*, Veḷukaṇṭakī Nandamātā along with Khujjuttarā is said to be a model of a female lay-follower (*AN* I.89). In the commentaries, she is described as an *anāgāmī* (non-returner; that is someone who has achieved the third level of awakening), and able to recite the Pāli canon (*Sn-a* I.369).

Of course, we do not know whether the textual structure of *Soḷasapañha* and the fact that this text was recited by an outstanding lay woman influenced Khunying Yai in her decision to refer to it so often. But it is certainly worthwhile to point out these similarities. In fact, there are other canonical elements she was integrating in her texts that combine outstanding spiritual practice by women with the status of lay disciple. In her *Aṭṭhadhammapañha* text, apart from referring to the Buddha, she refers to only three other Pāli figures, all of whom are female lay-followers.[23] For Khunying Yai, these three

20 Collins, 1992, 126.

21 Gethin, 1992, 166.

22 In the West, this text is more widely known as *Pārāyanavagga*.

23 Khunying Yai Damrongthammasan, 2474 [1931], 7.

female figures are examples of persons with unshakable confidence in the dhamma. One of them is Mallikā, the wife of the Senāpati (general) and also later judge, Bandhula. The other one is Uttarā, who hired the prostitute Sirimā for her husband so that she could keep the eight precepts.[24] The third one is Queen Sāmāvatī, who was the mistress of another remarkable figure, Khujjuttarā.[25] Khujjuttarā is said to have been able to memorize sermons by the Buddha which later became the canonical book *Ittivuttaka*. She memorized what the Buddha taught in order to teach Queen Sāmāvatī and her 500 ladies-in-waiting. The Buddha praised Khujjuttarā as the foremost of his laywomen disciples in terms of her learning (*AN* I.26).

These biographies of Pāli canonical figures clearly resemble a number of elements in Khunying Yai's own biography. In particular, the resemblances in terms of memory, orality, and recitation of Buddhist texts as an important part of female Buddhist teaching and learning are noteworthy. Despite the relatively frequent references to female canonical figures in the *Aṭṭhadhammapañha*, her texts do not discuss matters related to gender at all. This is of course not surprising, given her understanding of the dhamma.

From our interviews with Khunying Yai's adopted son, Khun Prasop Wisetsiri, we know that the *Dhammānudhammapaṭipatti* texts were to a large extent, if not entirely, produced orally: while she dictated these texts from memory, Khunying Yai's servant Khun Phueng Chuenjit noted them down. This is remarkable in that even though she must have possessed at least basic writing skills and was able to read, she preferred to dictate these rather complex texts. That this method of text production seems to have been quite normal for her is shown by the fact that Khunying Yai even dictated private letters.[26] We do of course not know, and probably never will, exactly how the *Dhammānudhammapaṭipatti* texts were produced, and it seems likely that Khunying Yai read the texts (or had them read out) once Khun Phueng had noted them down, and edited them. Not only did she produce her texts orally but she also had a servant read out Buddhist texts to her, sometimes

[24] See the story of Uttara and Sirimā on pages 150–1.
[25] See the discussion of Khujjuttara in Chapter 7, page 108.
[26] Seeger and Naris, 2556b [2013b], 142.

for large parts of the day. In addition, she received a significant amount of her knowledge through listening to the teachings of her main teacher Somdet Phra Buddhaghosajarn Jaroen Ñāṇavaro (1872–1951), a highly revered and high-ranking monk who was abbot of the famous Bangkok monastery Wat Thepsirin. For a certain period of time, probably for several years, she visited him in his monastery Wat Thepsirin almost daily in order to learn from his oral instructions and explanations.

Despite the enormous memory that an oral production of the *Dhammānudhammapaṭipatti* texts would require, in the light of what I have described above this does make perfect sense. We not only know that she must have possessed an enormously precise and highly developed memory, but she also grew up in an oral culture in which the memorization of long texts seems to have been rather common. We also know that the people she knew, or must have been close to, memorized long texts as an integral part of their Buddhist practice.

Another interesting aspect of Khunying Yai's life is that she was a member of an extensive (probably informal) network of female practitioners. This network allowed its members to exchange knowledge and experience. They were travelling the country extensively as part of their ascetic practice (*dhutaṅga*) or/and in the search of a teacher. Wat Saneha in Nakhon Pathom, Wat Sattanartpariwat in Ratburi, Wat Thammikaram in Prajuapkhirikhan and the Bangkok temples Wat Somanaswiharn, Wat Prok and Wat Thepsirin, to name only a few, seem to have been important monasteries for female practice, knowledge exchange, and networking. In these monastic centres, female practitioners were actively supported by monks in their pursuit of acquiring Buddhist knowledge (pariyatti) and spiritual practice (paṭipatti). During my research, I discovered links between the outstanding female practitioners and teachers Khunying Yai, Ki Nanayon, Khunying Rabiap Sunthornlikhit, and Ajarn Naep Mahaniranon.[27] What Khunying Yai's and other female

[27] Ajarn Naep (1898–1983) is the first famous female Abhidhamma teacher in Thailand. It seems that Wat Prok has been another important centre for the networking of female practitioners of that time. But further research is needed on the extensive networking between these women.

practitioners' biographies show is that the religious roles of women and the relations between the (male) saṅgha and female practitioners in Thai Buddhism are much more multi-faceted and complex than is often assumed. The absence of a bhikkhunī order has undoubtedly had a major impact on women's religious roles in Thai Buddhism. It is also clear from my study of Thai Buddhist women's biographies that women had to face barriers in their religious learning and practice that men did not have to. Nonetheless, what has also become apparent in my long-term study on female practitioners is that in Thai Buddhism,[28] there have been numerous women who have pursued the path to awakening while being highly revered for their knowledge and genuine practice by sometimes a large number of Thai Buddhists, both male and female. At the same time, these women were intensively and generously supported by (sometimes high-ranking, revered, and famous) monks. In fact, I conclude that in many respects, the biographies of Khunying Yai and other Thai women contain many elements that seem to be remarkably similar to textual and spiritual practices in early Buddhism.

Epilogue

In 1944, Khunying Yai attended the funeral of her long-term spiritual friend (*sahadhammika*) Khun Nai Thang Kotchasut, who was also a highly respected female practitioner, at the Ratburi monastery Wat Sattanartpariwat. There—it is, at the moment, not entirely clear why—she was examined by a famous physician who attested to her: 'You will live for a long time.' Khunying Yai replied: 'There is no need to console me, doctor!' Shortly afterwards, she invited a learned Pāli scholar monk to recite her favourite Pāli texts and discuss the dhamma with her. Then she prostrated in front of him three times and collapsed. The monk could not believe that Khunying Yai had died. The way she died combines what had been important to her throughout her life: respect for and closeness to

[28] I would not be surprised if this also is the case in other Theravāda Buddhist countries.

the saṅgha, to listen to the dhamma (*dhammassavanaṃ*), and to discuss the dhamma (*dhammasākacchā*).
From the famous canonical text *Maṅgalasuttaṃ*:

> *... kālena dhammassavanaṃ, etaṃ maṅgalam uttamaṃ.*
>
> *.... Samaṇānañca dassanaṃ;*
> *kālena dhammasākacchā, etaṃ maṅgalam uttamaṃ.*
>
> ... listening to the *dhamma* on due occasions—this is the greatest blessing.
> ... seeing recluses and having religious discussions on due occasions—this is the greatest blessing.[29]

Martin Seeger
University of Leeds

References

Cremation books

Cremation Book of Phra Ajan Man Bhūridatto, 31 January 2493, Wat Pa Sutthawat Sakon Nakhorn.

Cremation Book of Noi Paurohit, 26 November 2474(1), *atthammapanha phutthamamaka pen phu-top phra jau boromwongthoe krom muen wiwitwanpricha song tatsin* [Eight Questions on the *Dhamma*—Buddhists gave an Answer and Prince Krom Muen Wiwitwanpricha Decided Who Answered Best], Phra Nakhon: Rongphim Phra Jan.

Cremation Book of Noi Paurohit, 26 November 2474(2), Phra Nakhon: Rongphim Lahuthot.

Texts by Khunying Yai Damrongthammasan

Khunying Yai Damrongthammasan, 2474 [1931], [Essays on Eight Questions on the *Dhamma*] *Aṭṭhadhammapañha*, in the Cremation Book of Noi Paurohit, 26 November 2474(1), pp. 1–10.

[No author mentioned], 2475a [1932a], *patipattiwiphak wa duai khamtham khamtop thammapatibat* [*paṭipattivibhāga* on Questions and Answers about the Practice of the Dhamma], Phra Nakhon: Rongphim Phra Jan.

[29] I thank Bhikkhu Anālayo for his comments on this translation.

[No author mentioned], 2475b [1932b], *patipattinithet wa duai khwam-patipatti thang phraphutthasatsana* [*paṭipattinidesa* on the Buddhist Practice], Phra Nakhon: Rongphim Phra Jan.

[No author mentioned], 2476a [1933a], *patipattiwiphang wa duai khwam-patipatti thang phraphutthasatsana* [*paṭipattivibhaṅga* on the Buddhist Practice], Phra Nakhon: Rongphim Phra Jan.

[No author mentioned], 2476b [1933b], *nangsue patipatti putcha wisatchana* [*paṭipattipucchā-visajjanā*], Phra Nakhon: Rongphim Sophonphiphanthanakon.

[No author mentioned], 2477 [1934], *patipattiwiphat wa duai khwampa-tibat thang phraphutthasatsana* [*paṭipattivibhajhana* on the Buddhist Practice], no further details.

Glossary

abhidhamma	higher *dhamma*—used as a category to describe works that extract teachings from the *sutta* literature, and provide expositions of them
āgama	a type of text, the Sanskrit equivalent of *nikāya*
apadāna	a biography, autobiography or story
arahant or *arahantship*	a person who has achieved the state of Awakening
aṭṭhakathā	a Pāli commentary on the Pāli canon
bodhisatta	the Buddha in a previous life
brahmin	a member of the highest Brahmanical/Hindu caste
caṇḍala	a low-class person
deva	a god
devatā	a divine being
dhamma	this word usually refers to one of two things—the teachings of the Buddha, or the truth realized by him
dhammakathikā	a teacher of the *dhamma*
dharmaśāstra	a set of books that prescribe Hindu duty (*dharma*)
duggati	a low or bad rebirth
gahapati	a householder
gāndharva	a heavenly being
gaṇikā	a courtesan

garudhammas	eight rules that nuns (but not monks) must adhere to
iddhi	psychic powers
janapada	region
jātaka	story of the previous life of the Buddha
kamma	action
khattiya	the second caste/class of Hinduism/Brahmanism; the warrior or sovereign class
kula	family or group
kuṭi or *kuṭika*	hut
mahājanapada	the sixteen city-state principalities of ancient India
nāga	a class of mythical being—a serpent
nagarasobhiṇī	a type of prostitute
nibbāna (Pāli) or *nirvāṇa* (Sanskrit)	the quintessential religious experience for Buddhism
nikāya	the literal meaning of the term is 'a collection', however, it is used as either the title of a text (whose contents were collected long ago) or to refer to a group or collection of texts
pācittiya	a class of monastic rule entailing confession
pāda	the fourth part (or 'foot') of a verse
pārājika	the most serious class of monastic rule—breach of these often leads to permanent expulsion from the community
paribbājikā	a renouncer
paṭisambidhā	a type of knowledge/realization
petī/peta	a class of mythical being—a hungry ghost
rūpājīvā	a type of prostitute
samaṇa (male) or *samaṇī* (female) (Pāli)/ *śramaṇī* (Skt)	a renouncer
saṅgha	the Buddhist community
saṅghadisesa	a class of monastic rule; the second class, entailing a formula meeting to be called
seṭṭhikula	a merchant family
stūpa	a Buddhist monument

sutta (Pāli) or *sūtra* (Skt)	the literal meaning of the word is 'thread', and it is used in Buddhism for a type of text, usually narrative texts that contain teachings
svayaṃvara	a marriage ceremony, traditionally one during which the woman chooses her own husband
tāpasī	an ascetic
vaṇṇa	class
vesīyā/vesī	a low-class prostitute
vibhaṅga	the nuns' section of the Pāli *Vinaya*
vihāra or *vihāraka*	a monastic dwelling
vinaya	part of the Buddhist canon, the section on monastic rules
vinayadhārā/ vinayadhārī	someone who knows/understands the monastic rules

Bibliography

Ali, Daud. 2004. *Courtly Culture and Political Life in Early Medieval India*. Cambridge: Cambridge University Press/Cambridge Studies in Indian History and Society.

Allchin, F.R. 1995. *The Archeology of Early Historic South Asia: The Emergence of Cities and States*. Cambridge: Cambridge University Press.

Allen, Nicholas. 2007. 'Bhīṣma as Matchmaker'. In *Gender and Narrative in the Mahābhārata*, edited by Simon Brodbeck and Brian Black, pp. 176–88. Abingdon: Routledge.

Allon, Mark. 2001. *Three Gāndhārī Ekottarikāgama-Type Sūtras: British Library Kharoṣṭhī Fragments 12 and 14*. Seattle: University of Washington Press.

Anālayo. 2007. 'Oral Dimensions of Pali Discourses: Pericopes, other Mnemonic Techniques and the Oral Performance Context'. *Canadian Journal of Buddhist Studies* VI(3): 5–33.

———. 2008. 'Theories on the Foundation of the Nuns' Order—A Critical Evaluation'. *Journal of the Centre for Buddhist Studies, Sri Lanka* 6: 105–42.

———. 2010a. 'Attitudes towards Nuns: A Case Study of the Nandakovāda in the Light of its Parallels'. *Journal of Buddhist Ethics* 17: 332–400.

———. 2010b. *The Genesis of the Bodhisattva Ideal*. Hamburg: Hamburg University Press.

———. 2010c. 'Women's Renunciation in Early Buddhism: The Four Assemblies and the Foundation of the Order of Nuns'. In *Dignity and*

Discipline: The Evolving Role of Women in Buddhism, edited by T. Mohr and J. Tsedroen, pp. 65–97. Boston: Wisdom.
———. 2011a. *A Comparative Study of the Majjhima-nikāya*, 2 vols. Taipai: Dharma Drum Publishing Corporation.
———. 2011b. 'Chos sbyin gyi mdo, Bhikṣuṇī Dharmadinnā Proves Her Wisdom'. *Chung-Hwa Buddhist Journal* 24: 3–33.
———. 2011c. 'Mahāprajāpatī's Going Forth in the Madhyama-āgama'. *Journal of Buddhist Ethics* 18: 268–317.
———. 2012. 'The Historical Value of the Pāli Discourses'. *Indo-Iranian Journal* 55(3): 223–53.
———. 2013a. 'Aṅguttara-nikāya/Ekottarika-āgama: Outstanding Bhikkhunīs in the Ekottarika-āgama'. In *Women in Early Indian Buddhism: Comparative Textual Studies*, edited by Alice Collett, pp. 97–115. Oxford and New York: Oxford University Press.
———. 2013b. 'Mahāyāna in the Ekottarika-āgama'. *Singaporean Journal of Buddhist Studies* 1: 5–43.
———. 2013c. 'Saṃyutta-nikāya / Saṃyukta-āgama: Defying Māra in the Saṃyukta-āgama'. In *Women in Early Indian Buddhism: Comparative Textual Studies*, edited by Alice Collett, pp. 116–39. Oxford and New York: Oxford University Press.
———. 2014a. 'Karma and Female Rebirth'. *Journal of Buddhist Ethics* 21: 108–41.
———. 2014b. 'The Brahmajāla and the Early Buddhist Oral Tradition'. *Annual Report of the International Research Institute for Advanced Buddhology at Soka University for the Academic Year 2013*, Vol. XVII: 41–60.
Apadāna. Mary E. Lilley (ed.). 2006 [1925–7]. *The Apadāna*, Parts I and II. London: The Pali Text Society.
Appleton, Naomi. 2009. *Jātaka Stories in Theravāda Tradition: Narrating the Bodhisatta Path*. Surrey: Ashgate.
Aṅguttara-nikāya. Vols I –VI. Vol. I ([1885] 1961) edited by Richard Morris and A. K. Warder; Vols II ([1888] 2008); III ([1897] 1994); IV ([1899] 1999); and V ([1900] 1999), edited by E. Hardy; Vol. VI ([1910] 2001) edited by Mabel Hunt, revised by C.A.F. Rhys Davids. London: The Pali Text Society.
Aṅguttara-nikāya-aṭṭhakathā. Published as *Manorathapūraṇī: Buddhaghosa's Commentary on the Aṅguttara-Nikāya*. Vol. I, edited by M. Walleser [1924] 1973. London: The Pali Text Society.
Asher, F. and W.M. Spink. 1989. 'Mauryan Figural Sculpture Reconsidered'. *Ars Orientalis* 19: 1–25.
Asher, Frederick M. 2006. 'Early Indian Art Reconsidered'. In *Between the Empires: Society in India 300 BCE to 400 CE*, edited by Patrick Olivelle, pp. 51–66. Oxford and New York: Oxford University Press.

Avadānaśataka. P.L. Vaidya (ed.). 1958. *Avadāna-śataka*. Darbhanga: Mithila Institute.

Bailey, Greg and Ian Mabbett. 2003. *The Sociology of Early Buddhism*. Cambridge: Cambridge University Press.

Barnes, Nancy J. 2000. 'The Nuns at the Stūpa: Inscriptional Evidence for the Lives and Activities of Early Buddhist Nuns in India'. In *Women's Buddhism, Buddhism's Women: Tradition, Revival, Renewal*, edited by Ellison Banks Findly, pp. 17–38. Somerville MA: Wisdom Publications.

Bechert, Heinz. 1958a. *Bruchstücke buddistischer Verssammlungen aus zentalasiatischen Sanskrithandschriften. 1 Die Anavaptagāthā und die Sthaviragāthā*. Berlin: Akademie Verlag.

———. 1958b. 'Über das Apadānabuch'. In *Wiener Zeitschrift für die Künde Süd- und Ostasiens und Archiv für Indische Philosophie*, edited by E. Frauwallner, pp. 7–9. Vienna: Verlag Brüder Hollinek.

———. 1961. *Bruchstücke buddistischer Verssammlungen aus zentalasiatischen Sanskrithandschriften. 1 Die Anavaptagāthā und die Sthaviragāthā*. Berlin: Akademie Verlag.

Bellina, Bérénice. 2003. 'Beads, Social Change and Interaction between India and South-east Asia'. *Antiquity* 77(296): 285–97.

Berkwitz, Stephen C., Juliane Schober, and Claudia Brown (eds). 2009. *Buddhist Manuscript Cultures: Knowledge, Ritual, and Art*. London and New York: Routledge.

Bhattacharji, Sukumari. 1999. 'Prostitution in Ancient India'. In *Women in Early Indian Societies*, edited by Kumkum Roy. New Delhi: Manohar Publishers.

Bingenheimer, Marcus. 2008. 'The Bhikṣuṇī Saṃyukta in the Shorter Chinese Saṃyukta Āgama'. *Buddhist Studies Review* 25(1): 5–26.

———. 2011. *Studies in Āgama Literature: With Special Reference to the Shorter Chinese Saṃyuktāgama*. Taiwan: Shi Weng Feng Print Co.

Black, Brian. 2007a. 'Eavesdropping on the Epic: Female Listeners in the *Mahābhārata*'. In *Gender and Narrative in the Mahābhārata*, edited by Simon Brodbeck and Brian Black, pp. 53–78. Abingdon: Routledge.

———. 2007b. *The Character of the Self in Ancient India: Priests, Kings and Women in the Early Upaniṣads*. New York: State University of New York Press.

Blackstone, Kathryn R. 2000. *Women in the Footsteps of the Buddha: Struggle for Liberation on the Therīgāthā*. Delhi: Motilal Banarsiddass.

Bode, Mabel. 1893. 'Women Leaders of the Buddhist Reformation'. *Journal of the Royal Asiatic Society of Great Britain and Ireland* 25: 517–66 and 763–98.

Bodhi, Bhikkhu. 2000. *The Connected Discourses of the Buddha: A New Translation of the Saṃyutta Nikāya*. Boston: Wisdom Publication.

———. 2012. *The Numerical Discourses of the Buddha: A Translation of the Aṅguttara Nikāya*. Bristol: The Pali Text Society.

Brekke, Torkel. 2003. 'Conversion in Buddhism?' In *Religious Conversion in India: Modes, Motivations and Meanings*, edited by Rowena Robinson and Sathianathan Clarke, pp. 181–91. New Delhi: Oxford University Press.

Brockington, John L. 2006. 'Epic Svayaṃvaras'. In *Voice of the Orient: A Tribute to Prof. Upendranath Dhal*, edited by Raghunath Panda and Madhusudan Mishra, pp. 35–42. Delhi: Eastern Book Linkers.

Brodbeck, Simon Pearce. 2009. *The Mahābhārata Patriline: Gender, Culture, and the Royal Hereditary*. Surrey: Ashgate.

Bucknell, Roderick S. 2008. 'The Two Versions of the Other Translation of the Saṃyuktāgama'. *Chung-Hwa Buddhist Journal* 21: 23–54.

———. 2011. 'The Historical Relationship between the Two Chinese Saṃyuktāgama Translations'. *Chung-Hwa Buddhist Journal* 24: 35–70.

Buddhavaṃsa. N.A. Jayawickrama (ed.). 1995 [1974]. *Buddhavaṃsa and Cariyāpiṭaka*. London: The Pali Text Society.

Burgess, James, and Bhagvānlal Indrājī Pandit. 1881. *Inscriptions from the Cave-temples of Western India: With Descriptive Notes, &c.* Archeological Survey of Western India, Volume 10. Bombay: Government Central Press.

Burgess, J.A.S. [1886] 1996. *The Buddhist Stupas of Amaravati and Jaggayyapeta*. New Delhi: Archaeological Survey of India.

Burlingame, Eugene Watson (ed.). [1921] 1995–2009. *Buddhist Legends, Translated from the Original Pali Text of the Dhammapada Commentary*, 3 vols. London: The Pali Text Society.

Chakravarti, Uma. [1987] 2008. *The Social Dimensions of Early Buddhism*. New Delhi: Munshiram Manoharlal.

Clarke, Shayne. 2014. *Family Matters in Indian Buddhist Monasticisms*. Hawai'i: University of Hawai'i Press.

Collett, Alice. 2006. 'Buddhism and Gender: Reframing and Refocusing the Debate'. *Journal of Feminist Studies in Religion* 22(2): 55–84.

———. 2009. 'Somā, the Learned Brahmin'. *Religions of South Asia* 3(1): 93–109.

———. 2010. 'Review of *A Bull of a Man: Images of Masculinity, Sex and the Body in Indian Buddhism*. Cambridge MA: Harvard University Press'. *Buddhist Studies Review* 27(1): 115–17.

———. 2011. 'The Female Past in Early Indian Buddhism: The Shared Narrative of the Seven Sisters in the Therī-Apadāna'. *Religions of South Asia* 5(1): 209–26.

———. 2013a. 'Nandā, Female Sibling of Gotama Buddha'. In *Women in Early Indian Buddhism: Comparative Textual Studies,* edited by Alice Collett, pp. 140–59. Oxford and New York: Oxford University Press.

———. 2013b. 'Reconceptualising Female Sexuality in Early Buddhism'. In *Women in Early Indian Buddhism: Comparative Textual Studies,* edited by Alice Collett, pp. 62–79. Oxford and New York: Oxford University Press.

———. 2015 (forthcoming). 'Women as Teachers and Pupils in Early Buddhist Communities: The Evidence of Epigraphy'. *Religions of South Asia.*

Collett, Alice and Anālayo. 2014. 'Bhikkhave and Bhikkhu as Gender-Inclusive Terminology in Early Buddhist Texts'. *Journal of Buddhist Ethics,* 21.

Collins, Steven. 1992. 'Notes on Some Oral Aspects of Pali Literature'. *Indo-lranian Journal* 35(2–3): 121–135.

Cone, Margaret. 2001 and 2010. *A Dictionary of Pāli, Parts I and II.* Oxford and Bristol: The Pali Text Society.

Cowell, Edward B. (ed.), and H.T. Francis, R. Chalmers, W. H. D. Rouse, and R. A. Neil (trans). [1895–1913] 1969. *Jātaka or Stories of the Buddha's Former Births,* 6 vols. Cambridge: Cambridge University Press. Cited after reprint, London: Luzac for the Pali Text Society.

Cousins, Lance. 2012. 'The Teachings of the Abhayagiri School'. In *How Theravāda Is Theravāda: Exploring Buddhist Identities,* edited by Peter Skilling, Jason A. Carbine, Claudio Cicuzza, and Santi Pakdeekham, pp. 67–164. Chiang Mai: Silkworm Books.

Crosby, Kate (trans.). 2009. *Mahabharata, Book Ten: Dead of Night and Book Eleven: The Women, by Valmīki.* New York: JCC Foundation.

Cutler, Sally Mellick. 1994. 'The Pāli Apadāna Collection'. *Journal of the Pali Text Society* XX: 1–42.

Damsteegt, Th. 1978. *Epigraphical Hybrid Sanskrit: Its Rise, Spread, Characteristics, and Relationship to Buddhist Hybrid Sanskrit.* Leiden: E. J. Brill.

Das Gupta, C. C. 1949–50. 'Shelarwadi Cave Inscriptions'. *Epigraphica Indica* 28: 76–7.

Deegalle, Mahinda. 2006. *Popularizing Buddhism: Preaching as Performance in Sri Lanka.* Albany, NY: State University of New York Press.

Dehejia, Vidya. 2009. *The Body Adorned: Dissolving Boundaries between Sacred and Profane in India's Art.* New York: Columbia University Press.

Deloche, Jean. 2007. *Studies in Fortification in India.* Paris: Ecole Française d'Extreme-Orient.

Dhammapada-aṭṭhakathā. H. C. Norman (ed.). [1906–15] 1992, 1993, 2007. *The Commentary on the Dhammapada*, 5 vols. Oxford: The Pali Text Society.

Dhand, Arti. 2008. *Woman as Fire, Woman as Sage: Sexual Ideology in the Mahābhārata*. Albany, NY: State University of New York Press.

Dīgha Nikāya. Published as *Dīgha Nikāya*, 3 vols. Vols I ([1889] corrected reprint 2007) and II ([1903] 1995) edited by T. W. Rhys Davids and J.E. Carpenter; Vol. III ([1910] corrected reprint 2006) edited by J.E. Carpenter. Oxford: The Pali Text Society.

Dīgha Nikāya-aṭṭhakathā. Published as *The Sumaṅgalavilāsinī: Buddhaghosa's Commentary on the Dīgha-nikāya*, 3 vols. Vol. I ([1886] 1968) edited by T.W. Rhys Davids and J.E. Carpenter; Vols. II and III ([1931] 1971 and [1932] 1971) edited by W. Stede from materials left unfinished by T.W. Rhys Davids and J.E. Carpenter. London: The Pali Text Society.

Dissanayake, Samanthi. 2013. 'Buddhist Text's True Author Identified as Thai Woman'. BBC News Online, http://www.bbc.co.uk/news/world-asia-21936656, accessed 22 July 2014.

Divyāvadāna. 1886. E.B. Cowell and R. A. Neil (eds). *The* Divyāvadāna*: A Collection of Early Buddhist Legends*. Now First Edited from the Nepalese Sanskrit Mss. in Cambridge and Paris. Cambridge: Cambridge University Press.

Doniger, Wendy. 1995. 'Begetting on Margin: Adultery and Surrogate Pseudomarriage in Hinduism'. In *From the Margins of Hindu Marriage: Essays on Gender, Religion, and Culture*, edited by Lindsey Harlan and Paul B. Courtright, pp. 160–183. New York: Oxford University Press.

Doniger, Wendy and Brian Smith (trans). 1991. *The Laws of Manu*. London: Penguin.

Duggan, Anne E. 2005. 'Persecuted Wife, Motifs S410–S451'. In *Archetypes and Motifs in Folklore and Literature: A Handbook*, edited by Jane Garry and Hasan El-Shamy. New York: ME Sharpe.

Dundas, Paul. 2003. 'Conversion in Jainism: Historical Perspectives'. In *Religious Conversion in India: Modes, Motivations and Meanings*, edited by Rowena Robinson and Sathianathan Clarke, pp.125–48. New Delhi: Oxford University Press.

———. 2006. 'A Non-Imperial Religion? Jainism in its Dark Ages'. In *Between the Empires: Society in India 300 BCE to 400 CE*, edited by Patrick Olivelle, pp. 383–414. Oxford and New York: Oxford University Press.

Dutt, Nalinaksha. 1931. 'Notes on the Nagarjunikonda Inscriptions'. *The Indian Historical Quarterly* 7(3): 633–53.

———. 1939–59. *Gilgit Manuscripts*. Calcutta: Calcutta Oriental Press.
Fabri, C.L. 1930. 'A Graeco-Buddhist Sculpture Representing the Buddha's Descent from the Heaven of the Thirty-three Gods'. *Acta Orientalia* VIII: 288–93.
Finnegan, Damchö Diana. 2009. '"For the Sake of Women too": Ethics and Gender in the Narratives of the Mūlasarvāstivāda Vinaya'. Ph.D. Thesis, University of Wisconsin-Madison.
Fogelin, Lars. 2006. *Archeology of Early Buddhism*. Lanham: Altamira Press.
Foley, Caroline A. 1893. 'The Women Leaders of the Buddhist Reformation as Illustrated by Dharmapāla's *Commentary on the Therīgāthā*'. In *Transactions of the Ninth International Congress of Orientalists*, Vol. 1 of *Indian and Aryans Sections*, edited by Ed Morgan, pp. 344–61.
Freiberger, Oliver. 2006. *Asceticism and Its Critics: Historical Accounts and Comparative Perspectives*. New York: Oxford University Press.
———. 2009. 'Negative Campaigning: Polemics against Brahmins in a Buddhist Sutta'. *Religions of South Asia* 3(1): 61–76.
Gallagher, David. 2009. *Metamorphosis: Transformations of the Body and the Influence of Ovid's Metamorphoses on the Germanic Literature of the Nineteenth and Twentieth Centuries*. Amsterdam: Rodopi BV.
Garbutt, Kathleen (trans.). 2006. *Mahabharata, Book Four: Virāta*. New York: New York University Press and JCC Foundation.
Geiger, Wilhelm. [1916] 2005. *A Pāli Grammar*, translated by Balakrishna Ghosh, revised and edited by K. R. Norman. Oxford: The Pali Text Society.
Gerhardt, Mia I. 1963. *The Art of Storytelling*. Leiden: E.J. Brill.
Gethin, Rupert. 1992. 'The Mātikās: Memorization, Mindfulness and the List'. In *In The Mirror of Memory: Reflections on Mindfulness and Remembrance in Indian and Tibetan Buddhism*, edited by J. Gyatso, pp. 149–72. Albany: State University of New York.
———. 1998. *The Foundations of Buddhism*. New York: Oxford University Press.
———. 2012. 'Was Buddhaghosa a Theravādin? Buddhist Identity in the Pali Commentaries and Chronicles'. In *How Theravāda Is Theravāda: Exploring Buddhist Identities*, edited by Peter Skilling, Jason A. Carbine, Claudio Cicuzza, and Santi Pakdeekham, pp. 1–66. Chiang Mai: Silkworm Books.
Glass, Andrew. 2007. *Four Gāndhārī Saṃyuktāgama Sūtras: Senior Kharoṣṭhī Fragment 5*. Seattle and London: University of Washington Press.
Gnoli, Raniero (ed.). 1978. *The Gilgit Manuscript of the Śayanāsanavastu and the Adhikaraṇavastu: Being the 15th and 16th Sections of the Vinaya of*

the Mūlasarvāstivādin. Rome: Istituto Italiano per il Medio ed Estremo Oriente.
Gross, Rita. 1993. *Buddhism after Patriarchy: A Feminist History, Analysis, and Reconstruction of Buddhism*. Albany: State University of New York Press.
Hiltebeitel, Alf. 2001. *Rethinking the Mahabharata: A Reader's Guide to the Education of the Dharma King*. Chicago: University of Chicago Press.
Hirakawa, Akira. 1982. *Monastic Discipline for the Buddhist Nuns: An English Translation of the Chinese Text of the Mahāsāṃghika-Bhikṣuṇī-Vinaya*. Tibetan Sanskrit Works Series, 21. Patna: K.P. Jayaswal Research Institute.
Heirman, Ann. 2001. 'Chinese Nuns and their Ordination in Fifth Century China'. *Journal of the International Association for Buddhist Studies* 24(4): 275–304.
———. 2002: *'The Discipline in Four Parts': Rules for Nuns According to the Dharmaguptakavinaya*. Delhi: Motilal Banarsidass.
von Hinüber, Oskar. 1996. *A Handbook of Pāli Literature*. Berlin: Walter de Gruyter.
———. 2008. 'The Foundation of the Bhikkhunīsaṅgha: A Contribution to the Earliest History of Buddhism'. *Annual Report of the International Research Institute for Advanced Buddhology at Soka* 11: 3–29.
Horner, I.B. [1930] 1990. *Women under Primitive Buddhism, Laywomen and Almswomen*, Delhi: Motilal Banarsidass.
Horner, I.B (trans.). [1938–52] 2001–7. *The Book of the Discipline*, 5 vols. Oxford and Lancaster: The Pali Text Society.
———. [1924] 2005. *The Minor Anthologies of the Pāli Canon IV: Vimanavatthu: Stories of the Mansions, New Translations of the Verses with Commentarial Excerpts*. Oxford: The Pali Text Society.
Hüsken, Ute. 2010. 'The Eight Garudhammas'. In *Dignity and Discipline: Reviving Full Ordination for Buddhist Nuns*, edited by Thea Mohr and Jampa Tsedroen, pp. 143–8. Boston: Wisdom Publications.
Huyen-Vi, Thich 1985–2004. 'Ekottarāgama'. *Buddhist Studies Review*, various volumes, in collaboration with Bhikkhu Pasadika for various volumes.
Jacobi, Hermann (trans.). 1968. *Jaina Sutras*, Part 1*: The Akaranga Sutra and the Kalpa Sutra*. New York: Dover Publications.
Jaini, Padmanabh S. [1970] 2001. 'Sramaṇas: Their Conflict with Brahmanical Society'. In *Collected Papers on Buddhist Studies*, edited by Padmanabh S. Jaini, pp. 47–96. New Delhi: Motilal Banarsiddass.
Jamison, Stephanie W. 1996. *Sacrificed Wife/Sacrificer's Wife: Women, Ritual, and Hospitality in Ancient India*. New York: Oxford University Press.

———. 2001. 'The Rigvedic Svayamvara? Formulaic Evidence'. In *Vidyārṇavavandanam: Essays in Honour of Asko Parpola*, edited by Klaus Karttunen and Petteri Koskikallio, pp. 303–15. Helsinki: Finnish Oriental Society.

Jātakatthavaṇṇanā. [1877–1896] 1990–1, 7 vols, edited by V. Fausboll; [1895–1907 and Index 1913] 1990, translated by various translators, under the editorship of E. B. Cowell, 6 vols. London and Oxford: The Pali Text Society.

Jyväsjärvi, Mari. 2007. 'Parivrājikā and Pravrajitā: Categories of Ascetic Women'. *Indologica Taurinensia*, 33: 73–92.

Kangle, R.P. (ed. and trans.). [1965–72] 1992–2003. *Kautilīya Arthaśāstra*, 3 vols. Delhi: Motilal Banarsidass [originally published by Bombay University, Bombay].

Kieffer-Pülz, Petra. 2013. 'Buddhist Nuns in South India as Reflected in the *Andhakaṭṭhakathā* and in Vajrabuddhi's *Anugaṇṭhipada*'. *Annual Report of the International Research Institute for Advanced Buddhology at Soka University* 16: 29–46.

Krey, Gisela. 2010. 'On Women as Teachers in Early Buddhism: Dhammadinnā and Khemā'. *Buddhist Studies Review* 27(1): 17–40.

Lamotte, Étienne. [1958] 1976. *Historie du bouddhisme indien: Des origins à l'ère Śaka*. Bibliothèque du Muséon, vol. 43. Louvian: Université de Louvain. (English translation by Sara Webb-Boin titled *History of Indian Buddhism from the Origins to the Śaka Era* was published in 1988. Publications de l'Institut Orientaliste de Louvain, 36. Louvain-la-Neuve: Université catholique de Louvain, Institut Orientaliste.)

Lang, Karen Christina. 1986. 'Lord Death's Snare: Gender-Related Imagery in the *Theragāthā* and the *Therīgāthā*'. *Journal of Feminist Studies in Religion* 2 (2): 63–79.

Langenberg, Amy. 2013. 'Mahāsāṃghika-Lokottaravāda Vinaya: The Intersection of Womanly Virtue and Buddhist Asceticism'. In *Women in Early Indian Buddhism: Comparative Textual Studies*, edited by Alice Collett, pp. 81–96. Oxford and New York: Oxford University Press.

Larzul, Sylvette. 2004. 'Further Considerations of Galland's *Mille et une Nuits*: A Study of the Tales told by Hanna'. *Marvels and Fairy-Tales: Journal of Fairy-Tale Studies* 18(2): 258–71.

Lenz, Timothy J. 2003. *A New Version of the Gāndhārī Dharmapada and a Collection of Previous-Birth Stories: British Library Kharoṣṭhī Fragments 16+25*. Seattle: University of Washington.

Legge, James (trans.). [1886] 1965. *A Record of Buddhistic Kingdoms: Being an Account by the Chinese Monk Fa-Hien of His Travels in India and Ceylon (A.D. 399–414)*. London: Constable and Company.

Lindquist, Steven. 2008. 'Gender at Janaka's Court: Women in the Bṛhadāraṇyaka Upaniṣad Reconsidered'. *Journal of Indian Philosophy* 36(3): 405–26.

Lienhard, Siegfried. 1984. *A History of Classical Poetry: Sanskrit, Pali, Prakrit*. Verlag: Otto Harrassowitz.

Lüders, H. 1912. *A List of Brahmi Inscriptions from the Earliest Times to about AD 400 with the Exception of Those of Asoka: Appendix to Epigraphia Indica and Record of the Archaeological Survey of India*. Calcutta: Superintendent Government Print.

———. 1961. *Mathura Inscriptions*, nos 1.65: 136, edited by K.L. Janert. Gottingen.

Majjhima-nikāya. Published as *Majjhima Nikāya*, 4 vols. Vol. I ([1888] 1993), edited by V. Trenckner; Vols II ([1896–98] reprinted with corrections, 2004) and III ([1899–1902] 1994), edited by R. Chalmers; Vol. IV (2006), index by M. Yamazaki and Y. Ousaka. Oxford: The Pali Text Society.

Majjhima-nikāya-aṭṭhakathā. Published as *Papañcasūdanī, Majjhimanikāyaṭṭhakathā of Buddhaghosācariya*, 3 vols. Vol. I ([1922] 1977), edited by J.H. Woods and D. Kosambi; Vols II and III ([1933] 1976 and [1937] 1977), edited by I.B. Horner. London: The Pali Text Society.

Mahāsāṅghika-Lokottaravāda Vinaya. Gustav Roth. 1970. *Bhikṣuṇī-Vinaya: Including Bhikṣuṇī-prakīrṇaka and a Summary of the Bhikṣu-Prakīrṇaka of the Ārya-Mahāsāṅghika-Lokottaravādin*. Patna: K.P. Jayaswal Research Institute.

Malalasekera, G. P. [1937] 2003. *Dictionary of Pali Proper Names*, 2 vols. London: Luzac for the Pali Text Society.

———. [1928] 1994. *The Pāli Literature of Ceylon*. Sri Lanka: Buddhist Publication Society.

———. Vol. I ([1937]1995) and Vol. II ([1938] 1998). *Dictionary of Pāli Proper Names*. Delhi: Munshiram Manoharlal.

Manné, Beatrice Joy. 1992. *Debates and Case Histories in the Pāli Canon*. PhD Thesis Rijkuniversiteit te Utrecht.

Marshall, John, and Alfred Foucher. [1939] 1983. *The Monuments of Sanchi*, 3 vols. New Delhi: Swati Publications.

Marzolph, Ulrich (ed.). 2006. *The Arabian Nights Reader*. Detroit: Wayne State University Press.

Marzolph, Ulrich, Richard Van Leeuwen, and Hassan Wassouf. 2004. *The Arabian Nights Encyclopedia*, I. Santa Barbara: ABC-CLIO.

McDaniel, Justin Thomas. 2008. *Gathering Leaves and Lifting Words: Histories of Buddhist Monastic Education in Laos and Thailand*. Seattle and London: University of Washington Press.

Menski, Werner F. 1991. 'Marital Expectations as Dramatised in Hindu Marriage Rituals'. In *Roles and Rituals for Hindu Women*, edited by Julia Leslie, pp. 47–67. London: Pinter Publications.

Minh Chau, Thich. [1964] 1991. *The Chinese Madhyama Āgama and the Pāli Majjhima Nikāya*. Delhi: Motilal Banarsidass.

Mirashi, Vishnu Vasudev (ed.). 1977. *Inscriptions of the Śilāhāras*, Vol. VI *Corpus Inscriptionum Indicarum*. New Delhi: Archeological Survey of India.

Monius, Anne E. 2001. *Imagining a Place for Buddhism: Literary Culture and Religious Community in Tamil-Speaking South India*. Oxford and New York: Oxford University Press.

Mori, Sodō. 1989. 'Chronology of the 'Sīhala Sources' for the Pāli Commentaries (II)'. In *Studies of the Pāli Commentaries: A Provisional Collection of Articles*, edited by S. Mori, pp. 57–105. Tokyo: Tokyo Press.

———. 1989. 'The Value of the Pāli Commentaries as Research Material'. In *Studies of the Pāli Commentaries: A Provisional Collection of Articles*, edited by S. Mori, pp. 3–20. Tokyo: Tokyo Press.

Muldoon-Hules, Karen. 2009. 'Of Milk and Motherhood: The Kacaṅgalā Avadāna Read in a Brahmanical Light'. *Religions of South Asia* 3(1): 111–24.

———. 2013. '*Avadānaśataka*: The Role of Brahmanical Marriage in a Buddhist Text'. In *Women in Early Indian Buddhism: Comparative Textual Studies*, edited by Alice Collett, pp. 192–220. Oxford and New York: Oxford University Press.

Ñāṇamoli, Bhikkhu. 1982. *The Path of Discrimination*, translated by A. K. Warder. Oxford: The Pali Text Society.

Nyanaponika Thera and Hellmuth Hecker. 2003. *Great Disciples of the Buddha: Their Lives, Their Works, Their Legacy*. Edited and with an introduction by Bhikkhu Bodhi. Somerville: Buddhist Publication Society.

Neelis, Jason. 2007. 'Passages to India: Śaka and Kuṣāṇa Migrations in Historical Context'. In *On the Cusp of an Era: Art in the Pre-Kuṣāṇa World*, edited by Doris Meth Srinivasan, pp. 55–94. Koninklije Brill: Leiden.

Neumann, Karl Eugen. 1899. *Die Lieder der Mönche und Nonnen Gotamo Buddho's, aus dem Theragäthä und Therigäthä zum erstenmal übersetzt.* Berlin: Ernst Hofmann & Co.

Nichols, Michael. 2009. 'The Two Faces of Deva: The Marā/Brahmā Tandem'. *Religions of South Asia* 3(1): 45–60.

Nīlakēci. [1936] 1994. Published as *Neelakesi*, edited by A. Chakravarti. Madras: Vijayalakshmi Swarnabadhran Jain Trust.

Norman, K. R. 1983. *Pāli Literature*. Wiesbaden: Otto Harrassowitz.
———, (trans.). [1969] 2007. *The Elders' Verses I: Theragāthā*. London: Luzac.
———, (trans.). [1971] 2007. *The Elders' Verses II. Therīgāthā*. London: Luzac.
Obeyesekere, Ranjini. 2001. *Portraits of Buddhist Women: Stories from the Saddharmaratnāvaliya*. Albany, NY: State University of New York Press.
Ohnuma, Reiko. 2012. *Ties That Bind: Maternal Imagery and Discourse in Indian Buddhism*. Oxford: Oxford University Press.
Okubo, Yusen. 1982. 'The Ekottara-agama Fragments of the Gilgit Manuscript'. *Buddhist Seminar*, No. 35, May, 1982.
Olivelle, Patrick (trans.). 1996a. *Dharmasūtras: The Law Codes of Ancient India*. Oxford: Oxford University Press.
——— (trans.). 1996b. *Upaniṣads*. Oxford: Oxford University Press.
——— (trans.). 1997. *The Pañcatantra: The Book of India's Folk Wisdom*. Oxford: Oxford University Press.
———(trans.). 1999. *Dharmasutras: The Law Codes of Ancient India*. New York: Oxford University Press.
———. 2004. 'Rhetoric and Reality: Women's Agency in the Dharmaśāstras'. In *Encounters with the Word: Essays in Honour of Aloysius Pieris on his 70th Birthday*, edited by Robert Cruz, Marshal Fernando, and Asanga Tilakaratne, pp. 489–505. Colombo: Ecumenical Institute for Study and Dialogue; Aachen: Missionswissenschaftliches Institut Missio, e V.; Nurnberg: Missionsprokur der Jesuiten.
Orr, Leslie. 1998. 'Jain and Hindu "Religious Women" in Early Medieval Tamilnadu'. In *Open Boundaries: Jain Communities and Cultures in Indian History*, edited by John E. Cort, pp. 187–212. New York: State University of New York Press.
Pāli Vinaya. H. Oldenburg (ed.). [1879–82] 1999–2001. *Vinaya Piṭakaṃ*, 4 vols. Oxford: The Pali Text Society. And I. B. Horner (trans.). *The Book of the Discipline (vinaya-piṭaka)*, 5 vols; [1938–66] 1992–3. London and Oxford: The Pali Text Society.
Parasher-Sen, Aloka. 2006. 'Naming and Social Exclusion: The Outcast and the Outsider'. In *Between the Empires: Society in India 300 BCE to 400 CE*, edited by Patrick Olivelle, pp. 415–56. Oxford and New York: Oxford University Press.
Pecenko, Primoz. 2002. 'Līnatthapakāsinī and Sāratthamañjūsā: The Purāṇaṭīkās and the Ṭīkās on the Four Nikāyas'. *Journal of the Pali Text Society* 27: 82–5.
———. 2007. 'The Theravāda Tradition and Modern Pāli Scholarship: A Case of "Lost" Manuscripts Mentioned in Old Pāli Bibliographical Sources'. *Chung-Hwa Journal* 20: 331–48.

Pollock, Sheldon (trans.). 2008. *Mahabharata, Book Three: The Forest, by Valmīki.* New York: New York University Press and JCC Foundation.
Powers, John. 2009. *A Bull of a Man: Images of Masculinity, Sex and the Body in Indian Buddhism.* Cambridge, MA: Harvard University Press.
Praphot Setthakanon (ed.). [No date]. *jet wan banlu tham* [Achieving Awakening within Seven Days]. Nonthaburi: Sipanya.
Prasop Pasāro, Phra and Khunying Yai Damrongthammasan, 2527 [1984]. *tat buang kam* [Cutting the Karmic Fetters]. Bangkok: Kanphim Phra Nakhon.
Pruitt, William (trans.). 1999 [1998]. *The Commentary on the Verses of the Therīs (Therīgāthā-aṭṭhakathā, Paramatthadīpanī VI) by Ācariya Dhammapāla.* Oxford: The Pali Text Society.
Quintanilla, Sonya Rhie. 2007. *History of Early Stone Sculpture at Mathura: Ca. 150 BCE 100 CE.* Leiden: E.J. Brill.
Rāmāyaṇa. Robert P. Goldman (trans.) 2005. *Rāmāyaṇa, Book One: Boyhood, by Vālmiki.* New York: New York University Press and JCC Foundation.
Rhys Davids, C.A.F., (trans.). [1909] 2000. *Psalms of the Early Buddhists.* Oxford: The Pali Text Society.
Rhys Davids, C.A.F., and K.R. Norman (trans). 1989. *Poems of Early Buddhist Nuns (Therīgāthā).* Oxford: The Pali Text Society.
Richman, Paula. 1988. *Women, Branch Stories, and Religious Rhetoric in a Tamil Buddhist Text.* Maxwell School of Citizenship and Public Affairs, Syracuse University.
Roswell, Lewis Eugene. 1992. *Music and Musical Thought in Early India.* Chicago: University of Chicago Press.
Roy, Kumkum. 1988. 'Women and Men Donors at Sanchi: A Study of the Inscriptional Evidence'. In *Position and Status of women in Ancient India (Seminar Papers)*, Vol. 1, edited by L.K. Tripathi, pp. 209–23. Varanasi: Banaras Hindu University.
———. [2003] 2010. 'Of Theras and Theris: Visions of Liberation in the Early Buddhist Tradition'. In *The Power of Gender, and the Gender of Power: Explorations in Early Indian History, Oxford Collected Essays*, edited by Kumkum Roy, pp. 17–37. New Delhi: Oxford University Press.
Salomon, Richard. 1998. *Indian Epigraphy: A Guide to the Study of Inscriptions in Sanskrit, Prakrit, and Other Indo-Aryan Languages.* New York: Oxford University Press.
Salomon, Richard, with contributions from Andrew Glass. 2008. *Two Gāndhārī Manuscripts of the Songs of Lake Anavatapta (Anavatapta-gāthā), British Library Kharoṣṭhī Fragment 1 and Senior Scroll 14.* Seattle and London: University of Washington Press.

Saṃyutta-nikāya. M. Léon Feer (ed.). [1881–98] 2000–08. *Saṃyutta-nikāya*, 5 vols. Oxford: The Pali Text Society.
Sattar, Arshia (trans.). 1994. Somadeva. *Tales from the Kathāsaritsāgara*. London: Penguin Books.
Schalk, Peter, and Āḷvāpiḷḷai Vēluppiḷḷai (eds). 2002. *Buddhism among Tamils in Pre-Colonial Tamiḻakam and Īḻam. Part 1. Prologue: The Pre-Pallava and Pallava Period*. Uppsala: Acta Universitatis Upsaliensis (AUU).
Schalk, Peter, and Astrid van Nahl (eds). 2012. *Buddhism among Tamils. Part 3. Extension and Conclusions*. Uppsala: AUU.
Schober, Juliane (ed.). 1997. *Sacred Biography in the Buddhist Traditions of South and Southeast Asia*. Honolulu: University of Hawai'i Press.
Schopen, Gregory. 1985. 'Two Problems in the History of Buddhism: The Layman/Monk Distinction and the Doctrine of the Transference of Merit'. *Studien zur Indologie und Iranistik*, 10: 9–47.
———. 1997. *Bones, Stones and Buddhist Monks: Collected Papers on the Archaeology, Epigraphy, and Texts of Monastic Buddhism in India*. Honolulu: University of Hawai'i Press.
———. 2004. *Buddhist Monks and Business Matters: Still More Papers on Monastic Buddhism in India*. Honolulu: University of Hawai'i Press.
———. 2007. 'Art, Beauty and the Business of Running a Buddhist Monastery in Early Northwest India'. In *On the Cusp of an Era: Art in the Pre-Kuṣāṇa World*, edited by Doris Meth Srinivasan, pp. 287–317. Koninklije Brill: Leiden.
———. 2010. 'On Incompetent Monks and Able Urbane Nuns in a Buddhist Monastic Code'. *Journal of Indian Philosophy* 38(2): 107–31.
Schüler, Barbara. 2009. *Of Death and Birth: Icakkiyamman, a Tamil Goddess in Ritual and Story*. Wiesbaden: Otto Harrassowitz Verlag.
Seeger, Martin. 2009. 'The Changing Roles of Thai Buddhist Women: Obscuring Identities and Increasing Charisma'. *Religion Compass* 3: 806–22.
———. 2010. '"Against the Stream": The Thai Female Buddhist Saint Mae Chi Kaew Sianglam (1901–1991)'. *South East Asia Research* 18(3): 555–95.
———. 2013. 'Reversal of Female Power, Transcendentality, and Gender in Thai Buddhism: The Thai Buddhist Female Saint Khun Mae Bunruean Tongbuntoem (1895–1964)'. *Modern Asian Studies* 47(5): 1488–1519.
———. 2014. 'Orality, Memory, and Spiritual Practice: Outstanding Female Thai Buddhists in the Early 20th Century'. *Journal of the Oxford Centre for Buddhist Studies* 7: 153–90.

———. Forthcoming. '"The (Dis)appearance of an author": Some Observations and Reflections on Authorship in Modern Thai Buddhism'. *Journal of International Association of Buddhist Studies* 36.

Seeger, Martin and Charaschanyawong Naris. 2556a [2013a]. 'tam ruean-grau khong nakpatibat tham ying dot den thi thuk luem Khunying Yai Damrongthammasan (2429–87) lae panha wa duai khwampenjauk-hong phon-ngan praphan choeng phut an samkhan' [Researching the biography of a forgotten, outstanding female Buddhist practitioner: Khunying Yai Damrongthammasan (1886–1944) and the question of authorship of an important Buddhist treatise]. *Sinlapawatthanatham* (Art and Culture Magazine) April 2556 [2013]: 154–69.

———. 2556b [2013b]. 'phutthamamika ek u haeng yuk 2475 Khunying Yai Damrongthammasan' ['Buddhamamika Ek-U' during the time of the 1932 Siamese Revolution: Khunying Yai Damrongthammasan]. *Sinlapawatthanatham* (Art and Culture Magazine), November 2556 [2013]: 136–45.

Senart, Émile. 1882. *Le Mahvastu, Texts sancrit publié pour la première fois et accompagné d'introductions et d'un commentaraire*, Vol. I. Paris: Imprimerie Nationale.

———. 1905–6. 'The Inscriptions in the Caves at Nāsik'. In *Epigraphica Indica*, VIII, edited by E. Hultzsch, pp. 59–97. Calcutta: Office of the Superintendent of Government Printing, India.

Shah, Kirit K. 2001. *The Problem of Identity: Women in Early Indian Inscriptions*. New Delhi: Oxford University Press.

Sharma, Arvind. 1977. 'How and Why Did Women in Ancient India Become Nuns?' *Sociological Analysis* 38(3): 239–51.

Sharma, Ramesh Chandra. 1984. *Buddhist Art of Mathurā*. Delhi: Agam Publishers.

Shaw, Julia. 2007. *Buddhist Landscapes in Central India: Sanchi Hill and Archaeologies of Religious and Social Change*. London: The British Association of South Asian Studies.

Silk, Jonathan A. 2007. 'Garlanding as Sexual Invitation: Indian Buddhist Evidence'. *Indo-Iranian Journal* 50(1): 5–10.

———. 2009. *Riven by Lust: Incest and Schism in Indian Buddhist Legend and Historiography*. Honolulu: University of Hawai'i Press.

Singh, Sarva Daman. 1999. 'Polyandry in the Vedic Period'. In *Women in Early Indian Societies*, edited by Kumkum Roy, pp. 175–95. New Delhi: Manohar Publishers.

Skilling, Peter. 2001a. 'Eṣā agrā: Images of Nuns in (Mūla-)Sarvāstivādin Literature'. *Journal of the International Association of Buddhist Studies* 24(2): 135–56.

———. 2001b. 'Nuns, Laywomen, Donors, Goddesses: Female Roles in Early Indian Buddhism'. *Journal of the International Association of Buddhist Studies* 24(2): 241–74.

Somphong Suthinsak (comp.). 2537 [1994]. *wat thammikaram jangwat prajuapkhirikhan* [The History of Wat Thammikaram in Prajuabkhirikhan Province]. Bangkok: Liang Chiang.

Srinivasan, Doris Meth. 2005. 'The Mauryan Gaṇikā from Dīdārgañj (Pāṭaliputra)'. *East and West* 55(1): 345–62.

———. 2006. 'Royalty's Courtesans and God's Mortal Wives: Keepers of Culture in Pre-colonial India'. In *The Courtesan's Arts: Cross-Cultural Perspectives,* edited by M. Feldman and B. Gordon, pp. 161–81. New York: Oxford University Press.

Sternbach, Ludwig. 1953. *Texts on Courtezans in Classical Sanskrit* (Vishveshvaranand Indological Series). Hosiarpur: Vishveshvaranand Institute Publications.

Strauch, Ingo. 2013. 'The Bajaur Collection of Kharoṣṭhī Manuscripts: Mahāprajāpatī Gautamī and the Order of Nuns in a Gandhāran Version of the Dakṣiṇāvibhaṅgasūtra'. In *Women in Early Indian Buddhism: Comparative Textual Studies,* edited by Alice Collett, pp. 18–45. Oxford and New York: Oxford University Press.

Sumaṅgalavilāsinī. [1886] 1968. Published as *The Sumaṅgalavilāsinī: Buddhaghosa's Commentary on the Digha Nikāya,* Pt I, edited by T. W. Rhys Davids and J. Estlin Carpenter. London: Pali Text Society.

Sutherland Goldman, Sally J. 2000. 'Anklets Away: Symbolism of Jewelry and Ornamentation in Vālmīki's Rāmāyaṇa'. In *A Varied Optic: Contemporary Studies of the Rāmāyaṇa,* edited by Mandakranta Bose, pp. 125–53. Vancouver: Institute of Asian Studies.

Thera-Therīgāthā. H. Oldenburg and R. Pischel (eds). [1883] 1999. *The Thera- and Therīgāthā: Stanzas Ascribed to Elders of the Buddhist Order of Recluses.* Oxford: The Pali Text Society.

Theragāthā-aṭṭhakathā. Published as *Paramatthadīpanī Theragāthā-aṭṭhakathā: The Commentary of Dhammapālācariya,* edited by F. L. Woodward, 3 vols, Vols I ([1940] 1995); II ([1952] 2013); and III ([1959] 1984). Oxford: The Pali Text Society.

Therīgāthā-aṭṭhakathā. William Pruitt (ed.). 1997. *Therīgāthā Commentary (Paramatthadīpanī VI).* Oxford: The Pali Text Society. Also William Pruitt (trans.). 1998. *The Commentary on the Verses of the Therīs.* Oxford: The Pali Text Society.

Todorov, Tzvetan. 'Narrative Men'. In *The Arabian Nights Reader,* edited by Ulrich Marzolph, pp. 226–38. Detroit: Wayne State University Press.

Udāna Commentary. F. L. Woodward (ed.). [1926] 1977. *Paramatthadīpanī Udānaṭṭhakathā of Dhammapālācariya*. London: The Pali Text Society.
Vēluppiḷḷai, Āḷvāpiḷḷai. 1997. 'A Negative Evaluation of Non-Buddhist Indian Religions in the Maṇimēkalai'. In *A Buddhist Woman's Path to Enlightenment: Proceedings of a Workshop on the Tamil̲ Narrative Maṇimēkalai*, edited by Peter Schalk, pp. 223–40. Uppsala University, May 25–29, 1995, Peter Schalk, ed.-in-chief. Uppsala: AUU.
Vimānavatthu and Petavatthu. N.A. Jayawickrama (ed.). 1999. *Vimānavatthu and Petavatthu*. Oxford: The Pali Text Society.
Wagle, Narendra. 1966. *Society at the Time of the Buddha*. Bombay: Popular Prakashan.
Waldschmidt, Ernst. 1980. 'Central Asian Fragments and the Relation to the Chinese Āgamas'. In *Die Sprache der ältesten buddhischen Überlieferung—The Language of the Earliest Buddhist Tradition*, edited by Heinz Bechert, pp. 136–74. Göttingen: Vandenhoeck & Ruprecht.
Walters, Jonathan S. 1995. 'Gotamī's Story: Introduction and Translation'. In *Buddhism in Practice*, edited by Donald S. Lopez Jr, pp. 113–38. Princeton: Princeton University Press.
———. 1997. 'Stupa, Story and Empire: Constructions of the Buddha Biography in Early Post-Aśokan India'. In *Sacred Biography in the Buddhist Traditions of South and Southeast Asia*, edited by Juliane Schober, pp. 160–92. Honolulu: University of Hawai'i Press.
———. 2013. 'Wives of the Saints: Marriage and Kamma in the Path to Arahantship'. In *Women in Early Indian Buddhism: Comparative Textual Studies*, edited by Alice Collett, pp. 160–91. Oxford and New York: Oxford University Press.
Warder, A. K. 1967. *Pali Metre*. London: The Pali Text Society.
Witzel, Michael. 1997. 'The Development of the Vedic Canon and its Schools: The Social and Political Milieu'. In *Inside the Texts beyond the Texts: New Approaches to the Study of the Vedas, Proceedings of the International Vedic Workshop, Harvard University, June 1989, Harvard Oriental Series, Opera Minora*, 2, edited by Michael Witzel, pp. 257–348. Cambridge, MA: Harvard University Department of Sanskrit and Indian Studies.
Woodward, F.L. (trans.). [1936] 2003. *The Book of Gradual Sayings (Aṅguttara-nikāya) or More Numbered Suttas*, Vol. V *(The Book of the Tens and Elevens)*. Oxford: The Pali Text Society.
Young, Serinity. 2004. *Courtesans and Tantric Consorts: Sexualities in Buddhist Narrative, Iconography, and Ritual*. New York: Routledge.
———. 2007. 'Female Mutability and Male Anxiety in an Early Buddhist Legend'. *Journal of History of Sexuality* 16(1): 14–39.

Index

queen, chief 30–1, 49, 74–5, 77, 86
Quintanilla, Sonya 5, 147

rag–robes 46, 137–8, 228
Rājagaha xxiv, 21–2, 24, 60–1, 70, 78, 143, 146, 180
rebirth 8, 30, 75, 140, 209, 216, 218, 236
recension 6–7, 29, 34, 72–5, 164, 201–2
recluses 15, 144, 172, 189
record xxxi, 30–1, 51, 54, 59, 105
  historical 127, 203, 230
Reformation x–xi
religion x–xi, xiv, 202
  historian of xxiii, 3
renouncers 104, 189
Rhys Davids, Caroline ix, xxi–xxii, xxiv, 10, 71, 95, 163
rice 51, 75–6
rivers 78, 85, 152, 154, 173
road 51–3, 121, 136, 154, 159
robes 42, 46, 58–9, 75, 119, 136–7, 157, 190, 215
rogues 71, 142, 153, 158
role xxvi, 19, 21, 31, 73, 81–3, 85, 87, 91–3, 100, 105–7, 109–10, 193, 199, 210
  religious 243
  rotational 105
Roswell, Eugene 115, 132–3
rules 106–7, 137, 143, 152–4, 158, 160, 183, 190, 212, 215–16, 221, 228
  monastic 48

Saccaka 48–9, 192
Sakka 46, 78, 83, 86, 151
Salomon, Richard 4, 147
Sāmā 65, 195
samaṇa tradition 188–90, 193
samaṇī 189–91
Saṃyutta–nikāya 26–7, 29, 35–6, 40, 67, 69, 93, 119, 125, 158, 190, 197, 207, 216
saṅgha 30–1, 76, 99, 105, 140–3, 156, 166–7, 187, 239, 243–4
saṅghādisesa (saṅghadisesa) 143, 152–4, 215
Sāriputta 49, 63, 67–8, 85–6, 93, 162, 193, 200, 207–9, 211
Sattuka 60–1, 64–5
Sāvatthī 43–4, 50, 52, 74–5, 79, 142
scenes 58, 67–8, 114
Schalk, Peter 40, 189, 202
scholars xi, xiv, xxii, 5, 7, 94, 203
scholarship iv, x, xii–xiv, 193
Schopen, Gregory 5–6, 101, 104, 107–8, 126–7
Seeger, Martin 229, 231–3, 237, 241
sensual pleasures 9, 20, 28, 70–1, 117, 131, 134, 173, 181, 195, 216
servants 6, 21, 29, 50–1, 57, 64, 127, 167–8, 170–2, 175, 178, 212, 241
services 21, 139–40, 143–4, 146, 150
sex 129, 135, 144, 149, 155, 215–16, 219–21
sexual assault xxviii, 67, 81, 152–6, 228
  incidents of 153
Sirimā 150–1, 241
sisters xxii, 22, 43, 49, 54, 72–3, 76, 81, 83, 85, 126, 154, 163–4, 210, 219–20
sister's husband 154
slaves 6, 34, 78, 83, 176, 178–9
social exclusion 128, 131, 167

About the author

Alice Collett teaches in the Department of Theology and Religious Studies, York St John University, UK. She has published several articles and book chapters on women in early Indian Buddhism, and her edited volume, *Women in Early Indian Buddhism: Comparative Textual Studies*, was published in 2013. She is the co-editor of *Buddhist Studies Review*. She is currently working on a new project on women in early Buddhist inscriptions.